Copyright © 2012 by Abhisek Vyas

Sybase Developer (ASE 15) survival guide

Published by:
Sybaserays publications

ISBN: 978-1-300-37736-8

First Edition

www.sybaserays.com

All rights reserved. No part of this book may be reproduced or transmitted in any form or by any means, electronic or mechanical, including photocopying, recording, or by any information storage and retrieval system without the written permission of the author, except where permitted by law.

This book has been written with care, neither the author, nor the publisher, nor Sybase Inc are responsible for errors, nor do they accept any liabilities for damages resulting from the use of the information herein.

INTRODUCTION

The strongest reason for writing this book occurred to me when I decided to take up a certification exam for Sybase ASE SQL Developer professional ; partly to test myself and partly to enhance my theoretical knowledge about Sybase as a subject. During the preparation phase, I did realize that it wasn't easy to find structured and easily understandable study material that could suffice focusing on just the right topics so as to ace the examination while also providing a comprehensive view about the subject as a whole.

Though designed for both beginners and advanced level professionals, this book will also prove to be a useful tool for aspirants of *Sybase ASE SQL Developer Professional certification exam.* While beginners will find this book useful for RDBMS topics (including Logical and Physical design, normalization, primary key, constraints, DDL and DML); topics for intermediate and advanced level professionals cover Stored procedure, Triggers, Performance and Tuning Basics, Query optimization process, Index, Query optimization engine, Partition, locking etc. Also, this book covers all the topics in the same order as in the syllabus for *Sybase ASE SQL Developer Professional certification exam,* which will make the contents much easier to grasp when there is little time on hand for preparation.

Whats new in ASE 15:
In addition to the topics covered in previous version of Sybase ASE, this book includes details on new features of the ASE 15 version, including :
- Local and global index
- Scrollable cursor
- New join types
- ASE 15 optimization goals and
- New commands for getting optimizer information.

In this book, I have tried to incorporate easy examples and explain cases that a Sybase professional and/or student come across. For instances, a Syntax for a database command always follows with an example, so you get a glimpse of the real – life situation immediately after you see the syntax. Also, classified information is described in tabular from so that it is organized and easy to memorize. Since there can be number of methods one can write a code, I have tried to include as many ways as possible to implement a database logic with relevant examples. Apparently, what readers will find the most benefiting in terms of strengthening their concepts in Sybase is the Summary given at the end of every chapter followed by a couple of relevant practice questions.

ACKNOWLEDGMENT

Throughout the process of writing this book, many individuals have taken time out to help me. I would like to give a special thanks to the Deepak, Deb and Pankaj for actively participating in giving feedback and suggestions for this book.

Thanks to all my friends and colleagues for sharing my happiness when I started this project and following with encouragement when it seemed too difficult to be completed. I would have probably given up without their support and the belief that we can always find a way if we really want something.

DEDICATION

I dedicate this to my parents who always gave me hopes. And to my wife Pallavi , who always believed that I can do anything I put my mind to.

CONTENTS AT A GLANCE

Section 1 - What's New in ASE 15 13
    1.1   Describe local/global indexes on partitioned tables 13
    1.2   Identify aspects of insensitive/semi-sensitive scrollable cursors 16
    1.3   Describe metrics capture 22
    1.4   Identify and define new commands for getting optimizer information 25
    1.5   Describe ASE 15.0 optimization goals and their impact on query plans 28
    1.6   Describe the various join types (hash joins, merge joins, NLJ, N-ary NLJ) 31
    Summary 38
    Practice Test 39

Section 2 - ASE Performance and Tuning Basics 41
    2.1   Define tradeoffs of performance & tuning - with an emphasis on code 41
    2.2   Identify steps involved in executing a query 52
    2.3   List what query plan information can be viewed 53
    Summary 56
    Practice Test 57

Section 3 - Logical and Physical Design 59
    3.1   Define Entities, Relationships (subtype-supertype) & Attribute cardinality 59
    3.2   Assess a relational data model 60
    3.3   Create Associative Tables 62
    3.4   Identify qualities for Primary Key 63
    3.5   Represent relationships as Foreign keys 64
    3.6   Determine column data type and null/not null status, default values, rules & constraints 65
    3.7   Enforce domain integrity 69
    3.8   Define derived tables, intra-row derived columns and inter-row derived columns 70
    3.9   List advantages of normalization 76
    3.10   Understand First, Second and Third Normal Form 77

3.11	List denormalization techniques	79
	Summary	84
	Practice Test	85

Section 4 - ANSI SQL – DDL 87

4.1	Describe how to create tables, views, indexes, etc.	87
4.2	Define system and user-defined datatypes	95
4.3	Define column properties such as null and identity	95
4.4	Define temporary tables	98
4.5	Describe different partitioning strategies	100
4.6	Understand partitioning options with alter table	105
	Summary	108
	Pactice Test	109

Section 5 - ANSI SQL - DML 111

5.1	Describe the data manipulation commands: select, insert, update, and delete, and the use of cursors	111
5.2	Identify important clauses of DML statements, such as where, having, order by, etc.	122
	WHERE:	122
5.3	Identify the performance and tuning aspects of DML statements, such as direct and deferred updates, etc.	126
5.4	Identify techniques to promote the most efficient update method	130
5.5	Understand computed columns:	131
	Summary	136
	Practice Test	137

Section 6 - Query Access Methods 139

6.1	Define range queries, point queries, and covered queries	139
6.2	Explain how ASE accesses data in selects, inserts, deletes, and updates	140
6.3	Define I/O for a select using a non-clustered index	143
6.4	Define performance benefits of using indexes	143
6.5	Define bulk copy and BCP commands	143

6.6	Define logging & minimally-logged operations	145
Summary		147
Practice Test		148

Section 7 - Query Optimization 149

7.1	Define the 'Or Strategy' and showplan, plus options	149
7.2	Identify optimization 'set' command tools	171
7.3	Use of Abstract Plans	173
7.4	Determine if the optimizer selected serial or parallel access	179
7.5	Define Procedure Cache & explain how stored procedures are processed	184
7.6	Identify factors for setting Prefetch at the Query-Level	185
7.7	Identify Query Degradation	186
7.8	Identify tasks for which internal working tables are created in tempdb or in memory	187
7.9	Design queries to take maximum advantage of optimizer features	188
7.10	Identify guidelines to minimize join related performance problems	188
7.11	Identify factors of Subquery Optimization	189
Summary		191
Practice Test		192

Section 8 - Stored Procedures and Triggers 193

8.1	Write and tune stored procedures and triggers	193
8.2	Define query plans and the procedure cache	200
8.3	Define triggers and their usage	202
Summary		209
Practice Test		210

Section 9 - Transact-SQL Statements 211

9.1	Use of Sybase-specific Transact-SQL commands, such as functions, programming commands such as if and while, local and global variables	211
9.2	Describe 'scrollable cursors'	218
Please read following sections:		218
9.3	Identify guidelines for SARGs	218

Summary 225

Practice Test 226

Section 10 - Data Integrity and Constraints 227

10.1   Identify and define both the ANSI-standard constraints, such as check constraints and primary key constraints 227

10.2   Describe traditional Sybase data integrity mechanisms such as rules and defaults 228

Summary 233

Practice Test 234

Section 11 - Transaction Management and Locking 235

11.1   Describe the behavior of transactions and transaction management commands 235

11.2   Describe behavior of locks 237

11.3   Describe transaction logging; lock blocking, diagnosis and resolution of deadlocks 242

11.4   Describe the effect of transaction isolation levels 244

11.5   Define methods for reducing lock contention 248

11.6   Describe how ASE resolves a deadlock 249

Summary 250

Practice Test 251

Section 12 - Joins, Subqueries, and Unions 253

12.1   Define the different types of joins 253

12.2   Describe the union and union all command 257

12.3   Describe subqueries 258

12.4   Describe join costing and subquery optimization 264

Summary 265

Practice Test 266

Section 13 - Optimizer Statistics 267

13.1   Describe table-level and distribution statistics 267

13.2 Define the different types of statistics, such as cluster ratios, density values, and histograms 270

13.3 Describe simulated statistics 273

Summary 274

Practice Test 275

Practice Test Answers 277

INDEX 284

Section 1 - What's New in ASE 15

1.1 Describe local/global indexes on partitioned tables

Indexes, like tables, can be partitioned. Prior to Adaptive Server 15.0, all indexes were global. With Adaptive Server 15.0, you can create local as well as global indexes.

An index partition is an independent database object identified with a unique combination of index ID and partition ID; it is a subset of an index, and resides on a segment or other storage device.

Adaptive Server supports local and global indexes.
- A *local index* – spans data in exactly one data partition. For semantically partitioned tables, a local index has partitions that are equipartitioned with their base table; that is, the table and index share the same partitioning key and partitioning type. For all partitioned tables with local indexes, each local index partition has one and only one corresponding data partition.
  Each local index spans just one data partition. You can create local indexes on range-, hash-, list-, and round-robin–partitioned tables. Local indexes allow multiple threads to scan each data partition in parallel, which can greatly improve performance.
- A *global index* – spans all data partitions in a table. Sybase supports only unpartitioned global indexes. All unpartitioned indexes on unpartitioned tables are global.

- A partitioned table can have partitioned and unpartitioned indexes.
- An unpartitioned table can have only unpartitioned, global indexes.

Local versus global indexes
- Local indexes can increase concurrency through multiple index access points, which reduces root-page contention.
- You can place local nonclustered index subtrees (index partitions) on separate segments to increase I/O parallelism.
- You can run reorg rebuild on a per-partition basis, reorganizing the local index sub-tree while minimizing the impact on other operations.
- Global nonclustered indexes are better for covered scans than local indexes, especially for queries that need to fetch rows across partitions.

Creating global indexes:
You can create global, clustered indexes only for round-robin–partitioned tables. Adaptive Server supports global, nonclustered, unpartitioned indexes for all types of partitioned tables.
You can create clustered and nonclustered global indexes on partitioned tables using syntax supported in Adaptive Server version 12.5.x and earlier.
When you create an index on a partitioned table, Adaptive Server automatically creates a global index, if you:

- Create a nonclustered index on any partitioned table, and do not include the local index keywords. For example, on the hash-partitioned table mysalesdetail.
  create nonclustered index ord_idx on mysalesdetail (au_id)
- Create a clustered index on a round-robin–partitioned table, and do not include the local index keywords. For example, on currentpublishers table.
  create clustered index pub_idx on currentpublishers

Creating local indexes:
Adaptive Server supports local clustered indexes and local nonclustered indexes on all types of partitioned tables. A local index inherits *the partition types, partitioning columns, and partition bounds* of the base table.

For **range-, hash-, and list**-partitioned tables, Adaptive Server always creates local clustered indexes, whether or not you include the keywords local index in the create index statement.

This example creates a local, clustered index on the partitioned mysalesdetail table. In a clustered index, the physical order of index rows must be the same as that of the data rows; you can create only one clustered index per table.

create clustered index clust_idx
       on mysalesdetail(ord_num) local index

This example creates a local, nonclustered index on the partitioned mysalesdetail table. The index is partitioned by title_id. You can create as many as 249 nonclustered indexes per table.

create nonclustered index nonclust_idx
       on mysalesdetail(title_id)
    local index p1 on seg1, p2 on seg2, p3 on seg3

Global nonclustered index on partitioned table:

You can create global indexes that are nonclustered and unpartitioned for all partitioning table strategies.The index and the data partitions can reside on the same or different segments. You can create the index on any indexable column in the table. The example in Figure 1-1 is indexed on the pub_name column; the table is partitioned on the pub_id column.

For this example, we use alter table to repartition publishers with three range partitions on the pub_id column.
Alter table publishers partition by range(pub_id)
(a values <= ("100"),
b values <= ("200"),
c values <= ("300"))

To create a global nonclustered index on the pub_name column, enter:

create nonclustered index publish2_idx
on publishers(pub_name)

Figure 1-1: Global nonclustered index on a partitioned table

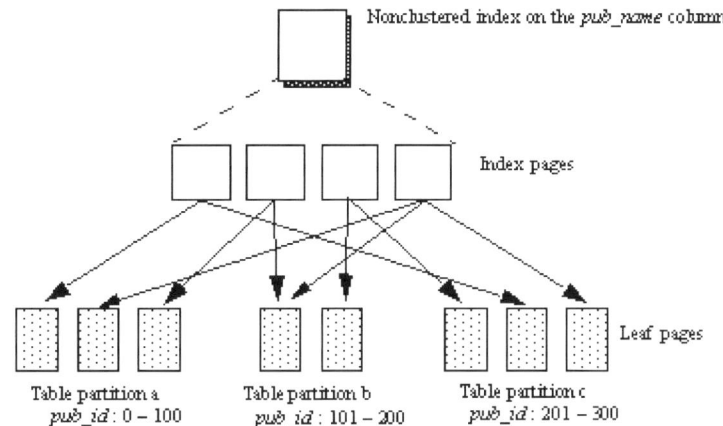

In Figure 1-2, the example is indexed on the pub_id column; the table is also partitioned on the pub_id column.

To create a global nonclustered index on the pub_id column, enter:

create nonclustered index publish3_idx
on publishers(pub_id)

Figure 1-2: Global nonclustered index on a partitioned table

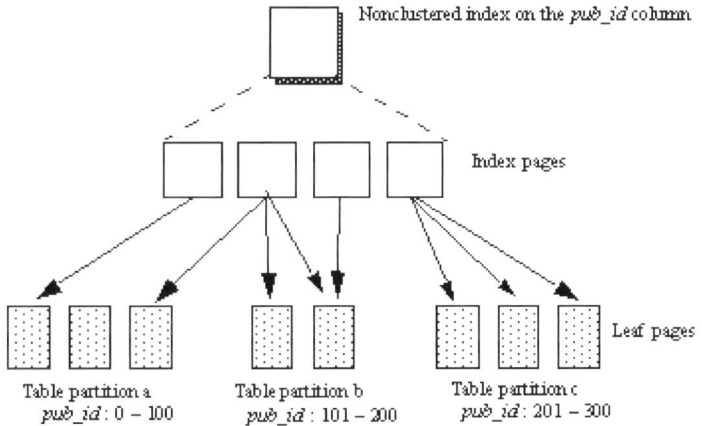

Local nonclustered indexes:

You can define local nonclustered indexes on any set of indexable columns. Using the *publishers* table partitioned by range on the *pub_id* column as in "Global nonclustered index on partitioned table", create a partitioned, nonclustered index on the *pub_id* and *city* columns:

create nonclustered index publish8_idx (A)
on publishers(pub_id, city) local index p1, p2, p3

You can also create a partitioned, nonclustered index on the *city* column:
create nonclustered index publish9_idx (B)
 on publishers(city)
 local index p1, p2, p3

Figure 1-3 shows both examples of nonclustered local indexes. The graphic description of each is identical. However, you can enforce uniqueness on example A; you cannot enforce uniqueness on example B.

Figure 1-3: Local nonclustered indexes

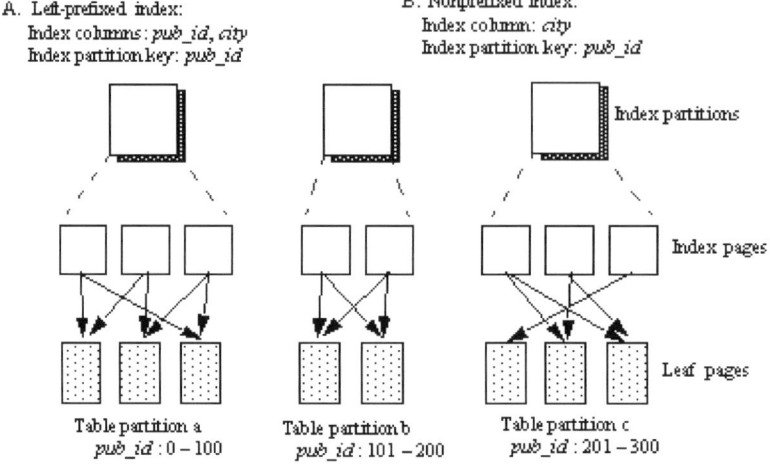

1.2 Identify aspects of insensitive/semi-sensitive scrollable cursors
Scrollable cursors:
Adaptive Server Enterprise allows both scrollable and nonscrollable cursors, which can be either ***semi-sensitive*** or ***insensitive***.

"Scrollable" means that you can scroll through the cursor result set by fetching any, or many, rows, rather than one row at a time; you can also scan the result set repeatedly. You must use **Transact-SQL or JDBC** to declare a scrollable cursor, and you must have the query engine provided in Adaptive Server 15.0 or later. When scrollable cursors are requested, either a server-side or client-side scrollable cursor may be invoked. Adaptive Server must support scrollable cursors in order for a server-side cursor to be invoked. If Adaptive Server does not support scrollable cursors, the desired functionality may be mimicked by the driver using **cached resultset**. This is known as client-side scrollable cursors.

- For scrollable cursors in ASE 15, the only valid cursor specifica- tion is "for read only."
- All update cursors are nonscrollable.

Section 1- What's New in ASE 15

- Non-scrollable, insensitive cursors are also supported on Open Server and are set with the **CS_NOSCROLL_INSENSITIVE** option.
- A new capability**, CS_REQ_CURINFO3**, is added to Open Server to support the new scrollable cursor feature. During login, **CS_REQ_CURINFO3** allows a remote client connecting to Open Server to request scrollable cursor support.
- The ASE ODBC Driver and the ASE OLE DB Provider can support both server-side and client-side scrollable cursors on ASE version 15.0 and later.

A scrollable cursor allows you to set the position of the cursor anywhere in the cursor result set for as long as the cursor is open, by specifying the option *first, last, absolute, next, prior,* absolute or *relative* in a fetch statement.

declare cursor_name
 [cursor_sensitivity]
 [cursor_scrollability] cursor
 for cursor_specification

Example:
declare CurSr scroll cursor for
 select emp_name from employees

Fetch extension	Description
first	Fetch the first row from the cursor result set.
last	Fetch the last row from the cursor result set.
next	Fetch the next row from the cursor result set. This is the default fetch performed when retrieving a row from a non-scrollable cursor. It is the only extension to the fetch command allowed in a non-scrollable cursor.
prior	Fetch the previous row in the cursor result set.
absolute n	Fetch the nth row in the cursor result set from the beginning of the cursor set.
relative n	Fetch the nth row in the cursor result set from the current cursor position.

Note: cursor_scrollability can be defined as **scroll** or no **scroll**. The default is **no scroll**. cursor_sensitivity can be defined as **insensitive** or **semi_sensitive**. The default for the cursor is **semi-sensitive**. No support for the concept of "sensitive" exists in ASE 15.

The **UseCursor** property must be set correctly in order to obtain the desired scrollable cursor.
Setting the UseCursor connection property:
- When you set the UseCursor connection property to 1, and the ASE version is 15.0 or later, server-side scrollable cursors are used. Server-side scrollable cursors are not available on all pre-15.0 ASE versions.
- When you set the UseCursor connection property to 0, client-side scrollable cursors (**cached resultsets**) are used, regardless of the ASE version.

Cursor related Global variables:

Cursor type	Variable @@rowcount works as
Forward only Cursor	Increments by one each time a row is fetched from a cursor until the number of rows in the cursor result set is equal to the rows fetched.
Scrollable Cursor	Can increment beyond the total count of rows in the cursor result set. There is no maximum value for @@rowcount. Regardless of the cursor direction specified in the fetch statement, @@rowcount will increment by one with each successful fetch. @@rowcount does not reflect the number of rows in the result set.

@@fatch_status:

Return value	Description
0	Successful fetch
-1	Failed fetch statement. Row requested is outside the result set, such as requesting the relative 20th row where cursor set contains only 15 rows.
-2	Reserved Value

@@cursor_rows:

Return value	Description
0	No rows qualified on the last open cursor, the last open cursor is closed or deallocated, or no cursors are open.
-1	The cursor is declared as scrollable and semi-sensitive, but the cursor's worktable is not fully populated. The number of rows the cursor worktable will contain is unknown.
-2	The last row in the scrollable sensitive cursor is reached, and the size of the worktable is known. @@cursor_rows will now reflect the number of rows contained by the cursor (n).

Rules for Scrollable Cursor:

next => A fetch utilizing the next extension when the cursor is already positioned in the last row of the cursor set will result in @@sqlstatus = 2, @@fetch_status = -1, and no data returned by the fetch. Cursor position will remain on the last row of the cursor set.

prior => A fetch utilizing the prior extension when the cursor is already positioned at the first row of the cursor result set will result in @@sqlstatus = 2, @@fetch_status = -1, and no data returned by the fetch. Cursor position will remain on the first row of the cursor set.

Note: A subsequent fetch of the next cursor row will fetch the first row of the cursor result set.

absolute => A fetch utilizing the absolute extension that calls a row that is greater than the rowcount in the cursor set will result in @@sqlstatus = 2, @@fetch_status of -1, and no data returned by the fetch.

Sensitivity and scrollability:
- **Insensitive:** The cursor shows only the result set as it is when the cursor is opened; data changes in the underlying tables are not visible
- **Semi-sensitive:** some changes in the base tables made since opening the cursor may appear in the result set. Data changes may or may not be visible to the semi-sensitive cursor.

Insensitive scrollable cursors:
When you declare and open an insensitive cursor, a worktable is created and fully populated with the cursor result set. Locks on the base table are released, and only the worktable is used for fetching.
To declare cursor CurSr_I as an insensitive cursor, enter:
declare CurSr_I insensitive scroll cursor for
select emp_id, fname, lname
from emp_tb
where emp_id > 2002000

open CurSr_I

The scrolling worktable is now populated with the data shown in Table 2-1. To change the name "Sam" to "Joe," enter:
update emp_tab set fname = "Joe"
where fname = "Sam"

Now four "Sam" rows in the base table emp_tab disappear, replaced by four "Joe" rows.

fetch absolute 2 CurSr_I

The cursor reads the second row from the cursor result set, and returns Row 2, "2002020, Sam, Clarac." Because the cursor is insensitive, the updated value is invisible to the cursor, and the value of the returned row—"Sam," rather than "Joe"—is the same as the value of Row 2 in Table 2-1.

Table 2-1

Row position	employee id	first name	last name
1	2002010	Mari	Cazalis
2	2002020	Sam	Clarac
3	2002030	Bill	Darby
4	2002040	Sam	Burke
5	2002050	Mary	Armand
6	2002060	Mickey	Phelan
7	2002070	Sam	Fife
8	2002080	Wanda	Wolfe
9	2002090	Nina	Howe
10	2002100	Sam	West

This next command inserts one more qualified row (that is, a row that meets the query condition in declare cursor) into table emp_tab, but the row membership is fixed in an cursor, so the added row is not visible to cursor CurSr_I. Enter:

insert into emp_tab values (2002101, "Sophie", "Chen", .., ..., ...)

The following fetch command scrolls the cursor to the end of the worktable, and reads the last row in the result set, returning the row value "2002100, Sam, West." Again, because the cursor is insensitive, the new row inserted in emp_tab is not visible in cursor CurSr_I's result set.

fetch last CurSr_I

Semisensitive scrollable cursors:
Semisensitive scrollable cursors are like insensitive cursors in that they use a worktable to hold the result set for scrolling purposes. But in **semi_sensitive** mode, the cursor's worktable materializes as the rows are fetched, rather than when you open the cursor. The membership of the result set is fixed only after all the rows have been fetched once.

To declare cursor CurSr_SS semisensitive and scrollable, enter:

declare CurSr_SS semi_sensitive scroll cursor for
select emp_id, fname, lname
from emp_tab
where emp_id > 2002000

open CurSr_SS

The initial rows of the result set contain the data shown in Table 2-1 (see above page). Because the cursor is semisensitive, none of the rows are copied to the worktable when you open the cursor. To fetch the first record, enter:

fetch first CurSr_SS

The cursor reads the first row from *emp_tab* and returns 2002010, Mari, Cazalis. This row is copied to the worktable. Fetch the next row by entering:

fetch next CurSr_SS

The cursor reads the second row from *emp_tab* and returns 2002020, Sam, Clarac. This row is copied to the worktable. To replace the name "Sam" with the name "Joe," enter:

update emp_tab set fname = "Joe"
where fname = "Sam"

The four "Sam" rows in the base table *emp_tab* disappear, and four "Joe" rows appear instead. To fetch only the second row, enter:

fetch absolute 2 CurSr_SS

The cursor reads the second row from the result set and returns employee ID 2002020, but the value of the returned row is "Sam," not "Joe." Because the cursor is semisensitive, this row was copied into the worktable before the row was updated, and the data change made by the **update** statement is invisible to the cursor, since the row returned comes from the result set scrolling worktable.

To fetch the fourth row, enter:

fetch absolute 4 CurSr_SS

The cursor reads the fourth row from the result set. Since Row 4, (2002040, Sam, Burke) was fetched after "Sam" was updated to "Joe," the returned employee ID 2002040 is Joe, Burke. The third and fourth rows are now copied to the worktable.

To add a new row, enter:

insert into emp_tab values (2002101, "Sophie", "Chen", .., ..., ...)

One more qualified row is added in the result set. This row is visible in the following **fetch** statement, because the cursor is semisensitive and because we have not yet fetched the last row. Fetch the updated version by entering:

fetch last CurSr_SS

The **fetch** statement reads 2002101, Sophie, Chen in the result set.

After using fetch with the **last** option, you have copied all the qualified rows of the cursor CurSr_SS to the worktable. Locking on the base table, *emp_tab*, is released, and the result set of cursor CurSr_SS is fixed. Any further data changes in *emp_tab* do not affect the result set of s.

Note: Locking schema and transaction isolation level also affect cursor visibility. The above example is based on the default isolation level, level 1.

1.3 Describe metrics capture

Query Processing Metrics:
Query processing (QP) metrics identify and compare empirical metric values in query execution. When a query is executed, it is associated with a set of defined metrics that are the basis for comparison in QP metrics.
Captured metrics include:
CPU execution time – the time, in milliseconds, it takes to execute the query.
Elapsed time – the time, in milliseconds, from after the compile to the end of the execution.
Logical I/O – the number of logical I/O reads.
Physical I/O – the number of physical I/O reads.
Count – the number of times a query is executed.
Abort count – the number of times a query is aborted by the resource governor due to a resource limit being exceeded.

Note: Each metric, except count and abort count, has three values: **minimum**, **maximum**, and **average**.

Enable QP metrics:
You can activate and use QP metrics at the **server level** or at the **session level**.
The QP metrics for ad hoc statements are captured directly into a system catalog, while the QP metrics for statements in a stored procedure are saved in a procedure cache. When the **stored procedure or query in the statement cache** is flushed, the respective captured metrics are written to the **system catalog**.
Enable at the Server Level :
sp_configure "enable metrics capture", 1

Enable at the Session Level:
set metrics_capture on/off

Restricting query metrics capture:

Section 1- What's New in ASE 15

There are four configuration parameters that set the query metrics threshold for capture into the catalog. These parameters are useful if you want to filter out trivial metrics before writing metrics information to the catalog. The syntax is:

sp_configure 'metrics lio max' | 'metrics pio max' |
'metrics elap max' | 'metrics exec max' , <value>

Configuration parameters:

parameters	Description
metrics elap max	If the elapsed time of the query is less than the value of metrics elap max, then the metrics associated with the query are not written to the system tables.
metrics exec max	If the execution time of the query is less than the value of metrics exec max, then the metrics associated with the query are not written to the system tables.
metrics lio max	If the logical IO time of the query is less than the value of metrics lio max, then the metrics associated with the query are not written to the system tables.
metrics pio max	If the physical IO time of the query is less than the value of metrics pio max, then the metrics associated with the query are not written to the system tables.

For example, the following will not capture those query plans for which lio is less than 10:
sp_configure 'metrics lio max', 10

If you **do not** set any of these configuration parameters, Adaptive Server captures the query metrics to the **system tables**. However, if you set any of these configuration parameters, Adaptive Server uses only those nonzero configuration parameters as thresholds for determining whether to capture query metrics.

For example, if you set metrics elap max to a non-zero value, but no others, query metrics are captured only if the elapsed time is bigger than the configured value. Because the other three configuration parameters are set to 0, they do not act as **thresholds** for capturing metrics.

Note: By default, these configuration parameters are set to 0 (off).

Clearing the metrics:
Use **sp_metrics 'flush'** to flush all aggregated metrics in **memory to the system catalog**. The aggregated metrics for all statements in memory are zeroed out.
The syntax of removing QP metrics from the system catalog is:
sp_metrics 'drop', '@gid' [, '@id']
To remove one entry, use:
sp_metrics 'drop', '<gid>', '<id>'

You can also use filter to remove QP metrics from the system catalog, based on some metrics conditions. The syntax is:
sp_metrics 'filter', '@gid', [, '@predicate']
For example:
sp_metrics 'filter','1','lio_max < 100'
deletes all QP metrics in group 1 where lio_max < 100.

Using sysquerymetrics and sp_metrics:

sp_metrics: Backs up, drops, and flushes QP metrics—always captured in the default running group, which is group 1 in each respective database—and their statistics on queries.
Syntax:
sp_metrics ['backup' backup_group_ID | 'drop', 'gid' [, 'id'] |
      'flush' | 'help', 'command']

Adaptive Server using sp_metrics to manage sysquerymetrics data. The data most currently collected is stored in sysquerymetrics with a global ID (GID) of 1. If you use the sp_metrics...backup parameter to save previous data, you must use a GID greater than 1 that is not already in use. To find the next available GID, select the max(gid) from sysquerymetrics and add one to the value.

sp_metrics examples:
To enable metrics capture, enter:
set metrics_capture on

To flush the metrics, enter:
sp_metrics 'flush'

To select a GID (if this returns a NULL value or 1, use a value of 2 or higher), enter:
select max(gid)+1 from sysquerymetrics

To back up the data, enter:
sp_metrics 'backup', '3'

To turn off metrics capture, enter:
set metrics_capture off

To analyze the data, enter:
*select * from sysquerymetrics where gid = 3*

To drop the data, enter:
sp_metrics 'drop', '2', '5'

Filtering the data in sysquerymetrics:
You can filter the data in sysquerymetrics by deleting data whose value is less than a predetermined value. You must enable allow updates before you delete data.
When you drop metrics, the begin range and end range must exist. For example, in this query, which attempts to drop the metrics from a group that starts with 3:
sp_metrics 'drop', '2', '5'
The drop fails because group 2 does not exist.
sysquerymetrics can consume a large amount of space in the system segment. However, to reduce the amount of space used:
1. Run **sp_metrics** capture.
2. At the end of the capture period, issue:
    Select max(gid) from sysquerymetrics
    sp_metrics 'backup', 'gid'
3. Start the next capture period.
4. Filter the previous results. For example, you can delete the rows that have an looming less than 10,000.
5. Repeat this sequence 10 to 15 times.

1.4 Identify and define new commands for getting optimizer information

How to create and maintain accurate statistics:
Statistics are kept up to date by regularly running the update statistics command, or by dropping and recreating indexes,which can be very time and resource consuming. In the past there were a number of 'rules of thumb' floating around among DBAs about when to update statistics.

The honest answer to the question was, is, and will always be—"It all depends on your data and your queries".

As we've seen, the 'why' of updating statistics is obvious and clear-cut; to provide the optimizer with the most accurate picture of your data as possible. The 'how' of maintaining accurate statistics offer you the opportunity to apply a little creativity to the process. By this point in your work with ASE you've likely developed your own statistics maintenance practices based on your system and experience. In most cases there shouldn't be a need to make many changes to this for ASE 15. One change that you should consider very seriously is putting and maintaining statistics on all columns of all your composite indexes, and on all columns that are referenced in queries (especially joins) that do not belong to any index.

Let's take a look at new ways in ASE 15 to make the statistics more accurate.

HistogramTuning Configuration Value:
This new configuration value was included in order to address an issue that appeared with the release of 11.9 – "How many steps should I use to make highly duplicated values visible to the optimizer?" and/or "How do I make sure data skew won't unexpectedly affect my performance?"

In past versions of ASE a DBA had to run problem queries against histograms with various numbers of steps before finding an optimal number to use with. Then the DBA had to make sure that all upstate statistics commands used the optimal requested steps for each column. For now it's important to understand that when a column contains some degree of data skew the histogram will be more accurate if it contains more steps. The greater the number of steps the more likely it is that the highly duplicated values will be represented by their own individual step or 'cell'. This in turn gives the optimizer very accurate information about the column and especially about the amount of duplication.

HistogramTuning Factor makes this complex tuning step automatic. No need to run test after test to find that 'sweet spot' number of steps.

Automatic Update Statistics:
To make life a little easier there are a few ways to automate update statistics. You can use **Job Scheduler** to run the job. You can set up automated update statistics as part of the **'self-management installation'** and you create your own **scripts** for the automation. All three of these methods use the new **datachange()** function. Automatic Update Statistics is simple and easy to set up and use. But, and there always seems to be one, keep in mind that having update statistics running on multiple table/indexes during the regular work day could have a nasty effect on overall performance.

See the 'ASE 15 Performance and Tuning Series: Query Processing and Abstract Plans' document in the manuals area of the Sybase web site for instructions on how to set up each option for Automatic Update Statistics.

New Datachange() function:
The datachange function is the key to identifying whether **update statistics** operations on a **table, index, partition, or column** is neces- sary. The datachange function returns a **value** to indicate how much the data has changed within a table, partition, index, or column. A value of 0% indicates no changes to the object are measured by the datachange function. As the data changes, the value returned will increase.

Syntax: *select datachange(object_name, partition_name, column_name)*

Measure the data changed at the table level:
select datachange("employees", null, null)
Measure the data change to the identification column of the employees table:
select datachange("employees ", null, "identification")
Measure the data change to the employees_part2 partition of the employees table:
select datachange("employee ", " employees part2", null)
Measure the data change to the identification column contained in the employees_part4 partition of the employees table:
select datachange("employees ", " employees_part4", "identification")

- The datachange function requires all three parameters.

- datachange is a measure of the inserts, deletes and updates but it does not count them individually. datachange counts an update as a delete and an insert, so each update contributes a count of 2 towards the datachange counter.
- The datachange built-in returns the datachange count as a percent of the number of rows, but it bases this percentage on the number of rows remaining, not the original number of rows. For example, if a table has five rows and one row is deleted, datachange reports a value of 25 % since the current row count is 4 and the datachange counter is 1.
- datachange is expressed as a percentage of the total number of rows in the table, or partition if you specify a partition. The percentage value can be greater than 100 percent because the number of changes to an object can be much greater than the number of rows in the table, particularly when the number of deletes and updates happening to a table is very high.
- The value that datachange displays is the in-memory value. This can differ from the on-disk value because the on-disk value gets updated by the housekeeper, when you run sp_flushstats, or when an object descriptor gets flushed.
- The datachange values is not reset when histograms are created for global indexes on partitioned tables.
- Instead of consuming resources, datachange discards the descriptor for an object that is not already in the cache.

datachange is reset or initialized to zero when:
- New columns are added, and their datachange value is initialized.
- New partitions are added, and their datachange value is initialized.
- Data-partition-specific histograms are created, deleted or updated. When this occurs, the datachange value of the histograms is reset for the corresponding column and partition.
- Data is truncated for a table or partition, and its datachange value is reset
- A table is repartitioned either directly or indirectly as a result of some other command, and the datachange value is reset for all the table's partitions and columns.
- A table is unpartitioned, and the datachange value is reset for all columns for the table.

datachange has the following restrictions:
- datachange statistics are not maintained on tables in system tempdbs, user-defined tempdbs, system tables, or proxy tables.
- datachange updates are non-transactional. If you roll back a transaction, the datachange values are not rolled back, and these values can become inaccurate.
- If memory allocation for column-level counters fails, Adaptive Server tracks partition-level datachange values instead of column-level values.
- If Adaptive Server does not maintain column-level datachange values, it then resets the partition-level datachange values whenever the datachange values for a column are reset.

Using set option show_missing_stats:
Prior to ASE 15 there were few methods that could be used to find columns that were missing statistics. The most common was to pour through optimizer related traceon outputs looking for missing statistics messages. This could become very time consuming to say the least.
Another time intensive method is to go through all your queries and all your table schemas matching queries to columns. Of course you could always use a shotgun approach by running 'update index statistics' on all your tables. This will put statistics on all columns in all indexes, but it will miss columns that are referenced by queries but not a part of an index. In that case, you could use the 'nuclear option' by running 'update all statistics' on all tables. Keep in mind that if you use this option it is likely to take days to complete and will be a major nightmare to maintain all the unnecessary statistics you'll create.

But in ASE 15 you can perform this chore quickly, easily and in a more focused way by using the new set option "show_missing_stats". Here's how it works – Identify a query that is causing a performance
problem and get its text. Then in ISQL or a script.
set option show_missing_stats on
go
dbcc traceon (3604)
go
set noexec on
go
your problem query here
go
NO STATS on column tableA.column1
NO STATS on column tableA.colum4
NO STATS on column tableB.colunm2
NO STATS on column tableB.column5
(This will be followed by your result set)
You can then easily compare this output to the table's schema to determine if you need to run 'update index statistics' and/or
'update statistics column_name' to put statistics on the columns where they're missing.

1.5 Describe ASE 15.0 optimization goals and their impact on query plans

Optimization goals:
The new "optimization goal" configuration parameter allows the user to choose the optimization strategy that best fits the query environment.

Optimization goals are a convenient way to match query demands with the best optimization techniques, thus ensuring optimal use of the optimizer's time and resources. The query optimizer allows you to configure three types of optimization goals, which you can specify at three tiers: **server level**, **session level**, and **query level**.

You can set the optimization goal at the desired level. The server-level optimization goal is overridden at the session level, which is overridden at the query level.

These optimization goals allow you to choose an optimization strategy that best fits your query environment:

parameter	Description
allrows_mix	The **default goal**, and the most useful goal in a mixed-query environment. allrows_mix balances the needs of **OLTP** and **DSS query environments**. allrows_mix is basically allrows_oltp + merge joins + parallelism.
allrows_dss	The most useful goal for **operational DSS queries of medium to high complexity**. Currently, this goal is provided on an experimental basis.
allrows_oltp	The optimizer considers only **nested-loop joins.** This option is basically allrows_mix + hash joins.

At the server level, use sp_configure. For example:
sp_configure "optimization goal", 0, "allrows_mix"
or
Modify the optimization goal configuration parameter in the Adaptive Server configuration file

At the session level, use set plan optgoal. For example:
set plan optgoal allrows_dss

At the query level, use a select or other DML command. For example:
select * from A order by A.col_name1 plan
  "(use optgoal allrows_dss)"

In general, you can set query-level optimization goals using **select, update, and delete** statements. However, you cannot set query-level optimization goals in pure insert statements, although you can set optimization goals in insert...select statements.

Limiting the time spent optimizing a query:
Long-running and complex queries can be time-consuming and costly to optimize. The timeout mechanism helps to limit that time while supplying a satisfactory query plan. The query optimizer provides a mechanism by which the optimizer can limit the time taken by long-running and complex queries; timing out allows the query processor to stop optimizing when it is reasonable to do so.

However, changing timeout values should be a last resort, as there are usually better alternatives to try. For example, make sure statistics exist (by using the show_missing_stats set command) and are up to date, since poor or missing statistics can result is overestimating costs which could result in excessive optimization time as the optimizer tries to find a better plan, even though the current best plan may actually execute quickly. Another solution for reducing compilation time, rather than reducing the timeout, is to turn on the statement cache so that queries that are re-executed frequently are only optimized once and cached. Another solution for complex queries could be to use allrows_oltp, which reduces the options considered during optimization. Yet another solution for reducing compilation time rather than reducing timeout is to use abstract plans. This effectively skips the optimizer and can be used if current performance is acceptable and it is anticipated that the data distribution changes are minimal or will not affect the query plans.

The optimizer triggers timeout during optimization when both these circumstances are met:
    At least one complete plan has been retained as the best plan.
    The user-configured timeout percentage limit has been exceeded.

You can limit the amount of time Adaptive Server spends optimizing a query at every level, setting the optimization timeout limit parameter to a value between 0 and 1000. The optimization timeout limit parameter represents the percentage of estimated query execution time that Adaptive Server must spend to optimize the query. For example, specifying a value of 10 tells Adaptive Server to spend 10% of the estimated query execution time in optimizing the query. Similarly, a value of 1000 tells Adaptive Server to spend 1000% of the estimated query execution time, or 10 times the estimated query execution time, in optimizing the query.

A separate configuration parameter, sproc optimize timeout limit, is used for stored procedures. It has a default value of 40 and a maximum value of 4000. Since a stored procedure is usually cached, it is worthwhile to spend more time looking for better plans for complex queries, since a procedure is optimized once and then cached for reuse.

A large timeout value may be useful for optimization of stored procedures with complex queries. It is expected that the longer optimization time of the stored procedures will yield better plans; the longer optimization time can be amortized over several executions of the stored procedure.

A small timeout value may be used when a faster compilation time is wanted from complex ad-hoc queries that normally take a long time to compile. However, for most queries, the default timeout value of 10 should suffice.

Use sp_configure to set the optimization timeout limit configuration parameter at the server level. For example, to limit optimization time to 10% of total query processing time, enter:

sp_configure "optimization timeout limit", 10

Use set to set optimization time at the session level:
set plan opttimeoutlimit <n>

Where n is any integer between 0 and 1000.

Use select to limit optimization time at the query level:
select * from <table> plan "(use opttimeoutlimit <n>)"

Where n is any integer between 0 and 1000. 0 is used to indicate that no timeout should be used, which could take hours to optimize queries with 20 or more tables if no low cost plan is found.
Default value: 10

Range of values: 0 – 1000

1.6 Describe the various join types (hash joins, merge joins, NLJ, N-ary NLJ)

Adaptive Server provides four primary JOIN operator strategies: NESTED LOOP JOIN, MERGE JOIN, HASH JOIN, and NARY NESTED LOOP JOIN, which is a variant of NESTED LOOP JOIN. In versions earlier than 15.0, NESTED LOOP JOIN was the primary JOIN strategy. MERGE JOIN was also available, but was, by default, not enabled

NESTED LOOP JOIN:
NESTED LOOP JOIN, the simplest join strategy, is a binary operator with the left child forming the outer data stream and the right child forming the inner data stream.
For every row from the outer data stream, the inner data stream is opened. Often, the right child is a scan operator. Opening the inner data stream effectively positions the scan on the first row that qualifies all of the searchable arguments. The qualifying row is returned to the NESTED LOOP JOIN's parent operator. Subsequent calls to the join operator continue to return qualifying rows from the inner stream.
After the last qualifying row from the inner stream is returned for the current outer row, the inner stream is closed. A call is made to get the next qualifying row from the outer stream. The values from this row provide the searchable arguments used to open and position the scan on the inner stream. This process continues until the NESTED LOOP JOIN's left child returns End Of Scan.
-- Collect all of the title ids for books written by "Bloom".
select ta.title_id
from titleauthor ta, authors a
where a.au_id = ta.au_id
and au_lname = "Bloom"
go
QUERY PLAN FOR STATEMENT 1 (at line 2).
STEP 1
The type of query is SELECT.
3 operator(s) under root
ROOT:EMIT Operator (VA = 3)
|NESTED LOOP JOIN Operator (Join Type: Inner Join)
|
| |SCAN Operator (VA = 0)
| | FROM TABLE
| | authors
| | a
| | Index : aunmind
| | Forward Scan.
| | Positioning by key.

| | Keys are:
| | au_lname ASC
| | Using I/O Size 2 Kbytes for index leaf pages.
| | With LRU Buffer Replacement Strategy for index leaf pages.
| | Using I/O Size 2 Kbytes for data pages.
| | With LRU Buffer Replacement Strategy for data pages.
| |
| | SCAN Operator (VA = 1)
| | FROM TABLE
| | titleauthor
| | ta
| | Using Clustered Index.
| | Index : taind
| | Forward Scan.
| | Positioning by key.
| | Keys are:
| | au_id ASC
| | Using I/O Size 2 Kbytes for data pages.
| | With LRU Buffer Replacement Strategy for data pages.

The authors table is joined with the titleauthor table. A NESTED LOOP JOIN strategy has been chosen. The NESTED LOOP JOIN operator's type is "Inner Join." First, the authors table is opened and positioned on the first row (using the aunmind index) containing an l_name value of "Bloom." Then, the titleauthor table is opened and positioned on the first row with an au_id equal to the au_id value of the current authors' row using the clustered index "taind." If there is no useful index for lookups on the inner stream, the optimizer may generate a reformatting strategy.

Note: Generally, a NESTED LOOP JOIN strategy is effective when there is a useful index available for qualifying the join predicates on the inner stream.

MERGE JOIN:
The MERGE JOIN operator is a binary operator. The left and right children are the outer and inner data streams, respectively. Both data streams must be sorted on the MERGE JOIN's key values. First, a row from the outer stream is fetched. This initializes the MERGE JOIN's join key values. Then, rows from the inner stream are fetched until a row with key values that match or are greater than (less than if key column is descending) is encountered. If the join key matches, the qualifying row is passed on for additional processing, and a subsequent next call to the MERGE JOIN operator continues fetching from the currently active stream.
If the new values are greater than the current comparison key, these values are used as the new comparison join key while fetching rows from the other stream. This process continues until one of the data streams is exhausted.

Section 1- What's New in ASE 15

> Note: Generally, the MERGE JOIN strategy is effective when a scan of the data streams requires that most of the rows must be processed, and that, if any of the input streams are large, they are already sorted on the join keys.

```
select ta.title_id
from titleauthor ta, authors a
where a.au_id = ta.au_id
and au_lname = "Bloom"
go
QUERY PLAN FOR STATEMENT 1 (at line 2).
STEP 1
The type of query is EXECUTE.
Executing a newly cached statement.
QUERY PLAN FOR STATEMENT 1 (at line 1).
STEP 1
The type of query is SELECT.
3 operator(s) under root
ROOT:EMIT Operator (VA = 3)
|MERGE JOIN Operator (Join Type: Inner Join)
| Using Worktable2 for internal storage.
| Key Count: 1
| Key Ordering: ASC
|
| |SORT Operator
| | Using Worktable1 for internal storage.
| |
| | |SCAN Operator
| | | FROM TABLE
| | | authors
| | | a
| | | Index : aunmind
| | | Forward Scan.
| | | Positioning by key.
| | | Keys are:
| | | au_lname ASC
| | | Using I/O Size 2 Kbytes for index leaf pages.
| | | With LRU Buffer Replacement Strategy for index leaf pages.
| | | Using I/O Size 2 Kbytes for data pages.
| | | With LRU Buffer Replacement Strategy for data pages.
|
| |SCAN Operator
| | FROM TABLE
| | titleauthor
| | ta
| | Index : auidind
| | Forward Scan.
| | Positioning at index start.
| | Using I/O Size 2 Kbytes for index leaf pages.
| | With LRU Buffer Replacement Strategy for index leaf pages.
```

| | Using I/O Size 2 Kbytes for data pages.
| | With LRU Buffer Replacement Strategy for data pages.

In this example, a sort operator is the left child, or outer stream. The data source for the sort operator is the authors table. The sort operator is required because the authors table has no index on au_id that would otherwise provide the necessary sorted order. A scan of the titleauthor table is the right child/inner stream. The scan uses the auidind index, which provides the necessary ordering for the MERGE JOIN strategy.
A row is fetched from the outer stream (the authors table is the original source) to establish an initial join key comparison value. Then rows are fetched from the titleauthor table until a row with a join key equal to or greater than the comparison key is found.
Inner stream rows with matching keys are stored in a cache in case they need to be refetched. These rows are refetched when the outer stream contains duplicate keys. When a titleauthor.au_id value that is greater than the current join key comparison value is fetched, the MERGE JOIN operator starts fetching from the outer stream until a join key value equal to or greater than the current titleauthor.au_id value is found. The scan of the inner stream resumes at that point.
The MERGE JOIN operator's showplan output contains a message indicating the worktable to be used for the inner stream's backing store. The worktable is written to if the inner rows with duplicate join keys no longer fits in cached memory. The width of a cached row is limited to 64 kilobytes.

HASH JOIN:
The HASH JOIN operator is a binary operator. The left child generates the build input stream. The right child generates the probe input stream. The build set is generated by completely draining the build input stream when the first row is requested from the HASH JOIN operator. Every row is read from the input stream and hashed into an appropriate bucket using the hash key. If there is not enough memory to hold the entire build set, then a portion of it spills to disk. This portion is referred to as a *hash partition* and should not be confused with table partitions. A hash partition consists of a collection of hash buckets. After the entire left child's stream has been drained, the probe input is read.
Each row from the probe set is hashed. A lookup is done in the corresponding build bucket to check for rows with matching hash keys. This occurs if the build set's bucket is memory resident. If it has been spilled, the probe row is written to the corresponding spilled probe partition. When a probe row's key matches a build row's key, then the necessary projection of the two row's columns is passed up for additional processing.
Spilled partitions are processed in subsequent recursive passes of the HASH JOIN algorithm. New hash seeds are used in each pass so that the data is redistributed across different hash buckets. This recursive processing continues until the last spilled partition is completely memory resident. When a hash partition from the build set contains many duplicates, the HASH JOIN operator reverts back to NESTED LOOP JOIN processing.
Generally, the HASH JOIN strategy is good in cases where most of the rows from the source sets must be processed and there are no inherent useful orderings on the join keys or there are no interesting orderings that can be promoted to calling operators (for example, an order by clause on the join key). HASH JOINs perform particularly well if one of the data sets is small enough to be

memory resident. In this case, no spilling occurs and no I/O is needed to perform that HASH JOIN algorithm.

```
select ta.title_id
from titleauthor ta, authors a
where a.au_id = ta.au_id
and au_lname = "Bloom"
QUERY PLAN FOR STATEMENT 1 (at line 2).
3 operator(s) under root
The type of query is SELECT.
ROOT:EMIT Operator
|HASH JOIN Operator (Join Type: Inner Join)
| Using Worktable1 for internal storage.
|
| |SCAN Operator
| | FROM TABLE
| | authors
| | a
| | Index : aunmind
| | Forward Scan.
| | Positioning by key.
| | Keys are:
| | au_lname ASC
| | Using I/O Size 2 Kbytes for index leaf pages.
| | With LRU Buffer Replacement Strategy for index leaf pages.
| | Using I/O Size 2 Kbytes for data pages.
| | With LRU Buffer Replacement Strategy for data pages.
|
| |SCAN Operator
| | FROM TABLE
| | titleauthor
| | ta
| | Index : auidind
| | Forward Scan.
| | Positioning at index start.
| | Using I/O Size 2 Kbytes for index leaf pages.
| | With LRU Buffer Replacement Strategy for index leaf pages.
| | Using I/O Size 2 Kbytes for data pages.
| | With LRU Buffer Replacement Strategy for data pages.
```

In this example, the source of the build input stream is an index scan of author.aunmind. Only rows with an au_lname value of "Bloom" are returned from this scan. These rows are then hashed on their au_id value and placed into their corresponding hash bucket. After the initial build phase is completed, the probe stream is opened and scanned. Each row from the source index, titleauthor.auidind, is hashed on the au_id column. The resulting hash value is used to determine which bucket in the build set should be searched for matching hash keys. Each row from the build set's hash bucket is compared to the probe row's hash key for equality. If the row matches, the titleauthor.au_id column is returned to the EMIT operator.

The HASH JOIN operator's showplan output contains a message indicating the worktable to be used for the spilled partition's backing store. The input row width is limited to 64 kilobytes.

NARY NESTED LOOP JOIN operator:

The NARY NESTED LOOP JOIN strategy is never evaluated or chosen by the optimizer. It is an operator that is constructed during code generation. If the compiler finds series of two or more left-deep NESTED LOOP JOINs, it attempts to transform them into a NARY NESTED LOOP JOIN operator. Two additional requirements allow for transformation scan; each NESTED LOOP JOIN operator has an "inner join" type and the right child of each NESTED LOOP JOIN is a SCAN operator. A RESTRICT operator is permitted above the SCAN operator.

NARY NESTED LOOP JOIN execution has a performance benefit over the execution of a series of NESTED LOOP JOIN operators. The example below demonstrates a fundamental difference between the two methods of execution.

With a series of NESTED LOOP JOIN, a scan may eliminate rows based on searchable argument values initialized by an earlier scan. That scan may not be the one that immediately preceded the failing scan. With a series of NESTED LOOP JOINs, the previous scan would be completely drained although it has no effect on the failing scan. This could result in a significant amount of needless I/O. With NARY NESTED LOOP JOINs, the next row fetched comes from the scan that produced the failing searchable argument value, which is far more efficient.

```
select a.au_id, au_fname, au_lname
from titles t, titleauthor ta, authors a
where a.au_id = ta.au_id
and ta.title_id = t.title_id
and a.au_id = t.title_id
and au_lname = "Bloom"
QUERY PLAN FOR STATEMENT 1 (at line 1).
STEP 1
The type of query is SELECT.
4 operator(s) under root
|ROOT:EMIT Operator (VA = 4)
|
|  |N-ARY NESTED LOOP JOIN Operator (VA = 3) has 3 children.
|  |  | SCAN Operator (VA = 0)
|  |  | FROM TABLE
|  |  | authors
|  |  | a
|  |  | Table Scan.
|  |  | Forward Scan.
|  |  | Positioning at start of table.
|  |  | Using I/O Size 2 Kbytes for data pages.
|  |  | With LRU Buffer Replacement Strategy for data pages.
|
|  |  |SCAN Operator (VA = 1)
|  |  | FROM TABLE
|  |  | titleauthor
|  |  | ta
```

| | | Table Scan.
| | | Forward Scan.
| | | Positioning at start of table.
| | | Using I/O Size 2 Kbytes for data pages.
| | | With LRU Buffer Replacement Strategy for data pages.
| |
| | | SCAN Operator (VA = 2)
| | | FROM TABLE
| | | titles
| | | t
| | | Index : titles_6720023942
| | | Forward Scan.
| | | Positioning by key.
| | | Index contains all needed columns. Base table will not be read.
| | | Keys are:
| | | title_id ASC
| | | Using I/O Size 2 Kbytes for index leaf pages.
| | | With LRU Buffer Replacement Strategy for index leaf pages.

Summary

In this section, you read about **What is new in ASE 15.**

- Adaptive Server supports local and global indexes.

    Local index – spans data in exactly one data partition

    Global index – spans all data partitions in a table.

- Adaptive Server Enterprise allows both scrollable and nonscrollable cursors, which can be either ***semi-sensitive*** or ***insensitive***.

- Query processing (QP) metrics identify and compare empirical metric values in query execution. When a query is executed, it is associated with a set of defined metrics that are the basis for comparison in QP metrics.

- The **datachange()** function is the key to identifying whether update statistics operations on a table, index, partition, or column is neces- sary.

- The query optimizer allows you to configure three types of optimization goals, which you can specify at three tiers: server level, session level, and query level.

- Adaptive Server provides four primary JOIN operator strategies: NESTED LOOP JOIN, MERGE JOIN, HASH JOIN, and NARY NESTED LOOP JOIN, which is a variant of NESTED LOOP JOIN. In versions earlier than 15.0, NESTED LOOP JOIN was the primary JOIN strategy. MERGE JOIN was also available, but was, by default, not enabled

Practice Test

1. What conditions must be met before altering the partition strategy of a table from round-robin to a range partitioned table?
    A. Additional partitions must be added to the round-robin table
    B. Table must be un-partitioned before changing partition strategy
    C. Table data must be truncated
    D. Table indexes must be dropped

2. Global indexes can be clustered on
    A. Round robin partitioned tables only.
    B. Round robin or range partitioned tables.
    C. Round robin, range or hash partitioned tables.
    D. List partitioned tables only.

3. Scrollable Cursor can NOT be
    A. semi-sensitive
    B. insensitive
    C. sensitive
    D. None of the above

4. Which of the following are TRUE about the cursor fetch statement? (Choose 2)
    A. The row number starts at 0.
    B. If fetch behavior is not specified, the next row is assumed by default.
    C. For a scrollable cursor, @@rowcount cannot exceed the total number of rows in the result set.
    D. @@fetch_status=0 implies the last fetch was successful.

5. Which of the following statement is NOT true?
    A. You can not use QP metrics at the server level.
    B. You can activate and use QP metrics at the session level.
    C. The QP metrics for ad hoc statements are captured directly into a system catalog
    D. QP metrics for statements in a stored procedure are saved in a procedure cache.

6. What is used to determine how many rows qualify for the search argument?
    A. Histogram
    B. Forwarded rows
    C. Data cluster ratio
    D. Index cluster ratio

7. If a query should use Nested Loop Joins, what optimization goal setting is recommended?
    A. None, use the default
    B. allrows_mix
    C. allrows_oltp
    D. allrows_dss

Section 2 - ASE Performance and Tuning Basics

2.1 Define tradeoffs of performance & tuning - with an emphasis on code

Performance and tuning is a vast topic to discuss. There is lot to read in Section 6 and 7. We will read only main topics in this section.

sp_configure:
Displays configuration parameters by group, their current values, their default values, the value to which they have most recently been set, and the amount of memory used by this setting. Displays only the parameters whose display level is the same as or below that of the user.
Syntax
sp_configure [configname [, configvalue] | group_name |
   non_unique_parameter_fragment]
sp_configure "configuration file", 0, {"write" | "read" | "verify" | "restore"}
   "file_name"

parameter	Description
Configname	Displays the current value, default value, most recently changed value, and amount of memory used by the setting for all parameters matching parameter.
Configvalue	Resets configname to configvalue and displays the current value, default value, configured value, and amount of memory used by configname. sp_configure configname, 0, "default" resets configname to its default value and displays current value, default value, configured value, and amount of memory used by configname.
group_name	Displays all configuration parameters in group_name, their current values, their default values, the value (if applicable) to which they have most recently been set, and the amount of memory used by this setting.
non_unique_parameter_fragment	Displays all parameter names that match non_unique_parameter_fragment, their current values, default values, configured values, and the amount of memory used.
Write	Creates file_name from the current configuration.
Read	Performs validation checking on values contained in file_name and reads those values that pass validation into the server. If any parameters are missing from file_name, the current running values for those parameters are used.
Verify	Performs validation checking on the values in file_name.

Restore	Creates file_name with the values in sysconfigures. This is useful if all copies of the configuration file have been lost and you need to generate a new copy
file_name	is the name of the file you want to use sp_configure on.

Examples:
Example 1
Displays all configuration parameters by group, their current values, their default values, the value (if applicable) to which they have most recently been set, and the amount of memory used by this setting:
sp_configure
Example 2
Displays all configuration parameters that include the word "identity":
sp_configure "identity"

Configuration option is not unique.

Parameter Name	Default	Memory Used	Config Value	Run Value	Unit	Type
identity burning set factor	5000	0	5000	5000	number	static
identity grab size	1	0	1	1	number	dynamic
identity reservation size	1	0	1	1	number	dynamic
size of auto identity column	10	0	10	10	bytes	dynamic

Example 3
Sets the system recovery interval in minutes to 3 minutes:
sp_configure "recovery interval in minutes", 3

Parameter Name	Default	Memory Used	Config Value	Run Value	Unit	Type
recovery interval in minutes	5	0	3	3	minutes	dynamic

Configuration option changed. The SQL Server need not be rebooted since the option is dynamic.

Example 4
Resets the value for number of devices to the Adaptive Server default:
sp_configure "number of device", 0, "default"
Example 5
Configures four databases to be recovered concurrently, enter:
sp_configure "max concurrently recovered db", 4
Example 6
Starts four checkpoint tasks, enter:
sp_configure "number of checkpoint tasks", 4
Example 7

Captures Query Processing metrics (qp metrics) at the server level:
sp_configure "enable metrics capture", 1
Example 8
Performs validation checking on the values in the file srv.config and reads the parameters that pass validation into the server. Current run values are substituted for values that do not pass validation checking:
sp_configure "configuration file", 0, "read", "srv.config"
Example 9
Runs validation checking on the values in the file restore.config:
sp_configure "configuration file", 0, "restore", "generic.config"
Example 10
Creates the file my_server.config and writes the current configuration values the server is using to that file:
sp_configure "configuration file", 0, "write",   "my_server.config"

Note: If file_name already exists, a message is written to the error log and the existing file is renamed using the convention file_name.001, file_name.002, and so on. If you have changed a static parameter but have not restarted your server, "write" gives you the currently running value for that parameter.

Example 11
Performs a validation check on the values in $SYBASE/backup_config.cfg:
sp_configure "configuration file", 0, "verify",   "$SYBASE/backup_config.cfg"

Adaptive Server uses the logical page size for the basic unit, other unit specifiers are p or P (page), m or M (megabytes), g or G (gigabytes) and t or T (terabytes).

When you execute sp_configure to modify a dynamic parameter:
- The configuration and run values are updated.
- The configuration file is updated.
- The change takes effect **immediately**.

When you execute sp_configure to modify a static parameter:
- The configuration value is updated.
- The configuration file is updated.
- The change takes effect only when you **restart** Adaptive Server.

Each configuration parameter has an associated display level. There are three display levels:
basic , intermediate and comprehensive
The default display level is "comprehensive". The syntax for showing your current display level is:
sp_displaylevel

The MDA Tables:

MDA is an acronym for Monitoring and Diagnostic Access. The Monitoring and Diagnostic Access "tables" are proxy tables on top of native server remote procedure calls (RPCs). These proxy tables can be materialized in any database or on another server, such as a monitoring repository. MDA tables can be accessed with regular SQL select statements, they're much easier to use than products like Monitor Server/Historical Server.

The MDA tables report information about ASE at a low level. Unlike the sp_sysmon process, which reports performance information at the server level, the MDA tables report data at the query and table level in addition to the server level. Further, the MDA tables provide information on current activity at the table, procedure, query, and process levels.

Before querying the MDA tables, they must have been installed first, and some ASE configuration parameters must have been set.
Follow these installation steps:

First, ensure that the configuration parameter 'enable cis' is set to 1 (if not, an ASE restart is needed)
sp_configure 'enable cis', 1
go

Next, within the $SYBASE (/Sybase) directory, under the ASE_15-0/scripts subdirectory, execute the following script to install the MDA proxy tables:

hostname:/sybase/ASE-15_0/scripts 1> isql -Usa –SSYBASE -iinstallmontables -oinstallmontables.out

Finally, grant the mon_role to any administrative user who will need access to the MDA tables:
exec sp_role 'grant','mon_role','sa'
go
exec sp_role 'grant','mon_role','mda_others'
go

Test basic MDA configuration: (note: you may need to disconnect/reconnect first to activate 'mon_role' when you just granted this role to the login you're currently using)
select * from master..monState
go

MDA tables in ASE 15:
select TableName, Description from master..monTables
go

Table-2-1

Name	Description

monTables	Provides a description of all of the available monitoring tables
monTableParameters	Provides a description of all of the optional parameters for each monitoring table
monTableColumns	Provides a description of all of the columns for each monitoring table
monState	Provides information regarding the overall state of the ASE
monEngine	Provides statistics regarding ASE engines
monDataCache	Provides statistics relating to data cache usage
monProcedureCache	Provides server-wide information related to cached procedures
monOpenDatabases	Provides state and statistical information for databases that are currently in use (i.e., open databases)
monSysWorkerThread	Provides server-wide statistics about worker threads
monNetworkIO	Provides server-wide statistics about network I/O
monErrorLog	Provides the most recent error messages raised by ASE. The maximum number of messages returned can be tuned by use of the "errorlog pipe max messages" configuration option.
monLocks	Provides information for all locks that are being held and those that have been requested by any process for every object
monDeadLock	Provides information about the most recent deadlocks that have occurred. The maximum number of messages returned can be tuned by use of the "deadlock pipe max messages" configuration option.
monWaitClassInfo	Provides a textual description for all of the wait classes, e.g., "waiting for a disk read to complete." All wait events (see the monWaitEventInfo table) have been grouped into the appropriate wait class.
monWaitEventInfo	Provides a textual description for every possible situation where a process is forced to wait for an event, e.g., "wait for buffer read to complete"
monCachedObject	Provides statistics for all objects and indexes that currently have pages cached within a data cache
monCachePool	Provides statistics for all pools allocated for all caches
monOpenObjectActivity	Provides statistics for all open objects
monIOQueue	Provides device I/O statistics, broken down into data and log I/O, for normal and temporary databases on each device
monDeviceIO	Provides statistical information about devices
monSysWaits	Provides a server-wide view of events that processes are waiting for
monProcess	Provides information about processes that are currently executing or waiting
monProcessLookup	Provides information enabling processes to be tracked to an application, user, client machine, etc.
monProcessActivity	Provides statistics about process activity
monProcessWorkerThread	Provides information about process use of worker threads
monProcessNetIO	Provides statistics about process network I/O activity

monProcessObject	Provides statistical information about process object access
monProcessWaits	Provides information about each event that a process has waited for or is currently waiting for
monProcessStatement	Provides statistics for currently executing statements
monSysStatement	Provides statistics for the most recently executed statements. The maximum number of statement statistics returned can be tuned by use of the "statement pipe max messages" configuration option.
monProcessSQLText	Provides the SQL text that is currently being executed. The maximum size of the SQLtext returned can be tuned by use of the "max SQL text monitored" configuration option.
monSysSQLText	Provides the most recently executed SQL text. The maximum number messages returned can be tuned by use of the "sql text pipe max messages" configuration option.
monCachedProcedures	Provides statistics about all procedures currently stored in the procedure cache
monProcessProcedures	Provides information about procedures that are being executed
monSysPlanText	Provides the most recently generated plan text. The maximum number of messages returned can be tuned by use of the "plan text pipe max messages" configuration option.
monOpenPartitionActivity	Provides statistics for all open partitions

New in ASE 15:
For ASE 15, one new MDA table was added, in addition to two modifications on existing MDA tables in order to add functionality for the monitoring of semantically partitioned tables. The following list briefly describes the MDA tables that have been modified or are new in ASE 15.
monProcessObject : Updated to provide information about each partition of an object a process is accessing rather than reporting at the object level.
Note the partition information presented when accessing a table with round-robin partitions:
select DBName, ObjectName, PartitionName, PartitionSize from monProcessObject

monCachedObject : Updated to provide information about each partition of an object found in cache rather than reporting at the object level.
The following query highlights current access to a partition. The query limits the search where ProcessesAccessing is greater than 0 in order to display objects currently accessed by users:
select PartitionID, CacheName, ObjectName, PartitionName from monCachedObject where ProcessesAccessing > 0

monOpenPartitionActivity — A new MDA table for ASE 15. This table is very similar to the monOpenObjectActivity table but at the partition level. For ASE 15 partitioned tables, this MDA table will show the monitoring information for each partition of the object. If the object is not partitioned beyond the single default partition (remember all tables in ASE 15 are considered partitioned) the table shows the same information as monOpenObjectActivity.

The following query highlights a range partitioned table undergoing a large insert:
select PartitionName, LogicalReads, PhysicalWrites, PagesWritten, RowsInserted from monOpenPartitionActivity
where ObjectName = "Employee_Trans"
go

Note: The monOpenObjectActivity table has not changed and will provide the same information as previous releases. For partitioned objects, the monitoring information is aggregated to provide monitoring information for the object as a whole.

Historical/Stateful MDA tables:
The complete list of stateful historical tables is:
- monDeadLock
- monErrorLog
- monSysPlanText
- monSysSQLText
- monSysStatement

Note: Avoid subqueries and joins on the MDA tables. Use the construct of the "permanent" MDA table database or copy the targeted MDA rows to tempdb as the first step of any query against the MDA data.

The MDA tables are memory resident. A join executed between MDA tables will result in performance degradation for the target instance of ASE. Additionally, two references to the same table in one query, as provided in a self join, will likely result in the comparison of result sets that are not identical.

Some useful queries:
select ObjectName, CacheName, CachedKB from monCachedObject where ObjectName = "Employee_Trans"
go
Above query will be, if table "Employee_Trans" is in cache or not

select SQLText from monSysSQLText where SQLText like "% Employee_Trans %"
go
Above query will display, "Employee_Trans" table has accessed by what SQLs.

Like above queries you can many things by using MDA tables listed in Table-2-1.
sp_sysmon:
A system procedure that produces Adaptive Server performance data. sp_sysmon output is most valuable when you have a good understanding of your Adaptive Server environment and its specific mix of applications. It displays statistics about the internal resource usage of the server.

In general, sp_sysmon produces valuable information when you use it:
- Before and after cache or pool configuration changes
- Before and after certain sp_configure changes
- Before and after the addition of new queries to your application mix
- Before and after an increase or decrease in the number of Adaptive Server engines
- When adding new disk devices and assigning objects to them
- During peak periods, to look for contention or bottlenecks
- During stress tests to evaluate an Adaptive Server configuration for a maximum expected application load
- When performance seems slow or behaves abnormally

It can also help with micro-level understanding of certain queries or applications during development.
Some examples are:
- Working with indexes and updates to see if certain updates reported as deferred_varcol are resulting direct vs. deferred updates
- Checking caching behavior of particular queries or a mix of queries
- Tuning the parameters and cache configuration for parallel index creation

There are two ways to invoke/use sp_sysmon:
1. Using a fixed time interval to provide a sample for a specified number of minutes
Syntax:
sp_sysmon interval [, section [, applmon]]
Note: ***interval*** must be in the form "hh:mm:ss"

Examples:
To run sp_sysmon for 5 minutes
sp_sysmon "00:05:00"

prints only the "Data Cache Management" report:
sp_sysmon "00:05:00", dcache

Note: See Table 2-2 for section parameters and Table 2-3 for applmon parameters.

2. Using the begin_sample and end_sample parameters to start and stop sampling

sp_sysmon begin_sample
execute proc1
execute proc2
select sum(amount) from Employee_Trans
sp_sysmon end_sample

Table 2-2

Section Parameter	Report section description

appmgmt	Application Management
dcache	Data Cache Management
diskio	Disk I/O Management
esp	ESP Management
housekeeper	Housekeeper Task Activity
indexmgmt	Index Management
kernel	Kernel Utilization
locks	Lock Management
memory	Memory Management
mdcache*	Metadata Cache Management
monaccess	Monitor Access to Executing SQL
netio	Network I/O Management
parallel	Parallel Query Management
pcache	Procedure Cache Management
recovery	Recovery Management
taskmgmt	Task Management
xactmgmt	Transaction Management
xactsum	Transaction Profile
wpm	Worker Process Management

Table 2-3

applmon Parameter	Information reported
appl_only	CPU, I/O, priority changes, and resource limit violations by application name.
appl_and_login	CPU, I/O, priority changes, and resource limit violations by application name and login name.
no_appl	Skips the application and login section of the report. This is the default.

Note: If you specify **applmon** parameter (third parameter), the report includes detailed information by application or by application and login name. This parameter is valid only when you print the entire report or when you request the "Application Management" section by specifying **appmgmt** as the section parameter. It is ignored if you specify it and request any other section parameter of the report for example pcache.

sp_monitor: Displays statistics about Adaptive Server.
Syntax
sp_monitor [connection, [cpu | diskio | elapsed time]]
  [event, [spid]] [procedure, [dbname, [procname,
  [, summary | detail]]]] [enable] [disable]
  [statement, [cpu | diskio | elapsed time]] [help],
  [connection | statement | procedure | event | deadlock | procstack]

The syntax for sp_monitor 'connection':

sp_monitor [connection, [cpu | diskio | elapsed time]]

The syntax for sp_monitor 'event':
sp_monitor [event, [spid]]

The syntax for sp_monitor 'procedure':
sp_monitor [procedure, [dbname , [procname, [, summary | detail]]]]

Parameters	Description
connection	Displays information on each connection. connection uses the following monitoring tables: • monProcessSQLText • monProcessActivity
cpu | diskio | elapsed time	These parameters order the output of **sp_monitor connection**. **cpu** indicates the amount of CPU time consumed by each different connection. **diskio** indicates the number of physical reads performed by each connection. **elapsed time** indicates the sum of the CPU time and the wait times for each connection.
event	Displays three possibilities. When you specify: • No option – only user tasks are displayed. • sp_monitor, event, "-1" – wait information about all tasks, both user and system, is displayed. • sp_monitor, event, "spid" – wait information pertaining to only the specified server process ID is displayed.
spid	Allows you to obtain event information for a specific task by entering its spid. You must specify the numeric value of spid within quotation marks.

procedure	Displays statistics about stored procedures:
	  ProcName – the stored procedure being monitored.
	  DBNAME – the database in which the stored procedure is located.
	  NumExecs – the approximate number of executions of this specific stored procedure.
	  AvgCPUTime – the average CPU time that it takes for the stored procedure to execute.
	  AvgPhysicalReads – the average number of disk reads performed by the stored procedure.
	  AvgLogicalReads – the average number of logical reads performed by the stored procedure.
	  AvgMemUsed_KB – the average amount of memory in KB used by the stored procedure.
	Note: procedure uses the **monSysStatement** monitoring table.

dbname	Displays information on procedures for the specified database.
procname	Displays information on the specified procedure
summary | detail	Displays either summary information, which provides an average of all instances of the procedure, or detailed information, which provides information on every instance of the stored procedure.
enable	Enables the new options for **sp_monitor**. It turns on the configuration

	parameter required to begin monitoring.
disable	Disables monitoring.
statement	Displays information on each statement. statement uses the following monitoring tables: • monProcessSQLText • monProcessStatement
cpu | diskio | elapsed time	These parameters help order the output of **sp_monitor** statement. **cpu** indicates the the cpu time consumed by different statements. **diskio** indicates the number of physical reads done by different statements. **elapsed time** indicates the sum of the CPU time and the wait times for different statements.
help	Displays the syntax and examples for sp_monitor, and also reports extensive information on using this procedure for deadlock analysis: sp_monitor 'help', 'deadlock'
deadlock	Tells **sp_monitor** to process historical data from the **monDeadlock** table, and prints out a **block** of output for each instance of deadlock\
Procstack	Examines the execution context of a task, including that of a deeply nexted stored procedure. The stack of procedures executed is extracted from the **monProcessProcedures** monitoring table.

Examples:
Identifies the connections performing the most physical reads:
sp_monitor "connection","diskio"

Displays the events each task spent time waiting for and the duration of the wait, reported in descending order of wait times:
sp_monitor "event"

Provides a summary of most recently run procedures, sorted in descending order of average elapsed time. This example provides historical monitoring information rather than the current state.
sp_monitor "procedure"

2.2 Identify steps involved in executing a query

The query processor is designed to process queries you specify. The processor yields highly efficient query plans that execute using minimal resources, and ensure that results are consistent and correct.
To process a query efficiently, the query processor uses:
- The specified query
- Statistics about the tables, indexes, and columns named in the query
- Configurable variables

The query processor has to execute several steps, using several modules, to successfully process a query:

Query Processor modules:

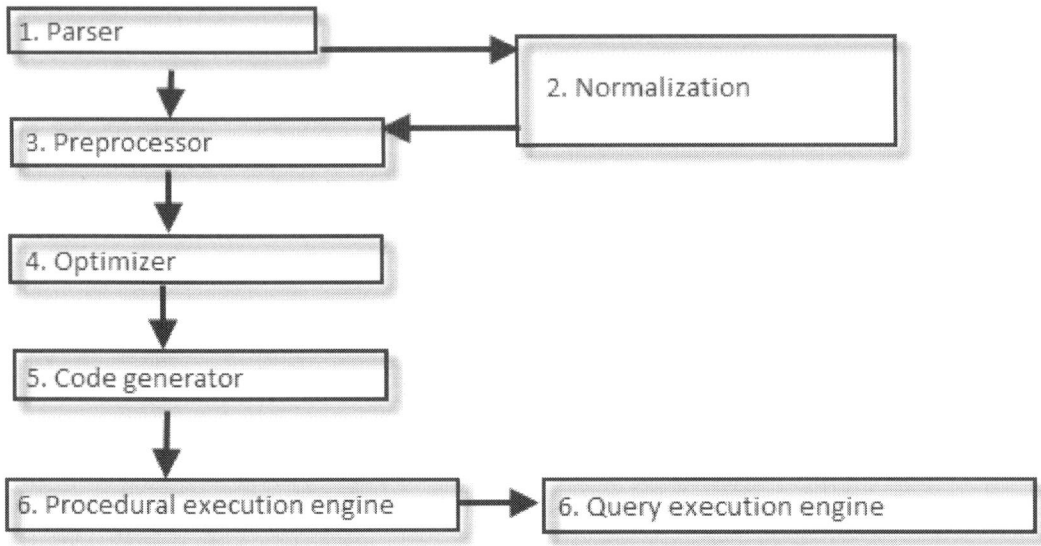

Above modules works as following:
1. The **parser** converts the text of the SQL statement to an internal representation called a **query tree**.
2. This query tree is **normalized**. This involves determining column and table names, transforming the query tree into **conjugate normal form (CNF)**, and resolving datatypes. At this point, you can determine if the statement may benefit from using the statement cache.
3. The **preprocessor** transforms the query tree for some types of SQL statements.
4. The **optimizer** analyzes the possible combinations of operations (join ordering, access and join methods, parallelism) to execute the SQL statement, and selects an efficient one based on the **cost estimates** of the alternatives.
5. The code generator converts the query plan generated by the **optimizer** into a format more suitable for the query **execution engine**.
6. The **procedural engine** executes command statements such as create table, execute procedure, and declare cursor directly. For data manipulation language (DML) statements, such as select, insert, delete, and update, the engine sets up the execution environment for all query plans and calls the query execution engine.
7. The query execution engine executes the ordered steps specified in the query plan provided by the code generator.

Query Processor Improvements:
Performance of index-based data access has been improved. Before ASE 15, the optimizer could not use the index if the join columns were of different datatypes. With ASE 15 there are no more issues surrounding mismatched datatypes and index usage. More than **one index** per table can be used to execute a query. This feature increases the performance of queries containing **ors and star joins**.

New optimization techniques now try to avoid creating worktables in the query scenario. Worktables were created in the tempdb to perform various tasks including sorting. The creation of worktables slows performance since they are typically resource intensive. ASE 15's new **hashing technique performs sorting and grouping in memory**, thus avoiding the necessity of a worktable. It is the buffer memory and not the procedure cache that is used for this operation. The elimination of the worktables has improved the performance of the queries containing order by and group by statements.

ASE 15 has enhanced the parallelism to handle large data sets. It now handles both **horizontal** and **vertical** parallelism. **Vertical parallelism** provides the ability to use **multiple CPUs** at the same time to run one or more operations of a single query. **Horizontal parallelism** allows the query to access different data located on different partitions or disk devices at the same time.

2.3 List what query plan information can be viewed
sp_showplan:
Syntax
sp_showplan spid, batch_id output, context_id output, stmt_num output
To display the showplan output for the current SQL statement without specifying the batch_id, context_id, or stmt_num:
sp_showplan spid, null, null, null

Parameters	Description
Spid	is the process ID for any user connection. Use sp_who to see spids.
batch_id	is a unique, nonnegative number for a batch.
context_id	is a unique number for every procedure (or trigger) executed in a batch.
stmt_num	is the number of the current statement within a batch. The stmt_num must be a positive number.

Displaying a query plan:

To see query plans, use:
set showplan on
To stop displaying query plans, use:
set showplan off

Query plans in Adaptive Server Enterprise 15.0 and later:
Adaptive Server traditionally classifies Transact-SQL statements into two groups:
- **Optimizable:** For example, this query is optimizable because it has many relations (tables):
  select * from t1, t2, t3, t4 where t1.c1 = t2.c1 and . . .
  order by t3.c4

The query processor requires the join order, type of join, search arguments, and ordering to be optimized.

- **Nonoptimizable:** Utility commands like update statistics and dbcc are not optimized.

Some of the new features of the query plans that showplan must display include:

new features	Description
Plan elements	query plans can be composed from over thirty different operators.
Plan shape	query plans are upside-down trees of operators. In general, more operators in a query plan result in more combinations of possible tree shapes. Query plans in version 15.0 and later can be more complex than those found in earlier versions. Nested indentation is provided to assist in visualizing the tree shape of these query plans.
Subplans	that are executed in parallel.

use set noexec with set showplan on to view a query plan without executing the query.
For example, this query prints the query plan but also executes the queries, which might be time consuming:

set showplan on
go
*select * from really_big_table*
*select * from really_really_big_table*
go

However, if you include set noexec, you can view the query plan without running the query.
Example:

set noexec on
go
set showplan on
go
*select * from really_big_table*
*select * from really_really_big_table*
go

Note: Stored procedures are compiled when they are first used, or if the resultant compiled plan is already in use by another session, so set noexec can have unexpected results, and Sybase® recommends that you use **set fmtonly on** instead. If you include a stored procedures inside another stored procedure, the second stored procedure is not run when you enable set noexec.

set showplan on
go

set fmtonly on
go
procedure_A
go

Summary

In this section, you read on tradeoffs of performance & tuning.

- **sp_configure** - Displays configuration parameters by group, their current values, their default values, the value to which they have most recently been set, and the amount of memory used by this setting. Displays only the parameters whose display level is the same as or below that of the user.

- MDA is an acronym for Monitoring and Diagnostic Access. The MDA tables report information about ASE at a low level. Unlike the sp_sysmon process, which reports performance information at the server level, the MDA tables report data at the query and table level in addition to the server level.

- For ASE 15, one new MDA table was added, in addition to two modifications on existing MDA tables in order to add functionality for the monitoring of semantically partitioned tables.
- **sp_monitor:** Displays statistics about Adaptive Server.
- The query processor has to execute several steps, using several modules, to successfully process a query, which are called Query Processor modules.
- Performance of index-based data access has been improved. Before ASE 15, the optimizer could not use the index if the join columns were of different datatypes. With ASE 15 there are no more issues surrounding mismatched datatypes and index usage. More than **one index** per table can be used to execute a query.
- ASE 15's new **hashing technique performs sorting and grouping in memory**, thus avoiding the necessity of a worktable.
- It now handles both **horizontal** and **vertical** parallelism.

    Vertical parallelism - Can use multiple CPUs at the same.

    Horizontal parallelism - Access different data located on different partitions or disk devices at the same time.

Practice Test

1. In sp_configure command, each configuration parameter has an associated display level and default is
    A. basic
    B. intermediate
    C. comprehensive
    D. None of the above

2. Which of the following statements are true about MDA tables (Choose 3)?
    A. MDA tables can be accessed with regular SQL select statements
    B. The MDA tables report information about ASE at a high level.
    C. MDA tables report data at the query and table level in addition to the server level.

D. MDA tables provide information on current activity at the table, procedure, query, and process levels.

3. Provides the SQL text that is currently being executed.
    A. monSysSQLText
    B. monSysStatement
    C. monProcessSQLText
    D. monSysPlanText

4. The parser converts the text of the SQL statement to an internal representation called a
    A. Query plan
    B. Query text
    C. Query tree
    D. Query sql

5. To see query plans, use:
    A. set queryplan on
    B. set displayplan 1
    C. set showplan on
    D. set displayplan on

Section 3 - Logical and Physical Design

3.1 Define Entities, Relationships (subtype-supertype) & Attribute cardinality

Entity:
An **entity** is the database equivalent of a noun. Distinguishable objects such as employees, order items, departments, and products are all examples of entities. In a database, a **table** represents each entity.

Attributes:
Each entity contains a number of **attributes**. Attributes are particular characteristics of the things that you would like to store. For example, in an employee entity, you might want to store an employee ID number, first and last names, an address, and other information that pertains to a particular employee. Attributes are also known as properties.

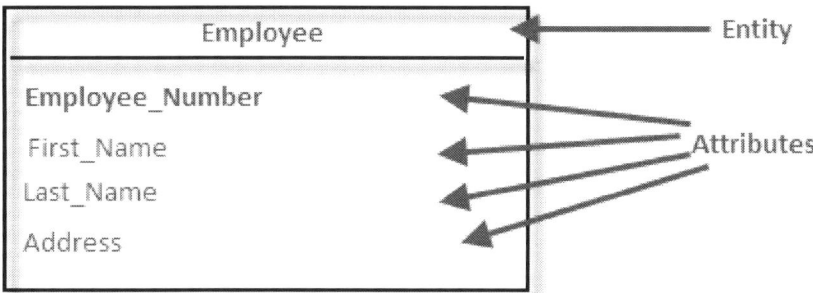

An **identifier** is one or more attributes on which all the other attributes depend. It uniquely identifies an item in the entity.

Relationships:
A **relationship** between entities is the database equivalent of a verb. An employee is a member of a department, or an office is located in a city. Relationships in a database may appear as foreign key relationships between tables, or may appear as separate tables themselves.
The relationships in the database are an encoding of rules or practices that govern the data in the entities. Once a relationship is built into the structure of the database, there is no provision for exceptions. Duplicate identifiers are not allowed.

Note: Strict database structure can benefit you because it can eliminate inconsistencies, such as a department with two managers. On the other hand, you as the designer should make your design flexible enough to allow some expansion for unforeseen uses.

Cardinality of relationships:
Relationships between data tables define cardinality when explaining how each table links to another.
There are three kinds of relationships between tables. These correspond to the **cardinality** (number) of the entities involved in the relationship.

- One-to-one relationship
- One-to-many relationships
- Many-to-many relationships

For example, consider a database designed to keep track of hospital records. Such a database could have many tables like:
a Doctor table full of doctor information
a Patient table with patient information and
a Department table with an entry for each department of the hospital.

In that model:
- There is a many-to-many relationship between the records in the doctor table and records in the patient table (Doctors have many patients, and a patient could have several doctors);
- a one-to-many relation between the department table and the doctor table (each doctor works for one department, but one department could have many doctors).
- one-to-one relationship is mostly used to split a table in two in order to optimize access or limit the visibility of some information. In the hospital example, such a relationship could be used to keep apart doctor's personal or administrative information.

In Cardinality (data modeling), collections of data elements are grouped into data tables. The data tables contain groups of data field names (known in the science world as database attributes). Tables are linked by key fields. A primary key assigns that field's special order to a table: for example, the DoctorLastName field might be assigned as the primary key of the Doctor table (#correction: PK are supposed to be unique. People can have same last name. Maybe introduce a new field called DoctorID). A table can also have a foreign key which indicates that that field is linked to the primary key of another table.

3.2 Assess a relational data model

Relational data models describe high-level logical data structure using several central data modeling concepts.
The purpose of the relational model is to provide a declarative method for specifying data and queries: users directly state what information the database contains and what information they want from it, and let the database management system software take care of describing data structures for storing the data and retrieval procedures for answering queries.

The Relation is the basic element in a relational data model.

Figure 3-1 Relations in the Relational Data Model

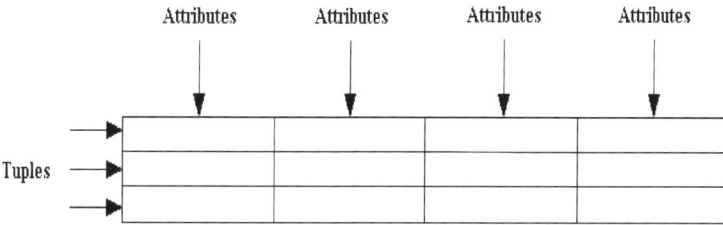

A relation is subject to the following rules:
- Relation (file, table) is a two-dimensional table.
- Attribute (i.e. field or data item) is a column in the table.
- Each column in the table has a unique name within that table.
- Each column is homogeneous. Thus the entries in any column are all of the same type (e.g. age, name, employee-number, etc).
- Each column has a domain, the set of possible values that can appear in that column.
- A Tuple (i.e. record) is a row in the table.
- The order of the rows and columns is not important.
- Values of a row all relate to some thing or portion of a thing.
- Repeating groups (collections of logically related attributes that occur multiple times within one record occurrence) are not allowed.
- Duplicate rows are not allowed (candidate keys are designed to prevent this).
- Cells must be single-valued (but can be variable length). Single valued means the following:

A relation may be expressed using the notation R(A,B,C, ...) where:
- R = the name of the relation.
- (A,B,C, ...) = the attributes within the relation.
- A = the attribute(s) which form the primary key.

3.3 Create Associative Tables

An associative entity is an element of the entity-relationship model. The database relational model does not offer direct support to many-to-many relationships, even though such relationships happen frequently in normal usage. The solution to this problem is the creation of another table to hold the necessary information for this relationship. This new table is called an associative entity.

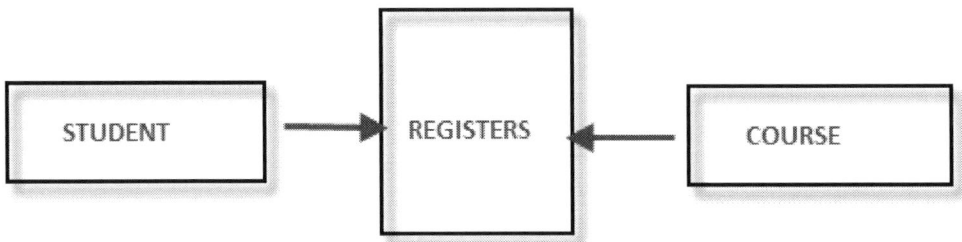

An associative entity
To create a relationship, a "child" entity must inherit the primary key of a "parent" entity. However, in a many-to-many relationship, neither entity is the "parent" or the "child"; the relationship is "unresolved". In order to work, these databases require an additional construct to "resolve" the relationship (which is why associative entities are also referred to as "resolving entities").
An associative entity can be thought of as both an entity and a relationship since it encapsulates properties from both. It is a relationship since it is serving to join two or more entities together, but it is also an entity since it may have its own properties. The associative entity must have identifiers, Primary Keys, for both adjoining tables, but may also contain its own unique identifier and other information about the relationship.

3.4 Identify qualities for Primary Key

Primary key does enforce entity integrity.

A primary key is the primary identifier for a table, and is attached to one or more columns whose values uniquely identify every row in the table.

Each table in a relational database may or may not have a primary key. The primary key is a column, or set of columns, that allows each row in the table to be uniquely identified. No two rows may have the same value of a primary key.

You can select a primary key from all of the available columns. Keep your primary key for each table as compact as possible.

Example for creating Primary key on a table while creating a table:

```
CREATE TABLE employee
(emp_id  int  PRIMARY KEY ,
emp_name char(50),
emp_addess varchar(255))
Or
CREATE TABLE employee
emp_id  int  CONSTRAINT pk_emp_id PRIMARY KEY ,
emp_name char(50),
emp_addess varchar(255))
Or
CREATE TABLE employee
(emp_id  int ,
emp_name char(50),
emp_addess varchar(255),
CONSTRAINT pk_emp_id PRIMARY KEY (emp_id)
 )
```

Example for creating Primary key on a table after creating a table:

Add primary key 'pk_emp' to table 'employee' on column name 'emp_id'

```
ALTER TABLE employee
ADD CONSTRAINT pk_emp
PRIMARY KEY CLUSTERED (emp_id)
```
Or
```
ALTER TABLE employee ADD CONSTRAINT pk_emp PRIMARY KEY CLUSTERED (emp_id)
```

Insert a record in 'employee' table:
```
INSERT INTO employee (emp_id, emp_name, emp_addess)
VALUES (1, 'ABHI', 'Singapore')
```

Try to insert another record with already inserted emp_id .i.e emp_id = 1
```
INSERT INTO employee (emp_id, emp_name, emp_addess)
  VALUES (1, 'ABHI', 'Singapore')
```
It will give below error because 'employee' table has primary key on column 'emp_id' and primary key will not allow to insert emp_id = 1 again as its duplicate.

> Error: Attempt to insert duplicate key row in object 'employee' with unique index 'pk_emp'.

Note:
- Default type of Primary is a type of **unique clustered** type of index.
- If you drop a table, associate primary key will be dropped automatically.
- We can not insert 'NULL' value to a primary key column.
- We can not create primary key on a NULL type of column/columns.

3.5 Represent relationships as Foreign keys

A **Foreign key** is a field (or fields) that points to the primary key of another table. The purpose of the foreign key is to ensure **referential integrity** of the data. In other words, only values that are supposed to appear in the database are permitted.
Let's create two tables for example: -
CREATE TABLE employee
(emp_id int CONSTRAINT pk_emp_id PRIMARY KEY,
 emp_name char(50),
 emp_address varchar(255)
)

CREATE TABLE emp_transactions
(tran_id int CONSTRAINT pk_dept_id PRIMARY KEY,
 emp_id   int ,
 amout   numeric(16,4),
 date   datetime,
 type   char(1),
 CONSTRAINT fk_emp_id FOREIGN KEY(emp_id)
 REFERENCES employee (emp_id)
)
emp_id column in the emp_department table is a **foreign key** pointing to the emp_id column in the employee table.
Note: There are many ways to create foreign key on a table. Above method is one of them.

Assume there are records in employee and emp_transactions table for your understanding.

emp_id	emp_name	emp_country
1	ABHI	Singapore
2	Mike	London
3	Thomas	Singapore

tran_id	emp_id	amount	date	type
1	1	10000.00	19/12/2011	C
2	1	20000.00	20/12/2011	C
3	2	15000.00	20/12/2011	D
4	3	17000.00	20/12/2011	C

In above Image you can see records for emp_id 1,2,3 exists in the emp_transaction table. Now try to delete a record from employee table for a emp_id, which exists in emp_transaction table.
DELETE FROM employee WHERE emp_id = 3

Section 3- Logical and Physical Design

It will prompt you error and won't allow deleting this record. It makes sense, because if there is no employee with emp_id 3 in employee table but exists in emp_transactions then how would you find employee detail like 'emp_name', 'emp_address' etc.?

If you want to delete any record from employee (parent) table, which exists in emp_transactions (child) table, you need to delete it from emp_transactions (child) table first.

Note: Creating an index on a foreign key is often useful for the following reasons:
- Changes to PRIMARY KEY constraints are checked with FOREIGN KEY constraints in related tables.
- Foreign key columns are frequently used in join criteria when the data from related tables is combined in queries by matching the column or columns in the FOREIGN KEY constraint of one table with the primary or unique key column or columns in the other table. An index enables the Database Engine to quickly find related data in the foreign key table. However, creating this index is not required. Data from two related tables can be combined even if no PRIMARY KEY or FOREIGN KEY constraints are defined between the tables, but a foreign key relationship between two tables indicates that the two tables have been optimized to be combined in a query that uses the keys as its criteria.
- A FOREIGN KEY constraint can reference columns in tables in the same database or within the same table. These are called *self-referencing* tables. For example, consider an employee table that contains three columns: **employee_number**, **employee_name**, and **manager_employee_number**. Because the manager is also an employee, there is a foreign key relationship from the **manager_employee_number** column to the **employee_number** column.

3.6 Determine column data type and null/not null status, default values, rules & constraints

New Datatypes:
bigint — Supports signed integers from –9,223,372,036,854,775,808 to +9,223,372,036,854,775,807
unsigned <xx> — Allows for range extension on the ASE integer datatypes of smallint, int, and bigint
Ranges for unsigned datatypes:

Datatype	Range
unsigned smallint	0 to 65,535
unsigned int	0 to 4,294,967,295
unsigned bigint	0 to 18,446,744,073,709,551,615

For unsigned datatypes, it is valid to also use unsigned tinyint, as this is syntactically supported. However, unsigned tinyint will function as a standard tinyint.
Note: The range for each of the unsigned datatypes doubles on the positive side of zero since it is not possible to declare a negative number with unsigned integer variables. The storage size for

each of the unsigned datatypes remains the same as the signed version of the corresponding datatype.

Basic Data Types:

Datatype	Value From	Value To	Storage*
Bit	0	1	1
Tinyint	0	+255	1
Smallint	-32,768	+32767	2
unsigned smallint	0	+65535	2
Int	-2,147,483,648	+2147483647	4
unsigned int	0	+4294967295	4
Bigint	-9,223,372,036,854,770,000	9,223,372,036,854,770,000.00	8
unsigned bigint	0	+18446744073709500000	8

Decimal Data Types:

Datatype	Value From	Value To	Storage*
numeric (p, s)	-1038	1038	2-17
decimal (p, s)	-1038	1038	2-17
float (precision)	machine dependent	machine dependent	4+
double precision	machine dependent	machine dependent	8
Real	machine dependent	machine dependent	4

Money Data Types:

Datatype	Value From	Value To	Storage*
smallmoney	-214,748.36	+214748.3647	4
Money	-922,337,203,685,477.00	+922337203685477	8

Date/Time Data Types:

Datatype	Value From	Value To	Storage*
Smalldatetime	01-Jan-90	65537	4
Datetime	1 January 1753	2958465	8
Date	1 January 0001	2958465	8
Time	12:00:00AM	11:59:59:999PM	4

Character Data Types:

Datatype	Description	Value To	Storage*
char(n)	Character	pagesize	n
varchar(n)	character varying	pagesize	actual entry
Unichar	unicode character	pagesize	n * @@unicharsize
Univarchar	unicode character varying	pagesize	actual entry * @@unicharsize
nchar(n)	national character	pagesize	n * @@ncharsize
nvarchar(n)	national char varying	pagesize	actual entry * @@ncharsize
Text		<2,147,483,647	multiples of 2k

Section 3- Logical and Physical Design

| Unitext | | 1073741823 | multiples of 2k |

Binary Data Types:

Datatype	Value From	Value To	Storage*
binary(n)		pagesize	n
varbinary(n)		pagesize	actual entry
Image		<2,147,483,647	multiples of 2k

Default Constraint:

The DEFAULT constraint is used to insert a default value into a column. The default value will be added to all new records, if no other value is specified.
Let's understand how to create default constraint on a table and how does it work.

CREATE TABLE employee
(emp_id int ,
 emp_name char(50),
 emp_address varchar(255),
 join_date   datetime DEFAULT getdate()
)
Or
ALTER TABLE employee REPLACE join_date DEFAULT getdate()

Other way to define default for a column on a table

Syntax: CREATE DEFAULT <default_name> AS <default>

Example: CREATE DEFAULT todays_date AS getdate()

Bind created default to a column of a table as below

Syntax: sp_bindefault <default_name> , "<table_name>.<column_name>"

Example: sp_bindefault todays_date , "employee.join_date"

NOTE: getdate() is system function to get system date.

INSERT INTO employee (emp_id, emp_name, emp_address)
VALUES (1, 'Mike', 'London')

In above insert statement we didn't provide column name 'join_date', lets see what value got inserted for 'join_date' column in *employee* table for this record.

emp_id	emp_name	emp_address	join_date
1	Mike	London	22/12/2011 5:54:40.760 AM

It inserted getdate() (system currentdate and time).

If you run below insert instead of above insert:
INSERT INTO employee (emp_id, emp_name, emp_address,join_date)
VALUES (1, 'Mike', 'London', NULL

emp_id	emp_name	emp_address	join_date
1	Mike	London	NULL

As above statement if you provide column name 'join_date' and NULL value for this column, it will insert NULL instead of getdate() (current system date and time)

Note:
- You can include only one **default** clause per column in a table.
- You can bind a new default to a datatype without unbinding the old one. The new default overrides and unbinds the old one.

Remove default from a column (if default is created in CREATE Table statement):
ALTER TABLE employee REPLACE join_date DEFAULT NULL

Note: In above statement you can define NOT NULL as well (it depends on column type .. if its NULL you have to REPLACE default as NULL, if its NOT NULL then you have to REPLACE default as NOT NULL)
Or
Remove default from a column (if default is created by 'CREATE DEFUALT' command and bind to column by 'sp_bindefault' command):

sp_unbindefault "employee.join_date"

DROP a default:
DROP DEFAULT todays_date

Note: You must unbind a default with **sp_unbindefault (**sp_unbindefault "<table_name>.<column_name> "**),** before you drop it otherwise it will give below error
Error: The default 'todays_date' cannot be dropped because it is bound to one or more column.

3.7 Enforce domain integrity

An **integrity constraint** is one which does not allow invalid data entry into the database.
Domain Integrity Rules are existing ASE server-enforced integrity mechanisms that can be used in conjunction with Access Rules to provide security policy control over the flow of information into and through the server

Domain Integrity Constraints are:
- Not null constraint
- Check constraint
- Rule constraint

3.8 Define derived tables, intra-row derived columns and inter-row derived columns

A derived table is defined by the evaluation of a query expression and differs from a regular table in that it is **neither** described in **system catalogs nor stored on disk**. In Adaptive Server, a derived table may be a **SQL derived table** or **an abstract plan derived table**.

A SQL derived table: defined by one or more tables through the evaluation of a query expression. A SQL derived table is used in the query expression in which it is defined and exists only for the duration of the query. See the Transact-SQL User's Guide.

How SQL derived tables work:
A SQL derived table is created with a derived table expression consisting of a nested select statement, as in the following example, which returns a list of cities in the publishers table of the pubs2 database:
select city from (select city from publishers)
cities
The SQL derived table is named cities and has one column titled city. The SQL derived table is defined by the nested select statement and persists only for the duration of the query, which returns the following:

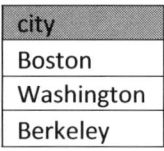

Advantages of SQL derived table:
- The SQL derived table persists only for the duration of the query, in contrast with a temporary table, which exists for the entire session.
- SQL derived tables eliminate this overhead by enabling queries to spontaneously create nonpersistent tables without needing to drop the tables or make insertions into the system catalog. Consequently, no administrative tasks are required.
- A SQL derived table used multiple times performs comparably to a query using a view with a cached definition.

SQL derived tables and optimization:
Queries expressed as a single SQL statement exploit the optimizer better than queries expressed in two or more SQL statements. SQL derived tables allow you to express concisely, in a single step, what might otherwise require several SQL statements and temporary tables, especially where intermediate aggregate results must be stored. For example:
select dt_1.* from
    (select sum(total_sales) from titles_west group by total_sales)
        dt_1(sales_sum),
    (select sum(total_sales) from titles_east group by total_sales)
        dt_2(sales_sum)
where dt_1.sales_sum = dt_2.sales_sum

Aggregate results are obtained from the SQL derived tables dt_1 and dt_2, and a join is computed between the two SQL derived tables. Everything is accomplished in a single SQL statement.

SQL derived table syntax:
The query expression for a SQL derived table is specified in the from clause of the select or select into command in place of a table or view name.
A derived table expression is similar to the select in a create view statement and follows the same rules, with the following exceptions:
- **Temporary tables** are permitted in a derived table expression except when it is part of a create view statement.
- **A local variable** is permitted in a derived table expression except when it is part of a create view statement. You cannot assign a value to a variable within a derived table expression.
- **A correlation_name**, which must follow the derived table expression to specify the name of the SQL derived table, may omit a derived column list, whereas a view cannot have unnamed columns:

*select * from*
(select sum(advance) from total_sales) dt

Derived column lists:
If a derived column list is not included in a SQL derived table, the names of the SQL derived table columns must match the names of the columns specified in the target list of the derived table expression. If a column name is not specified
in the target list of the derived table expression, as in the case where a constant expression or an aggregate is present in the target list of the derived table expression, the resulting column in the SQL derived table has no name.

If a derived column list is included in a SQL derived table, it must specify names for all columns in the target list of the derived table expression. These column names must be used in the queroy block in place of the natural column names of the SQL derived table. The columns must be listed in the order in which they occur in the derived table expression, and a column name cannot be specified more than once in the derived column list.

Correlated SQL derived tables:
Correlated SQL derived tables, which are not ANSI standard, are not supported. For example, the following query is not supported because it references the SQL derived table dt_publishers2 inside the derived table expression for dt_publishers1:
*select * from*
    *(select * from titles where titles.pub_id =dt_publishers2.pub_id)*
       dt_publishers1,
    *(select * from publishers where city = "Boston")*
       dt_publishers2
where dt_publishers1.pub_id = dt_publishers2.pub_id

Similarly, the following query is not supported because the derived table expression for dt_publishers references the publishers_pub_id column, which is outside the scope of the SQL derived table:

*select * from publishers*
where pub_id in (select pub_id from
(select pub_id from titles
where pub_id = publishers.pub_id)
dt_publishers)

The following query illustrates proper referencing and is supported:
*select * from publishers*
where pub_id in (select pub_id from
(select pub_id from titles)
dt_publishers
where pub_id = publishers.pub_id)

Use of SQL derived tables:
Queries expressed as a single SQL statement exploit the query processor better than queries expressed in two or more SQL statements. SQL-derived tables enable you to express, in a single step, what might otherwise require several
SQL statements and temporary tables, especially where intermediate aggregate results must be stored.
For example:
select dt_1. from*
(select sum(total_sales) from titles_west group by total_sales)
dt_1(sales_sum),
(select sum(total_sales) from titles_east group by total_sales)
dt_2(sales_sum)
where dt_1.sales_sum = dt_2.sales_sum

Here, aggregate results are obtained from the SQL derived tables dt_1 and dt_2, and a join is computed between the two SQL derived tables. Everything is accomplished in a single SQL statement.

Using SQL derived tables:
You can use SQL derived tables to form part of a larger integrated query using assorted SQL clauses and operators.

Nesting: A query can use numerous nested derived table expressions, which are SQL expressions that define a SQL derived table. Example:
select postalcode
from (select postalcode
from (select postalcode
from authors) dt_1) dt_2

Section 3- Logical and Physical Design

> **Note: The degree of nesting is limited to 25.**

Subqueries using SQL derived tables: You can use a SQL derived table in a subquery from clause
Example:
select pub_name from publishers
    where "business" in
        (select type from
            (select type from titles, publishers
                where titles.pub_id = publishers.pub_id)
        dt_titles)

A union clause is allowed within a derived table expression:
Example:
select * from
    (select stor_id, ord_num from sales
    union
    select stor_id, ord_num from sales_east)
dt_sales_info

Unions in subqueries: A union clause is allowed in a subquery inside a derived table expression.
select title_id from salesdetail
    where stor_id in
        (select stor_id from
            (select stor_id from sales
            union
            select stor_id from sales_east)
        dt_stores)

Renaming columns with SQL derived tables: If a derived column list is included for a SQL derived table, it follows the name of the SQL derived table and is enclosed in parentheses
Example:
select dt_b.book_title, dt_b.tot_sales
    from (select title, total_sales
        from titles) dt_b (book_title, tot_sales)
    where dt_b.book_title like "%Computer%"

Here the column names title and total_sales in the derived table expression are respectively renamed to book_title and tot_sales using the derived column list. The book_title and tot_sales column names are used in the rest of the query.

> **Note:** SQL derived tables cannot have unnamed columns.

Constant expressions:
If a column name is not specified in the target list of the derived table expression, as in the case where a constant expression is used for the column name, the resulting column in the SQL derived table has no name:
select * from
    (select title_id, (lorange + hirange)/2
    from roysched) as dt_avg_range
go

title_id	
BU1032	2500
BU1032	27500
PC1035	1000
PC1035	2500

You can specify column names for the target list of a derived table expression using a derived column list:
select * from
    (select title_id, (lorange + hirange)/2
    from roysched) as dt_avg_range (title, avg_range)
go

title_id	avg_range
BU1032	2500
BU1032	27500
PC1035	1000
PC1035	2500

avg_range is constants expression in above SQL.

Alternately, you can specify column names by renaming the column in the target list of the derived table expression:
select * from
    (select title_id, (lorange + hirange)/2 avg_range
    from roysched) as dt_avg_range
go

Note: If you specify column names in both a derived column list and in the target list of the derived table expression, the resulting columns are named by the derived column list. The column names in a derived column list take precedence over the names specified in the target list of the derived table expression.

Note: If you use a constant expression within a create view statement, you must specify a column name for the constant expression results.

Aggregate functions: Derived table expressions may use aggregate functions, such as sum, avg, max, min, count_big, and count.
Example:
select dt_a.pub_id, dt_a.adv_sum
  from (select pub_id, sum(advance) adv_sum
    from titles group by pub_id) dt_a

Joins with SQL derived tables:
Example: Between a SQL derived table and an existing table.
select dt_c.title_id, dt_c.pub_id
  from (select title_id, pub_id from titles) as dt_c,
    publishers
  where dt_c.pub_id = publishers.pub_id

Example: Between two SQL derived tables.
select dt_c.title_id, dt_c.pub_id
  from (select title_id, pub_id from titles)
    as dt_c,
    (select pub_id from publishers)
    as dt_d
  where dt_c.pub_id = dt_d.pub_id

Example: Outer joins involving SQL derived tables are also possible.
select dt_c.title_id, dt_c.pub_id
  from (select title_id, pub_id from titles)
    as dt_c,
    (select title_id, pub_id from publishers)
    as dt_d
  *where dt_c.title_id *= dt_d.title_id*

Note: Sybase supports both left and right outer joins.

Creating a table from a SQL derived table:
Example:
select pubdate into pub_dates
  from (select pubdate from titles) dt_e
    where pubdate = "450128 12:30:1PM"

Here, data from the SQL derived table dt_e is inserted into the new table pub_dates.

Using views with SQL derived tables:
create view view_colo_publishers (Pub_Id, Publisher,
City, State)
as select pub_id, pub_name, city, state
from
*(select * from publishers where state="CO")*

dt_colo_pubs
Data can be inserted through a view that contains a SQL derived table if the insert rules and permission settings for the derived table expression follow the insert rules and permission settings for the select part of the create view
statement. For example, the following insert statement inserts a row through the view_colo_publishers view into the publishers table on which the view is based:
insert view_colo_publishers values ('1799', 'Gigantico Publications', 'Denver', 'CO')

You can also update existing data through a view that uses a SQL derived table:
update view_colo_publishers set Publisher = "Colossicorp Industries"
where Pub_Id = "1699

> **Note: You must specify the column names of the view definition, not the column names of the underlying table.**

Correlated attributes: Correlated attributes that exceed the scope of a SQL derived table cannot be referenced from a SQL derived table expression

An abstract plan derived table: a derived table used in query processing, the optimization and execution of queries. An abstract plan derived table differs from a SQL derived table in that it exists as part of an abstract plan and is invisible to the end user.

3.9 List advantages of normalization

Normalization is the process of efficiently organizing data in a database. There are two main goals of the normalization process: eliminating redundant data (for example, storing the same data in more than one table) and **ensuring data dependencies make sense** (only storing related data in a table). Both of these are worthy goals as they reduce the amount of space a database consumes and ensure that data is logically stored.

When a table is normalized, the non-key columns depend on the key used. From a relational model point of view, it is standard to have tables that are in **Third Normal Form**. Normalized physical design provides the greatest ease of maintenance, and databases in this form are clearly understood by developers.

Advantages:
Normalization produces smaller tables with smaller rows:
- More rows per page (less logical I/O)
- More rows per I/O (more efficient)
- More rows fit in cache (less physical I/O)
- Searching, sorting, and creating indexes is faster, since tables are narrower, and more rows fit on a data page.
- You usually have more tables. You can have more clustered indexes (one per table), so you get more flexibility in tuning queries.

Section 3- Logical and Physical Design 77

- Index searching is often faster, since indexes tend to be narrower and shorter.
- More tables allow better use of segments to control physical placement of data.
- You usually have fewer indexes per table, so data modification commands are faster.
- Fewer null values and less redundant data, making your database more compact.
- Triggers execute more quickly if you are not maintaining redundant data.
- Data modification anomalies are reduced.
- Normalization is conceptually cleaner and easier to maintain and change as your needs change.
- While fully normalized databases require more joins, joins are generally very fast if indexes are available on the join columns.

Adaptive Server is optimized to keep higher levels of the index in cache, so each join performs only one or two physical I/Os for each matching row. The cost of finding rows already in the data cache is extremely low.

3.10 Understand First, Second and Third Normal Form

Fist Normal Form:
The rules for First Normal Form are:
- Every column must be atomic. It cannot be decomposed into two or more sub columns.
- You cannot have multivalued columns or repeating groups.
- Each row and column position can have only one value.

The table in Figure 3-10-1 violates First Normal Form, since the dept_no column contains a repeating group:

Figure 3-10-1: A table that violates first Normal Form:

Employee

emp_num	emp_lname	dept_no
1001	Mike	A20 C20
1002	Abhi	D50

Normalization creates two tables and moves dept_no to the second table:

Figure 3-10-2: Correcting First Normal Form violations by creating two tables

Employee

emp_num	emp_lname	dept_no
1001	Mike	A20 C20
1002	Abhi	D50

Emp_dept

emp_num	dept_no
1001	A20
1001	C20
1002	D50

Second Normal Form:
- Every non-key field must depend on the entire primary key, not on part of a composite primary key.
- If a database has only single-field primary keys, it is automatically in Second Normal Form.
- Remove subsets of data that apply to multiple rows of a table and place them in separate tables.

In Figure 3-10-3, the primary key is a composite key on emp_num and dept_no. But the value of dept_name depends only on dept_no, not on the entire primary key.

Figure 3-10-3: A table that violates Second Normal Form

Emp_dept

emp_num	dept_no	dept_name
1001	A10	accounting
1002	A10	accounting
1002	D60	development

Depends on part of primary

Primary Key(Composite)

To normalize this table, move dept_name to a second table, as shown in Figure 3-10-4.

Emp_dept

emp_num	dept_no
1001	A10
1002	A10
1002	D60

Primary Key(Composite)

Dept

dept_no	dept_name
A10	accounting
D60	development

Primary Key

Third Normal Form:
- For a table to be in Third Normal Form, a non-key field cannot depend on another non-key field or in other words, remove columns that are not dependent upon the primary key.

The table in Figure 3-10-5 violates Third Normal Form because the mgr_lname field depends on the mgr_emp_num field, which is not a key field.

Figure 3-10-5: A table that violates Third Normal Form

Dept

dept_no	dept_name	mgr_emp_num	mgr_lname
A10	accounting	10073	Steve
D60	development	10089	John
M80	marketing	10035	Ajay

Primary Key   Depends on non-Key

The solution is to split the Dept table into two tables, as shown in Figure 3-10-6. In this case, the Employees table, already stores this information, so removing the mgr_lname field from Dept brings the table into Third Normal Form.

Figure 3-10-6: Correcting Third Normal Form violations by creating two tables

Dept

dept_no	dept_name	mgr_emp_num
A10	accounting	10073
D60	development	10089
M80	marketing	10035

↑ Primary Key

Employee

emp_num	emp_lname
10073	Steve
10089	John
10035	Ajay

↑ Primary Key

3.11   List denormalization techniques

Denormalizing for performance:
Once you have normalized your database, you can run benchmark tests to verify performance. You may have to denormalize for specific queries and/or applications.

Denormalizing:
- Can be done with tables or columns
- Assumes prior normalization
- Requires a thorough knowledge of how the data is being used

You may want to denormalize if:
- All or nearly all of the most frequent queries require access to the full set of joined data.
- A majority of applications perform table scans when joining tables.
- Computational complexity of derived columns requires temporary tables or excessively complex queries.

Disadvantages:
- It usually speeds retrieval but can slow data modification.
- It is always application-specific and must be reevaluated if the application changes.
- It can increase the size of tables.
- In some instances, it simplifies coding; in others, it makes coding more complex.

Performance advantages:
- Minimizing the need for joins.

- Reducing the number of foreign keys on tables.
- Reducing the number of indexes, saving storage space, and reducing data modification time.
- Precomputing aggregate values, that is, computing them at data modification time rather than at select time.
- Reducing the number of tables (in some cases)

Denormalization input:
When deciding whether to denormalize, you need to analyze the data access requirements of the applications in your environment and their actual performance characteristics. Often, good indexing and other solutions solve many performance problems rather than denormalizing. Some of the issues to examine when considering denormalization include:
- What are the critical transactions, and what is the expected response time?
- How often are the transactions executed?
- What tables or columns do the critical transactions use? How many rows do they access each time?
- What is the mix of transaction types: select, insert, update, and delete?
- What is the usual sort order?
- What are the concurrency expectations?
- How big are the most frequently accessed tables?
- Do any processes compute summaries?
- Where is the data physically located?

Techniques:
The most prevalent denormalization techniques are:
- Adding redundant columns
- Adding derived columns
- Collapsing tables
- Duplicating tables
- Splitting tables

Let's discuss in detail:
Adding redundant columns:
You can add redundant columns to eliminate frequent joins. For example, if you are performing frequent joins on the titleauthor and authors tables to retrieve the author's last name, you can add the au_lname column to titleauthor.

Adding redundant columns eliminates joins for many queries. The problems with this solution are that it:
- Requires maintenance of new columns. you must make changes to two tables, and possibly to many rows in one of the tables.
- Requires more disk space, since au_lname is duplicated

Adding derived columns:

Adding derived columns can eliminate some joins and reduce the time needed to produce aggregate values. The total_sales column in the titles table of the pubs2 database provides one example of a derived column used to reduce
aggregate value processing time.

Below query shows, Frequent joins are needed between the titleauthor and titles tables to provide the total advance for a particular book title.
select title, sum(advance) from titleauthor ta, titles t where ta.title_id = t.title_id group by title_id

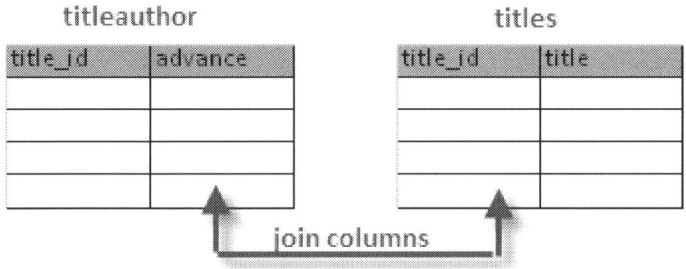

Figure 3-11-1 After adding derived column (sum_adv):
select title, sum_adv from titles

You can create and maintain a derived data column (sum_adv) in the titles table, eliminating both the join and the aggregate at runtime.
Note: This increases **storage** needs, and requires maintenance of the derived column whenever changes are made to the titles table.

Collapsing tables:

If most users need to see the full set of joined data from two tables, collapsing the two tables into one can improve performance by eliminating the join. For example, users frequently need to see the author name, author ID, and the
blurbs copy data at the same time. The solution is to collapse the two tables into one. The data from the two tables must be in a one-to-one relationship to collapse tables
Collapsing the tables eliminates the join, but loses the conceptual separation of the data. If some users still need access to just the pairs of data from the two tables, this access can be restored by using queries that select only the needed columns or by using views.

Duplicating tables:
If a group of users regularly needs only a subset of data, you can duplicate the critical table subset for that group.

Splitting tables:
Sometimes splitting normalized tables can improve performance. You can split tables in two ways:

Split type	Description
Horizontally	by placing rows in two separate tables, depending on data values in one or more columns
Vertically	by placing the primary key and some columns in one table, and placing other columns and the primary key in another table

Note: Splitting tables, either horizontally or vertically, adds complexity to your applications.

Horizontal splitting: Use horizontal splitting if:
- A table is large, and reducing its size reduces the number of index pages read in a query.
- The table split corresponds to a natural separation of the rows, such as different geographical sites or historical versus current data. You might choose horizontal splitting if you have a table that stores huge amounts of rarely used historical data, and your applications have high performance needs for current data in the same table.
- Table splitting distributes data over the physical media, however, there are other ways to accomplish this goal.

Generally, horizontal splitting requires different table names in queries, depending on values in the tables. In most database applications this complexity usually far outweighs the advantages of table splitting. If many queries perform table scans, horizontal splitting may improve performance enough to be worth the extra maintenance effort.

For example: if a table has records with 'active' and 'inactive' (assume it is **emp_status** column) and in application usyally only active records are accessed, so instead of accessing whole data all the time, we can split table horizontally into 'active' and 'inactive' data. That means, we can create to tables as Inactive_employee and Active_employee.

Vertical splitting: Use vertical splitting if:
- Some columns are accessed more frequently than other columns.
- The table has wide rows, and splitting the table reduces the number of pages that need to be read.

When a table contains very long columns that are accessed infrequently, placing them in a separate table can greatly speed the retrieval of the more frequently used columns. With shorter rows, more data rows fit on a data page, so for many queries, fewer pages can be accessed

Managing denormalized data:

Whatever denormalization techniques you use, you need to ensure data integrity by using:

	Description
Triggers	which can update derived or duplicated data anytime the base data changes
Application Logic	using transactions in each application that update denormalized data, to ensure that changes are atomic
Batch reconciliation	run at appropriate intervals, to bring the denormalized data back into agreement From an integrity point of view, triggers provide the best solution, although they can be costly in terms of performance.

Summary

In this section, you read about Logical and Physical Design.

- An **entity** is the database equivalent of a noun. Distinguishable objects such as employees, order items, departments, and products are all examples of entities. In a database, a **table** represents each entity. Attributes are particular characteristics of the things that you would like to store.
- The purpose of the relational model is to provide a declarative method for specifying data and queries: users directly state what information the database contains and what information they want from it, and let the database management system software take care of describing data structures for storing the data and retrieval procedures for answering queries.
- The Relation is the basic element in a relational data model.
- An associative entity is an element of the **entity-relationship model.**
- To create a relationship, a "child" entity must inherit the primary key of a "parent" entity.
- Primary key does enforce entity integrity.
- A Foreign key is a field (or fields) that points to the primary key of another table. The purpose of the foreign key is to ensure **referential integrity** of the data. In other words, only values that are supposed to appear in the database are permitted.
- The DEFAULT constraint is used to insert a default value into a column.
- An **integrity constraint** is one which does not allow invalid data entry into the database.
- There are two main goals of the normalization process: eliminating redundant data and ensuring data dependencies make sense.

Practice Test

Section 3- Logical and Physical Design   85

1. There are three kinds of relationships between tables. Those are [Choose 3]
    A. One-to-one
    B. One-to-many
    C. Many-to-many
    D. Many-to-one

2. Which of the following structures can be used to enforce entity integrity? (Choose 2)
    A. Trigger
    B. sp_primarykey
    C. Check constraint
    D. References constraint
    E. Primary key constraint

3. A **Foreign key** is a field (or fields) that points to the _____ of another table.
    A. Foreign key
    B. Primary Key
    C. Unique key
    D. No key

4. Which statements are TRUE. Defaults & rules... (Choose 2)
    A. can implement multi column checks.
    B. can be associated with user defined data types.
    C. can have associated messages.
    D. are not created when a table is created.

5. A derived table may be a [Choose 2]
    A. a permanent user table
    B. a SQL derived table
    C. an abstract plan derived table
    D a system table

6. What are not the advantages of normalization? [Choose 2]
    A. More rows per page
    B. More rows per I/O
    C. Less rows fit in cache
    D. Searching, sorting, and creating indexes is faster, since tables are narrower, and more rows fit on a data page.
    E. You usually have more indexes per table, so data modification commands are slow.

7. Whatever denormalization techniques you use, you need to ensure data integrity by using?
    A. Triggers
    B. Application Logic
    C. Batch reconciliation
    D. All of the above

Section 4 - ANSI SQL – DDL

4.1 Describe how to create tables, views, indexes, etc.

CREATE TABLE:

The simplest form of CREATE TABLE is:

create table table_name

(column_name datatype)

Note: Column names must be unique within a table, but you can use the same column name in different tables in the same database.
Note: If you have set quoted_identifier on, both the table name and the column names can be delimited identifiers. Otherwise, they must follow the rules for identifiers.

Delimited identifiers are object names enclosed in **double quotes**. Using delimited identifiers allows you to avoid certain restrictions on object names. You can use double quotes to delimit table, view, and column names. Delimited identifiers can be reserved words, can begin with nonalphabetic characters, and can include characters that would not otherwise be allowed. They cannot exceed 253 bytes. A pound sign (#) is illegal as a first character of any quoted identifier. Before you create or reference a delimited identifier, you must execute:
set quoted_identifier on
Each time you use the quoted identifier in a statement, you must enclose it in double quotes.
Example:
create table "1one"(col1 char(3))
*select * from "1one"*
- There can be as many as 2,000,000,000 tables per database.
- The limits for the length of object names or identifiers: 255 bytes for regular identifiers, and 253 bytes for delimited identifiers.
- The maximum number of columns in a table depends on many factors, including, among others, your server's logical page size and whether the tables are configured for allpages- or data only-locking.
- You can create temporary tables either by preceding the table name in a create table statement with a pound sign (#) or by specifying the name prefix "tempdb..".
- Different users can create tables of the same name.

Example: A user named "Abhisek" and a user named "Mike" can each create a table named employee. Users who have permissions on both tables must qualify them as Abhisek.employee and Mike.employee. Abhisek must qualify references to Mike's table as Mike.employee, but Abhisek can refer to her own table simply as employee.

Creating tables in different databases: You can create a table in another database from your current database. you must have create table permission in it.
Example: Assume your current databse is **olddb** (db name) and you want to create a table in database named **newdb**.
create table newdb..employee (emp_id int)

Note: You cannot create other database objects—**views, rules, defaults, stored procedures, and triggers**—in a database other than the current one.

CREATE INDEX:

The simplest form of create index is:

create index index_name
on table_name (column_name)

or

create [unique] [clustered | nonclustered] index index_name
on table_name (column_name)

Note: The index name must conform to the rules for identifiers.

- You cannot create indexes on columns with bit, text, or image datatypes.
- The owner of a table can create or drop an index at any time, whether or not there is data in the table. Indexes can be created on tables in another database by qualifying the table name.

If you create a index specifying more than a column, its called a composite index.

- You can specify up to 31 columns in a single composite index in Adaptive Server 11.9.2 and later.

Example: Composite Index

create index auth_name_ind
on authors(au_fname, au_lname)

Note: The columns in a composite index do not have to be in the same order as the columns in the create table statement.

unique option with index:

A unique index permits **NO** two rows to have the same index value, including NULL. The system checks for duplicate values when the index is created, if data already exists, and checks each time data is added or modified with an insert or update.

Including IDENTITY columns in nonunique indexes:

The identity in nonunique index database option automatically includes an IDENTITY column in a table's index keys so that all indexes created on the table are unique. This option makes logically nonunique indexes internally unique and allows them to process updatable cursors and isolation level 0 reads.

Command to enable identity in nonunique indexes:

sp_dboption <db_name>, "identity in nonunique index", true

Note: The table must already have an IDENTITY column for the identity in nonunique index database option to work,

Example:

create table sales_detail
(order_num numeric(16 ,0) identity,
item_name   varchar(50) not null)

create index idx1 on sales_detail (item_name)
We created index on only column *item_name*. now if we run sp_helpindex sales_detail it will return

index_name	index_keys
idx1	item_name, order_num

That means, it included column *order_num* as well (which is defined as IDENTITY column in table) automatically in idx1.

Ascending and descending index-column values: You can use the asc (ascending) and desc (descending) keywords to assign a sort order to each column in an index. By default, sort order is ascending.

Example:

*create index nonclustered cust_order_date
on Orders
(customer_ID asc,
date desc)*

Indexes on computed columns:

You can create indexes on computed columns as though they were regular columns, as long as the datatype of the result can be indexed. Computed column indexes and un provide a way to create indexes on complex datatypes like XML, text, image, and Java classes. Adaptive Server evaluates the computed columns and uses the results to build or update indexes when you create or update an index.

Indexing with function-based indexes:

Function-based indexes contain one or more expressions as index keys. You can create indexes on functions and expressions directly. Like computed column indexes, this feature is useful for user-defined ordering and DDS applications.

Syntax:

*create [unique] [clustered] | nonclustered] index index_name
on [[database.] owner.] table_name
(**column_expression** [asc | desc] [, **column_expression** [asc | desc]]...*

Example:
*CREATE INDEX generalized_index on parts_table
(general_key(part_no,listPrice,part_no>>version)*

Using clustered or nonclustered indexes:

Clustered Index	Nonclustered Index

Adaptive Server sorts rows on an ongoing basis so that their physical order is the same as their logical (indexed) order.	With a nonclustered index, the physical order of the rows is not the same as their indexed order.
The bottom or leaf level of a clustered index contains the actual data pages of the table.	The leaf level of a nonclustered index contains pointers to rows on data pages. More precisely, each leaf page contains an indexed value and a pointer to the row with that value.
There can be only one clustered index per table	Each of the up to 249 nonclustered indexes permitted on a table can provide access to the data in a different sorted order.
It is often created on the primary key—the column or columns that uniquely identify the row	

Finding data using a clustered index is almost always faster than using a nonclustered index. In addition, a clustered index is advantageous when many rows with contiguous key values are being retrieved—that is, on columns that are often searched for ranges of values.

Note: If neither the clustered nor the nonclustered keyword is used, Adaptive Server creates a **nonclustered index**.

Example: Create Clustered index
create clustered index idx1
on employee(emp_id)

Example: Create nonclustered index
create nonclustered index postalcodeind
on friends_etc(postalcode)

Creating clustered indexes on segments: The create index command allows you to create the index on a specified segment. Since the leaf level of a clustered index and its data pages are the same by definition, creating a clustered index and using the on segment_name extension moves a table from the device on which it was created to the named segment.

Specifying index options:

ignore_dup_key: If you try to insert a duplicate value into a column that has a unique index, the command is canceled. You can avoid this situation by including the ignore_dup_key option with a unique index.

Example: Create a table employee
```
CREATE TABLE employee
(emp_id      int         NOT NULL,
 emp_name    char(50)  NOT NULL,
 emp_city    char(20)        NULL)
```

Create a unique clustered index with ignore_dup_key index on employee
CREATE unique clustered index idx1 on employee (emp_id) with ignore_dup_key

Now insert following records in employee table

insert into employee values(101, 'Abhi', 'Singapore')
insert into employee values(102, 'Mike', 'Singapore')
insert into employee values(101, 'Abhi', 'Singapore')
insert into employee values(103, 'Vyas', 'Singapore')

It will give you following error message
(1 row affected)
(1 row affected)
Server Message: Number 3604, Severity 10
Server 'SERVER_NAME', Line 3:
Duplicate key was ignored.
(1 row affected)

Now run select * from employee and see the result set

emp_id	emp_name	emp_city
101	Abhi	Singapore
102	Mike	Singapore
103	Vyas	Singapore

It didn't insert row 3 because index is on key value and 101 is already inserted in 1st record in emp_id column (key column).

Note: The unique index can be either clustered or nonclustered.

ignore_dup_row and *allow_dup_row*: These are options for creating a nonunique, clustered index.

Example: Assuming we have created employee table as we created in above section and now create clustered index with **ignore_dup_row.**

CREATE clustered index idx1 on employee (emp_id) with ignore_dup_row

Now insert following records in employee table
insert into employee values(101, 'Abhi', 'Singapore')
insert into employee values(102, 'Mike', 'Singapore')
insert into employee values(101, 'Abhi', 'Singapore')
insert into employee values(101, 'Vyas', 'Singapore')

It will give you following error message
(1 row affected)
(1 row affected)
Server Message: Number 3605, Severity 10
Server ' SERVER_NAME ', Line 3:
Duplicate row was ignored.
(1 row affected)

Now run select * from employee and see the result set.
emp_id   emp_name   emp_city

101	Abhi	Singapore
101	Vyas	Singapore
102	Mike	Singapore

It didn't insert row 3 because same row (row 1) already inserted in 1st record. It inserted 4th record even key_value 101 (in emp_id column) is same.

Example: Assuming we have created employee table as we created in above section and now create clustered index with **allow_dup_row.**
CREATE clustered index idx1 on employee (emp_id) with allow_dup_row
Now insert following records in employee table
insert into employee values(101, 'Abhi', 'Singapore')
insert into employee values(102, 'Mike', 'Singapore')
insert into employee values(101, 'Abhi', 'Singapore')
insert into employee values(101, 'Vyas', 'Singapore')

It will not give any error message. Now run select * from employee and see the result set.

emp_id	emp_name	emp_city
101	Abhi	Singapore
101	Abhi	Singapore
101	Vyas	Singapore
102	Mike	Singapore

It inserted all the rows even there are duplicate rows.
Note: ignore_dup_row and allow_dup_row are mutually exclusive.

segment_name **option:** The on segment_name clause specifies a database segment name on which the index is to be created.
Example:
create index titleind on titles(title)
on seg1
- A nonclustered index can be created on a different segment than the data pages.
- If you use segment_name when creating a clustered index, the table containing the index moves to the segment you specify.

sp_helpindex: To see the indexes that exist on a table, you can use sp_helpindex.

Syntax: *sp_helpindex objectname*

Note: objectname can be any table name in the current database.

Example: sp_helpindex accounts

CREATE VIEW:

Syntax:

create view [owner .]view_name
[(column_name [, column_name]...)]
as
select [distinct] select_statement
[with check option]

Adaptive Server gives the columns of the view the same names and datatypes as the columns referred to in the select list of the select statement. The select list can be designated by the asterisk (*) or it can be a full or partial list of the column names in the base tables.

Note You cannot use **local variables** in view definitions.

Note: You can rename a view using **sp_rename**.

You can always supply column names, but they are required only:
- A column is derived from an arithmetic expression, function, string concatenation, or constant
- Two or more columns have the same name (usually because of a join)
- You want to give a column in a view a different name than the column from which it is derived

Note: If no column names are specified, the view columns acquire the same names as the columns in the select statement.

Advantage:
- Focus on the data that interests each user, and on the tasks for which that user is responsible.
- Define frequently used joins, projections, and selections as views so that users need not specify all the conditions and qualifications each time an operation is performed on that data.
- Display different data for different users, even when they are using the same data at the same time.
- Through a view, users can query and modify only the data they can see. The rest of the database is neither visible nor accessible.

select **statement with** *create view*: The select statement in the create view statement defines the view.

Example:
create view titles_view
as select title, type, price, pubdate
from titles

With check option: indicates that all data modification statements are validated against the view selection criteria. All rows inserted or updated through the view must remain visible through the view.

Example: The with check option clause validates each inserted or updated row against the view's selection criteria. Rows for which state has a value other than "CA" are rejected
create view stores_cal

as select * from stores
where state = "CA"
with check option

Create view with computed column:
Example:
create view accounts (title, advance, amt_due)
as select titles.title_id, advance,
(price * royalty /100) * total_sales
from titles, roysched
where price > $15
and advance > $5000
and titles.title_id = roysched.title_id

Create view with an aggregate or built-in function:
Example:
create view categories1 (category, average_price)
as select type, avg(price)
from titles
group by type

Views derived from other views:
Example:
create view author_codes
as select distinct au_id
from titleauthor

Views that include IDENTITY columns: You can define a view that includes an IDENTITY column by listing the
column name, or the syb_identity keyword, in the view's select statement.
Example:
create view sales_view
as select syb_identity, stor_id
from sales_daily

Multitable views: Adaptive Server prohibits delete statements on multitable views, but allows update and insert statements that would not be allowed in other systems. You can insert or update a multitable view if:
- The view has no with **check option** clause.
- All columns being inserted or updated belong to the **same base table**.

Note: Adaptive Server combines the statement with the stored definition of the view and translates it into a query on the view's underlying tables. This process is called **view resolution**
Restrictions on views:
- You can create a view only in the current database.
- The number of columns referenced by a view cannot exceed 1024.

- You cannot create a view on a temporary table.
- You cannot create a trigger or build an index on a view.
- You cannot use readtext or writetext on text or unitext, image columns in views.
- You cannot include **order by**, **compute** clauses or the keyword **into** in the select statements that define views.
- You cannot update, insert, or delete from a view with select statements that include the union operator.
- You can combine create view statements with other SQL statements in a single batch.
- You cannot insert directly to a computed column through a view.
- delete statements are not allowed on multitable views.
- You cannot update or insert into a view defined with the distinct clause.

Note: If you alter the structure of a view's underlying tables by adding or deleting columns, the new columns do not appear in a view defined with a select * clause unless the view is dropped and redefined. The asterisk shorthand is interpreted and expanded when the view is first created.
Note: If a view depends on a table or view that has been dropped, Adaptive Server produces an error message when anyone tries to use the view. If a new table or view with the same name and schema is created to replace the one that has been dropped, the view again becomes usable.

Permissions on objects at view creation: You can create a view successfully even if you do not have access to its objects. All permission checks occur when a user invokes the view.

Permissions on objects at view execution When a view is invoked, permission checks on its objects depend on whether the view and all referenced objects are owned by the same user.

4.2 Define system and user-defined datatypes

Adaptive Server supplies several system datatypes, and two user-defined datatypes, **timestamp and sysname**. You can use sp_addtype to build userdefined datatypes based on the system datatypes. You must specify a system datatype or user-defined datatype when declaring a column, local variable, or parameter.

Please see Section **Determine column data type and null/not null status, default values, rules & constraints** for system datatypes range.

4.3 Define column properties such as null and identity

Null values: Null specifies that Server assigns a null value if a user does not provide a value.
Syntax to define column property as NULL:

create table table_name
(column_name datatype NULL)

Example:

CREATE TABLE employee

(emp_id   int   NOT NULL,

 emp_name   char(50)   NOT NULL,

emp_city   char(20) NULL)

Note: A null value is *not* the same as "zero" or "blank." NULL means no entry has been made, and usually implies "value unknown"

If you omit null or not null in the create table statement, Adaptive Server uses the **null** mode defined for the database (by default, **NOT NULL**). Use **sp_dboption** to set the allow nulls by default option to true.

Using IDENTITY columns: An IDENTITY column contains a value for each row, generated automatically by Adaptive Server, that uniquely identifies the row within the table.
Each table can have only **one** IDENTITY column. You can define an IDENTITY column when you create a table with a **create table** or **select into statement**, or add it later with an **alter table statement**.
Syntax:
create table table_name
(column_name numeric(precision ,0) **identity**)

- IDENTITY columns must have a datatype of numeric and scale of 0, or any integer type.
- You can define the IDENTITY column with any desired precision, from 1 to 38 digits.
- You define an IDENTITY column by specifying the keyword identity, instead of **null** or **not null**.
- By default, Adaptive Server begins numbering rows with the value 1, and continues numbering rows consecutively as they are added. Some activities, such as manual insertions, deletions, or transaction rollbacks, and server shutdowns or failures, can create gaps in IDENTITY column values.

Example:
create table sales_detail
(order_num numeric(16 ,0) **identity**,
item_name   varchar(50) not null)

insert into sales_detail (item_name)
values('COMPUTER')
Above insert will insert numeric number automatically in **order_num** column.
order_num   item_name
------------------   ---------
          1   COMPUTER

Creating IDENTITY columns with user-defined datatypes:
Example: Create IDENTITY column with user-defined datatypes
sp_addtype ident, "numeric(5)", "identity"
This example shows an IDENTITY column based on the ident datatype:
create table sales_detail
(order_num ident, item_name varchar(50) NOT NULL)

- You cannot create an IDENTITY column from a user-defined datatype that allows null values.

Referring to IDENTITY columns with *syb_identity*:
Once you have defined an IDENTITY column, you need not remember the actual column name. You can use the syb_identity keyword, qualified by the table name where necessary, in a select, insert, update, or delete statement on
the table. Example:
select * from sales_detail
where syb_identity = 1

Creating "hidden" IDENTITY columns automatically:
System Administrators can use the auto identity database option to automatically include a 10-digit IDENTITY column in new tables. To turn this feature on in a database, use:
sp_dboption database_name, "auto identity", "true"

Note: If you create it like above, The IDENTITY column is not visible when you use select * to retrieve all columns from the table. You must explicitly include the column name, **SYB_IDENTITY_COL** (all uppercase letters), in the select list.
Example:
sp_dboption <database_name>, "auto identity", "true"
Note: you must be in master database while running this command to change database option.
Now create a table:
create table identit_test (col1 char(1))
run sp_help identit_test and check column names. It created table with 2 columns named as below
SYB_IDENTITY_COL
col1
Insert a value:
insert into identit_test values ('A')
run select SYB_IDENTITY_COL,* from identit_test
it will display following row:
SYB_IDENTITY_COL   col1
1   A

To set the precision of the automatic IDENTITY column, use the size of auto identity configuration parameter. For example, to set the precision of the IDENTITY column to 15 use:
sp_configure "size of auto identity", 15

4.4 Define temporary tables

Temporary tables are created in tempdb database (one of the default system database).
There are two types of Temporary tables:

- Tables that can be shared among Adaptive Server sessions
- Tables that are accessible only by the current Adaptive Server session or procedure

Tables that can be shared among Adaptive Server sessions:
Can be shared among server sessions. The table exists until the current session ends or until its owner drops it using drop table.
Example: Create global temporary table
CREATE TABLE tempdb..accounts
(id int)
Or
Use tempdb
Go
CREATE TABLE accounts
(id int)

Example: Drop temporary table
Drop table tempdb..accounts

Tables that are accessible only by the current Adaptive Server session or procedure:
Tables those are accessible only by the current Adaptive Server session or procedure. The table exists until the current session or procedure ends, or until its owner drops it using **drop table**. Create a nonshareable temporary table by specifying a **pound sign (#)** before the table name in the create table statement.
Example: Create local temporary table
CREATE table #accounts
(id int)
Or
Creating a temporary table from another table
*SELECT * into #accounts FROM accounts*

Above created table #accounts will be dropped if current session ends or if user drops it by using drop table command like
Drop table #accounts

To ensure that a temporary table name is unique for the current session, Adaptive Server:
- Truncates the table name to 238 bytes, including the pound sign (#)—if necessary
- Appends a 17-digit numeric suffix that is unique for an Adaptive Server session

Example: The following example shows a table created as #temptable and stored as #temptable00000050010721973:
use pubs2
go
create table #temptable (task char(30))
go
use tempdb

go
select name from sysobjects where name like
"#temptable%"
go

name

#temptable00000050010721973
(1 row affected)

Temporary tables in stored procedures:
- Stored procedures can reference temporary tables that are created during the current session.
- Temporary tables with names beginning with "#" that are created within stored procedures disappear when the procedure exits.
- You can create temporary tables without the # prefix, using create table tempdb..tablename from inside a stored procedure. These tables do not disappear when the procedure completes, so they can be referenced by independent procedures.

Note: You can use a user-defined datatype when creating a temporary table only if the datatype exists in tempdb..systypes

Note: To add an object to tempdb for the current session only, execute sp_addtype while using tempdb. To add an object permanently in tempdb, execute sp_addtype in model, then restart Adaptive Server so model is copied to tempdb.

Note: Temporary tables are not recoverable.

Rules that apply to both types of temporary tables:
- System procedures such as sp_help work on temporary tables only if you invoke them from tempdb.
- You cannot use user-defined datatypes in temporary tables unless the datatypes exist in tempdb; that is, unless the datatypes have been explicitly created in tempdb since the last time Adaptive Server was restarted.
- You can associate rules, defaults, and indexes with temporary tables. Indexes created on a temporary table disappear when the temporary table disappears.
- You do not have to set the select into/bulkcopy option on to select into a temporary table.

Rules that apply to only local temporary tables:
- You cannot create **views** on these tables.
- You cannot associate **triggers** with these tables.
- You cannot tell which **session** or **procedure** has created these tables.

4.5 Describe different partitioning strategies

Data partitioning breaks up large tables and indexes into smaller pieces that can reside on separate partitions.

Note: A segment is a portion of a device that is defined within ASE. It is used for the storage of specific types of data such as system data, log data, and the data itself.

Partitions can be placed on individual segments and multiple partitions can be placed on a single segment. In turn, a segment or segments can be placed on any logical or physical device, thus isolating I/O and aiding performance and data availability.

Note: Partitions are transparent to the end user, who can select, insert, and delete data using the same DML commands whether the table is partitioned or not.
Note: To view information about partitions use sp_helppartition.

Benefits of Partitioning:
- Improved scalability.
- Improved performance – concurrent multiple I/O on different partitions, and multiple threads on multiple CPUs working concurrently on multiple partitions.
- Faster response time.
- Partition transparency to applications.
- Very large database (VLDB) support – concurrent scanning of multiple partitions of very large tables.
- Range partitioning to manage historical data.

Data partitions: A data partition is an independent database object with a **unique partition ID**. It is a subset of a table, and shares the column definitions and referential and integrity constraints of the **base table**.
Note: Sybase recommends that you bind each partition to a different segment, and bind each segment to a different storage device to maximize I/O parallelism,
Each semantically partitioned table has a **partition key** that determines how individual data rows are distributed to different partitions.

Section 4- ANSI SQL - DDL

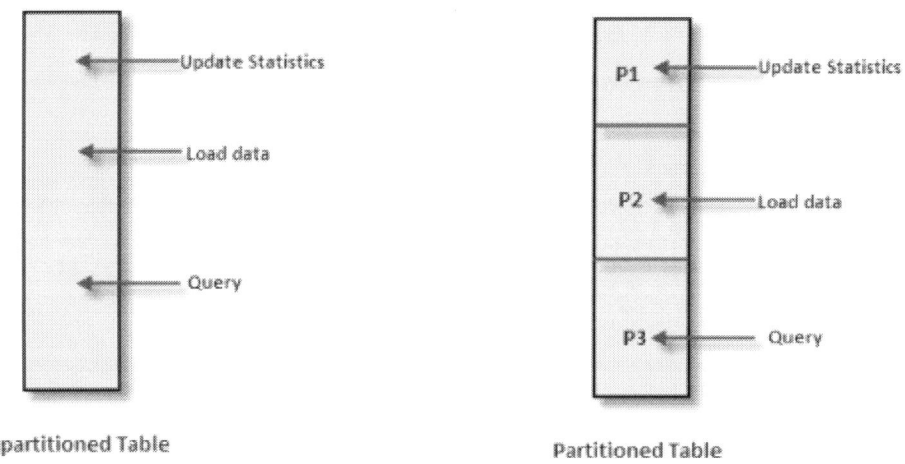

Unpartitioned Table   Partitioned Table

P1,P2,P3 are partitions for table

Above above shows a number of activities happening on a table like Update statistics, Load data, a large query. So many activities on a large and unpartitioned table will slow down performance. By partitioning a table or index into smaller pieces, DBAs can run utilities on a per partition basis. This results in the
utilities running faster, allowing other operations to work efficiently on data in other partitions and insuring that the
bulk of the data in the table is available for applications.

Index partitions: An index partition is an independent database object identified with a unique combination of index ID and partition ID; it is a subset of an index, and resides on a segment or other storage device.
(Please see section "Describe local/global indexes on partitioned tables" for more detail on Index partitions)

Partition IDs: A partition ID is a **pseudo-random number** similar to object ID. An index or data partition is identified with a unique combination of index ID and partition ID.

Partitioning types:
- Range partitioning
- Hash partitioning
- List partitioning
- Round-robin partitioning

Range partitioning: Rows in a range-partitioned table or index are distributed among partitions according to values in the partitioning key columns.
Example:

```
create table employees(emp_id int )
            partition by range(emp_id)
            (p1 values <=(100000),
            p2 values <= (200000))
```

Range partitioning is particularly useful for high-performance applications in both OLTP and decision-support environments like tables with constant updates, inserts, and deletes that contain a column or columns with sequential data in them such as a customer ID or a transaction date.Select ranges carefully so that rows are assigned equally to all partitions
Note: Range partitions are ordered; that is, each succeeding partition must have a higher bound than the previous partition.
Example: if you run below; it will give error **"Partition 'p2' -- Partition condition not in incremental order."**

```
create table employees(emp_id int )
            partition by range(emp_id)
            (p1 values <=(200000),
            p2 values <= (100000))
```

Hash partitioning: Uses a hash function to specify the partition assignment for each row. You select the partitioning key columns, but Adaptive Server chooses the hash function that controls the partition assignment. If you choose an appropriate partition key, hash partitioning distributes data evenly across all partitions. However, if you choose an inappropriate key—for example, a key that has the same value for many rows—the result may be skewed data, with an unbalanced distribution of rows among the partitions.

Hash partitioning is a good choice for:
- Large tables with many partitions—particularly in decision-support environments.
- Efficient equality searches on hash key columns.
- Data with no particular order, for example, alphanumeric product code keys

List partitioning: List partitioning is similar to range partitioning, but here the actual values to be placed on a partition are specified. List partitioning is useful for controlling where specific values are stored, even if the column itself is not sorted, and in cases where the order of values in the partition is not important.
Example of of the syntax used to create a table with list partitioning.
```
create table nation (nationkey integer not null, name char(25) not
null, regionkey varchar(30) not null, comment varchar(152) not null)
partition by list (regionkey)
(region1 values ('Americas'),
 region2 values ('Asia'),
 region3 values ('Europe'),
 region4 values ('Australia', 'Other'))
```

As with range partitioning, list partitioning distributes rows semantically; that is, according to the actual value in the partitioning key column. The value in the partitioning key column is compared with sets of user-supplied values to determine the partition to which each row belongs. The partition key must match exactly one of the values specified for
a partition.
A list partition has only one key column. The value list for each partition must contain at least one value, and value lists must be unique across all partitions. You can specify as many as 250 values in each list partition. List partitions are not ordered.

Round-robin partitioning:
In round-robin partitioning, Adaptive Server does not use partitioning criteria. Round-robin-partitioned tables have **no partition key**. Adaptive Server assigns rows in a round-robin manner to each partition so that each partition contains a more or less equal number of rows and load balancing is achieved. Because there is no partition key, rows are distributed randomly across all partitions.
Example:
create table emp_details
(emp_id int not null,
emp_name varchar(40) null,
city varchar(20) null,
state char(2) null)
partition by roundrobin 3 on (seg1)
Round-robin partitioning is supported primarily for compatibility with versions of Adaptive Server earlier than 15.0. In addition, round-robin partitioning offers:
- Multiple insertion points for future inserts.
- A way to enhance performance using parallelism.
- A way to perform administrative tasks, such as updating statistics and truncating data on individual partitions.

Partition type	Partition key allowed
Range	Upto 31 Keys
Hash	Upto 31 Keys
List(Semantically partitioned table)	One key
Round robin	No partition key

Note: You cannot specify a partition when using such DML commands as select, insert, and delete. Partitions are transparent when you access the table using DML commands.

Note: You can assign multiple partitions to a segment, but a partition can be assigned to only one segment. See below image to understand.

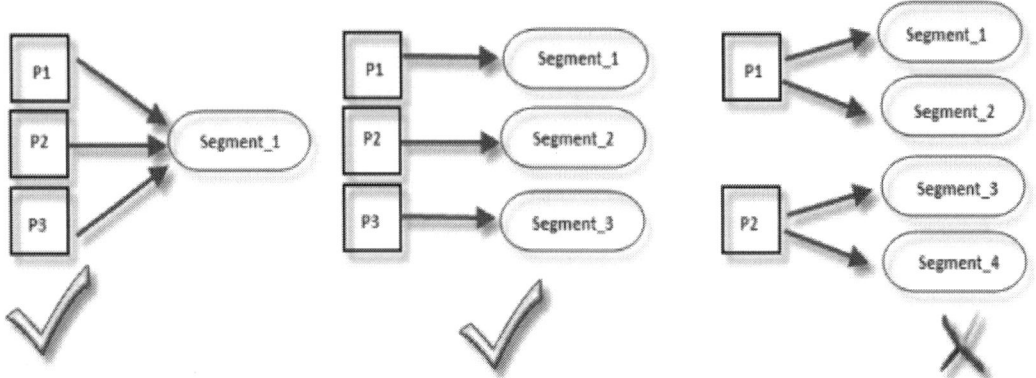

Order of partitioning tasks:
1. Maps a physical disk device or operating system file to a logical database device name (by using disk init):
Example:
use master
disk init
name ="data01",
physname = "SYB_DEV01/device_01 ",
size = "50M"
2. **A**ssign the new device to the database containing the table or index to partition (by using Alter table)
use master
alter database database_1 on data01
3. Define the segments in the database (This step is optional). Assuming data02 is also created as data01.
use database_1
sp_addsegment seg1, database_1, data01
sp_addsegment seg2, database_1, data02
4. Drop all indexes from the table to partition
Use database_1
drop index emp_transactions.emp_id
5. Using sp_dboption, enable the bulk copy of table or index data to the new partitions.
use master
sp_dboption database_1,"select into", true
6. Use alter table to repartition a table or create table to create a new table with partitions; use create index to create a new, partitioned index; or use select into to create a new, partitioned table from an existing table.
use database_1
alter table emp_transactions by range (emp_id)
(p1 values <= (1000) on seg1,
 p2 values <= (5000) on seg2)
7. Re-create indexes on the partitioned table. For example, on the emp_transactions table:
use database_1

create nonclustered index emp_idx
on emp_transactions (emp_id)

To create a partitioned table from an existing table, use the select into command:
Example:
*select * into emp_report partition by range (emp_id)*
(P1 values <= (100000) on seg1,
P2 values <= (200000) on seg2)
from emp_detail

Useful functions:
- **partition_id :** Returns partition ID for a specified table and partition
  Example: select partition_id("employee_transaction",""p1")
- **partition_name:** Returns partition name for the partition id
  Example: select partition_name(0, 1854303503)

4.6 Understand partitioning options with alter table

You can use the alter table command to:
- Change an unpartitioned table to a multipartitioned table.
- Add one or more partitions to a list- or range-partitioned tables.
- Repartition a table for a different partitioning type.
- Repartition a table for a different partitioning key or bound.
- Repartition a table for a different number of partitions.
- Repartition a table to assign partitions to different segments.

Repartitioning a table: procedure for repartitioning a table
1. If the partition key or type is to change during the repartition process, drop all indexes on the table.
2. Repartition the table using alter table.
3. If the partition key or type changed during the repartition process, recreate the indexes on the table.

Changing an unpartitioned table to a partitioned table:
Example:
alter table employee_transaction partition by range(emp_id)
(p1 values <= (100) on seg1,
p2 values <=(200) on seg2,
p3 values <= (300) on seg3)
Adding partitions to a partitioned table:
Example:
alter table employee_transaction add partition
(p4 values <= (500) on seg4)

Note: You can't add partitions to a hash or round-robin partitioned table. you can to list or range partitioned tables.

Changing partition type: Example:
alter table employee_transaction partition by hash(emp_id) 2
Note: You must drop all indexes before changing the partitioning type.
Changing the partitioning key:
alter table employee_transaction partition by hash(transaction_date) 2
Note: You must drop all indexes before changing the partitioning key.

Note: You can change partition type and partition key in a single alter command as well.
For example in above example table *employee_transaction* is hash partitioned and partition key is *transaction_date*, now we will change partition type and key in single alter command as follows:
alter table employee_transaction partition by range(emp_id)
(p1 values <= (100),
p2 values <=(200),
p3 values <= (300))
In above alter command, we changed partition type from **hash** to **range** and partition key from *transaction_date* to *emp_id*. (of course there should not be any index on the table if you want to do so).

Note: You can create an unpartitioned round-robin table from a partitioned roundrobin table using alter table with the unpartition clause—as long as all partitions are on the same segment, and there are no indexes on the table.
Example:
alter table employee_transaction unpartition

Note: alter table with the partition clause is supported only for the creation of round-robin partitions. It is not supported for the creation of other types of partitions.
Example: *alter table discounts partition 3*

Configuration partitions:
- number of open partitions – specifies the number of partitions that Adaptive Server can access at one time. The **default value is 500**.
- partition spinlock ratio – specifies the number of spinlocks used to protect against concurrent access of open partitions. The **default value is 10**.

You can delete all the information in a partition without affecting information in other partitions:
Example: *truncate table emp_detail partition p1*

Update statistics on partitions: You can action following tasks for a partition
- update statistics
- update table statistics
- update all statistics

- update index statistics
- delete statistics

Example: *update statistics employee_transaction partition p1*

Summary

We discussed about DDL (Data Definition Language) in this section.

- CREATE TABLE:

    create table table_name
    (column_name datatype)

- CREATE INDEX:

    create index index_name
    on table_name (column_name)

- You can create indexes on computed columns as though they were regular columns, as long as the datatype of the result can be indexed.

- CREATE VIEW:

    create view [owner.]view_name
    [(column_name [, column_name]...)]
    as
    select [distinct] select_statement
    [with check option]

- You must specify a system datatype or user-defined datatype when declaring a column, local variable, or parameter.

- An IDENTITY column contains a value for each row, generated automatically by Adaptive Server, that uniquely identifies the row within the table.

- Temporary tables are created in tempdb database (one of the default system database).

    There are two types of Temporary tables:

    - Tables that can be shared among Adaptive Server sessions
    - Tables that are accessible only by the current Adaptive Server session or procedure

- Data partitioning breaks up large tables and indexes into smaller pieces that can reside on separate partitions.

- An index partition is an independent database object identified with a unique combination of index ID and partition ID; it is a subset of an index, and resides on a segment or other storage device.

Pactice Test

1. Which of the following command can create a table in another database from your current database? (Assuming newdb is another database)
    A. create table newdb..employee (emp_id int)
    B. create table newdb.employee (emp_id int)
    C. create table employee (emp_id int) in newdb
    D. create table [newdb].employee (emp_id int)

2. Which of the following database object you can create in a database other than the current database?
    A. Views
    B. Tables
    C. stored procedures
    D. Triggers
    E. Rules and defaults
    F. Indexes

3. NULL value means?
    A. 0
    B. Blank
    C. value unknown
    D. " "

4. A _____ is a portion of a device that is defined within ASE. It is used for the storage of specific types of data such as system data, log data, and the data itself.
    A. segment
    B. table
    C. log
    D. disk

5. A data partition is an independent database object with a?
    A. unique partition ID
    B. unique disk ID
    C. unique part ID
    D. None of the above

6. You can specify maximum _____ values in each list partition?
    A. 1
    B. Depends on database size
    C. 250
    D. 255

Section 5 - ANSI SQL - DML

5.1 Describe the data manipulation commands: select, insert, update, and delete, and the use of cursors

Data Manipulation Commands: Data manipulation language (DML) commands query and manipulate data. Following are   DML commands
Select, Insert, Update, Delete

SELECT:
The select command retrieves data stored in the rows and columns of database tables using a procedure called a query. A query has three main parts: the select clause, the from clause, and the where clause.

A SQL query requests data from the database and receives the results. This process, also known as data retrieval, is expressed using the select statement. You can use it for selections, which retrieve a subset of the rows
in one or more tables, and you can use it for projections, which retrieve a subset of the columns in one or more tables.
A simple example of a select statement is:
select select_list from table_list
where search_conditions

The asterisk (*) selects all the column names in all the tables specified by the from clause. Use it to save typing time and errors when you want to see all the columns in a table. * retrieves the data in create table order.
The syntax for selecting all the columns in a table is:
*select **
from table_list

Note: You can also use "*" more than once in a query:
*select *, * from employee*

To select only specific columns in a table, use:
select column_name[, column_name]...
from *table_name*

You can rename a column heading for display purposes by using one of the following instead of only the column name in a select list.
column_heading = column_name
column_name column_heading
column_name as *column_heading*

Example:

select Publisher = pub_name, pub_id from publishers
select pub_name Publisher, pub_id from publishers
select pub_name as Publisher, pub_id from publishers

The select statement can also include one or more **expressions**, which allow you to manipulate the data retrieved.
select expression [, expression]...
from table_list

An expression is any combination of constants, column names, functions, subqueries, or case expressions, connected by arithmetic or bitwise operators and parentheses.
If any table or column name in the list does not conform to the rules for valid identifiers, set the quoted_identifier option on and enclose the identifier in double quotes

When a select list includes **text, unitext, image, and values**, the limit on the length of the data returned depends on the setting of the @@textsize global variable. The default setting for @@textsize depends on the software you use to access Adaptive Server; **the default value is 32K for isql.** To change the value, use the set command:
set textsize 25
With this setting of **@@textsize**, a select statement that includes a text column displays only the first 25 bytes of the data.
Note: When you select image data, the returned value includes the characters "0x", which indicates that the data is hexadecimal. These two characters are counted as part of @@textsize.
To reset @@textsize to the Adaptive Server default value, use:
set textsize 0

Note: local variables can not be declared in a select statement

INSERT: You can use the insert command to add rows to the database in two ways; with the values keyword or with a select statement:
- **The values keyword specifies values for some or all of the columns in a new row.**
  Syntax:
  insert *table_name*
  values (*constant1, constant2, ...*)
- **You can use a select statement in an insert statement to pull values from one or more tables**
  Syntax:
  insert *table_name*
  select *column_list*
  from *table_list*
     where *search_conditions*

Note: Limit is 50 tables in list (including table name in insert statement)
Note: You cannot use a compute clause in a select statement that is inside an insert statement, because statements that include compute do not generate normal rows.

When you add text, unitext, or image values with insert, all the data is written to the transaction log. You can use the writetext command to add these values without logging the long chunks of data that may comprise text, unitext, or

Example: Adding new rows with values
insert into employee
values ("101", "Abhi","Singapore")
Note: Data values should be typed in the same order as the column names in the original create table statement

Example: Inserting data into specific columns
insert into employee (emp_id, emp_name)
values ("101", "Abhisek")
Note: All other columns that are not included in the column list must be defined to **allow null values**. If you skip a column that has a default bound to it, the **default** is used.

Example: Using the NULL character string
insert into employee (emp_id, emp_name, city)
values ("101", "Abhisek", NULL)
Note: Only columns for which NULL was specified in the create table statement and into which you have explicitly entered NULL (no quotes), or into which no data has been entered, contain null values.
Note: NULL is not an empty string

Example: Inserting NULLs into columns that do not allow them
insert employee_transaction
select emp_id, isnull(salary, 0) from emp_salary
Note: Without the **isnull** function, this command inserts all the rows with non-null values into advances and produces error messages for all the rows where the advance column in titles contains NULL.

When you specify values for only some of the columns in a row, one of four things can happen to the columns with no values:
- If a default value exists for the column or user-defined datatype of the column, it is entered.
- If NULL was specified for the column when the table was created and no default value exists for the column or datatype, NULL is entered.
- If the column has the IDENTITY property, a unique, sequential value is entered.
- If NULL was not specified for the column when the table was created and no default exists, Adaptive Server rejects the row and displays an error message.

Example: Adaptive-Server-generated values for IDENTITY columns (table has emp_id an IDENTITY column and emp_name columns)
insert employee (emp_name)

values ("Abhisek")

> **Note:** When you insert a row into a table with an IDENTITY column, Adaptive Server automatically generates the column value. Do not include the name of the IDENTITY column in the column list or its value in the values list.

Example: Explicitly inserting data into an IDENTITY column
set identity_insert sales_daily on
insert sales_daily (syb_identity, stor_id) values (101, "1349")

Note: set identity_insert on for only one table at a time in a database within a session.
Note: After you set identity_insert off, you can insert IDENTITY column values automatically, without specifying the IDENTITY column, as before.

UPDATE: Use the update command to change single rows, groups of rows, or all rows in a table. As in all data modification statements, you can change the data in only one table at a time.
- If an update statement violates an integrity constraint, the update does not take place and an error message is generated. The update is canceled.
- if it affects the table's **IDENTITY** column, or if one of the values being added is the wrong datatype, or if it violates a rule that has been defined for one of the columns or datatypes involved.
- if an update statement modifies the same row twice, the second update is not based on the new values from the first update but on the **original values**. The results are unpredictable, since they depend on the **order of processing**.
- The update command is logged.
- If you are changing large blocks of text, unitext, or image data, try using the writetext command, which is not logged.
- You are limited to approximately 125K per update statement.

Syntax:
update table_name
set column_name = expression
where search_conditions

Set variables in an update statement:
update table_name
set variable_name = expression
where search_conditions

Example: Using the *set* clause with *update*
update Employee set Dept = "IT", Country = "Singapore"

Example: use computed column values in an update

*update titles
set price = price * 2*
Note: If you do not have a where clause, the specified columns of *all* the rows are updated with the values given in the set clause.

Example: Using the *where* clause with *update*
*update Employee
set Dept = "IT", Country = "Singapore"
where Dept = "Information Tech" and city = "India"*

Example: Using the *from* clause with *update*
Use the from clause to pull data from one or more tables into the table you are updating.
*update titleauthor set title_id = titles.title_id
from titleauthor, titles, authors where titles.title = "The Psychology of Computer Cooking"
and authors.au_id = titleauthor.au_id
and au_lname = "Stringer"*

Note: As an alternative to the from clause in the update statement, you can use a subquery.

Example: Updating IDENTITY columns
You can use the syb_identity keyword, qualified by the table name, where necessary, to update an IDENTITY column.
*update emp_transaction set emp_dept = "IT"
where syb_identity = 1*

DELETE: delete works for both single-row and multiple-row operations.
Basic Syntax:
*delete table_name
where column_name = expression*

Example: Using the *from and where* clause with *delete*
*delete titles
from authors, titles, titleauthor
where titles.title_id = titleauthor.title_id
and authors.au_id = titleauthor.au_id
and city = "Big Bad Bay City"*

Note: The where clause specifies which rows are to be removed. When no where clause is given in the delete statement, *all* rows in the table are removed.

Example: Deleting from IDENTITY columns
You can use the syb_identity keyword in a delete statement on tables containing an IDENTITY column.
delete sales_monthly

where syb_identity = 1

Deleting all rows from a table:
Use **truncate** table to delete all rows in a table. truncate table is almost always faster than a **delete** statement with no conditions, because the delete **logs each change**, while truncate table just logs the **deallocation of entire data pages**.

Note: You cannot use truncate table if another table has rows that reference it through a referential integrity constraint. Delete the rows from the foreign table, or truncate the foreign table and then truncate the primary table.

Syntax:
truncate table [[*database.*]*owner.*]*table_name*
[partition *partition_name*]

CURSORS:
A **cursor** accesses the results of a SQL select statement one or more rows at a time. Cursors allow you to modify or delete individual rows or a group of rows.

Cursor parts	Description
Cursor result set	The set (table) of qualifying rows that result from the execution of a query associated with the cursor.
Cursor position	The cursor position indicates the current row of the cursor. With an updatable cursor, you can explicitly modify or delete that row using update or delete statements, with a clause naming the cursor.

Two attributes specify the cursor's behavior:
• Sensitivity   • Scrollability
Adaptive Server offers two keywords to specify sensitivity and provides keywords for specifying scrollability:

Please see Section **Identify aspects of insensitive/semi-sensitive scrollable cursors for more info on Sensitivity and Scrollability**

Any sort command forces the cursor to become insensitive, even if you have declared it semi_sensitive, because it requires the rows in a table to be ordered before sort can be executed. A worktable, however, may be populated before any rows can be fetched.

Using cursors:

Declaring the cursor: When you declare the cursor, Adaptive Server creates the cursor structure. The server does not compile the cursor from the cursor declaration, however, until the cursor is open.

Syntax:

declare cursor_name cursor for select_statement
  [for {read only | update [of column_name_list]}]

- cusor name can not be more than **30 characters** and must be a valid Adaptive Server identifier containing, and must start with a letter, a pound sign (#), or an underscore (_).
- *select_statement* can not contain a compute, for browse, or into clause

Example:

declare emp_csr cursor for select emp_id, emp_name
from empployee where status = "Active"
for update of last_name

In above example *for update* clause used, so it can be used to update column *last_name* for any fetched row.

Unless you plan to update or delete rows through a cursor, you should declare a cursor **as read-only**. If you do not explicitly specify **read only** or **update**, the cursor is **implicitly updatable** when the **select** statement does *not* contain any of the following constructs:

distinct option , **group by** clause, Aggregate function, Subquery, **union** operator, **at isolation read uncommitted** clause

You cannot specify the **for update** clause if a cursor's *select_statement* contains one of the above constructs. Adaptive Server also defines a cursor as read-only if you declare certain types of cursors that include an **order by** clause as part of their *select_statement*.

Opening the cursor: If cursor declared

Outside of a stored procedure: Adaptive Server compiles the cursor and generates an optimized query plan. It then performs preliminary operations for executing the scan defined in the cursor and ready to returning a result row.

Within a stored procedure: If stored procedure is called for the first time, Adaptive Server compiles the cursor, generates an optimized query plan, and stores the plan for later use. If the stored procedure is called again later, the cursor already exists in compiled form. When the cursor is opened, Adaptive Server needs only to perform preliminary operations for executing a scan and returning a result set.

Note: Error messages related to declaring the cursor appear during the cursor open phase.

Syntax:

open cursor_name

Example:

open emp_csr

Note: You cannot open a cursor that is already open or that has not been defined with the **declare cursor** statement. You can reopen a closed cursor to reset the cursor position to the beginning of the cursor result set.

Fetching from the cursor: The fetch command executes the compiled cursor to return one or more rows meeting the conditions defined in the cursor. By default, a fetch returns only a single row.

if cursors is	
non-scrollable	The first fetch returns the first row that meets the cursor's search conditions, and stores the current position of the cursor. Each subsequent fetch uses the cursor position of the previous fetch to locate the next cursor row.
Scrollable	you can fetch any rows and set the current cursor position to any row in the result set, by specifying the fetch orientation option first, last, next, prior, absolute or relative in a fetch statement.

Note: Adaptive Server creates the cursor result set either by scanning the tables directly or by scanning a worktable generated by the query type.

Syntax:
fetch *cursor_name* [into *fetch_target_list*]
or
fetch [next | prior | first | last | absolute *fetch_offset* | relative *fetch_offset*] [from] cursor_name [into *fetch_target_list*]
Example: (First fetch)
fech emp_csr
emp_id   emp_name
----------   ----------------------
101   Abhisek

Note: After you **fetch** all the rows, the cursor points to the last row of the result set. If you **fetch** again, Adaptive Server returns a warning through the *@@sqlstatus* variable.
Note: By default, fetch retrieves only one row at a time. You can use the set cursor rows command to change the number of rows that are returned by fetch. However, this option does not affect a fetch containing an into clause.

Syntax:
set cursor rows number for cursor_name

Example:
set cursor rows 2 for emp_csr
After you set the number of cursor rows, each fetch of authors_crsr returns two rows from the cursor result set:
fetch emp_csr
emp_id   emp_name
----------   ----------------------
101   Abhisek

102	Mike

> **Note:** Use the *@@rowcount* global variable to monitor the number of rows of the cursor result set returned to the client up to the last fetch. This variable displays the total number of rows seen by the cursor at any one time.

Processing the row: By examining, updating, or deleting it through the cursor, Adaptive Server updates or deletes the data in the cursor result set (and in the corresponding base tables that derived the data) at the current cursor position after a fetch. This operation is optional.
The following update statement raises the salary of employee by 5 percent; it affects only the employees currently pointed to by the emp_csr cursor:
update employee
*set salary = salary * .05 + salary*
where current of emp_csr

Updating a cursor row involves changing data in the row or deleting the row completely. **You cannot use cursors to insert rows.** All updates through a cursor affect the corresponding **base tables** included in the cursor result set.

Closing the cursor: Adaptive Server closes the cursor result set, removes any remaining temporary tables, and releases the server resources held for the cursor structure. However, it keeps the query plan for the cursor so that it can be opened again. Closing the cursor does not change its definition. If you reopen a cursor, Adaptive Server creates a new cursor result set using the same query as before.
Syntax:
close *cursor_name*
Example:
close emp_csr

When you close a cursor and then reopen it, Adaptive Server recreates the cursor result, and positions the cursor before the first valid row. This allows you to process a cursor result set as many times as necessary. You can close the cursor at any time; you do not have to go through the entire result set.

Deallocating the cursor: Adaptive Server removes the query plan from memory and eliminates all trace of the cursor structure.
Syntax:
deallocate cursor *cursor_name*
Note: keyword cursor is optional in ASE 15.0 or later. Like
deallocate cursor_name

Note: You can not use deallocated cursor again. You need to declare it again.

Types of cursors: There are four types of cursors:

Type	Description
Client cursors	Declared through Open Client calls (or Embedded SQL). Open Client keeps track of the rows returned from Adaptive Server and buffers them for the application. Updates and deletes to the result set of client cursors can be done only through the Open Client calls.
Execute cursors	a subset of client cursors whose result set is defined by a stored procedure. The stored procedure can use parameters. The values of the parameters are sent through Open Client calls.
Server cursors	declared in SQL. If server cursors are used in stored procedures, the client executing the stored procedure is not aware of them. Results returned to the client for a fetch are the same as the results from a normal select.
Language cursors	declared in SQL without using Open Client. As with server cursors, the client is not aware of the cursors, and the results are returned to the client in the same format as a normal select.

Cursor scope:
- Within a user session, the cursor exists only until the user ends the session.
- If a declare cursor statement is part of a stored procedure or trigger, the cursor created within it applies to that scope and to the scope the stored procedure or trigger.
- cursors declared inside a trigger on an **inserted** or a **deleted** table are not accessible to any **nested** stored procedures or triggers.
- Once the stored procedure or trigger completes, Adaptive Server deallocates the cursors created within it.
- A cursor name must be unique within a given scope. Adaptive Server detects name conflicts within a particular scope only during **runtime**.

Cursor scans and the cursor result set:
The method create the cursor result set depends on the cursor and on the query plan for the cursor select statement.
- If a worktable is not required, Adaptive Server performs a fetch by positioning the cursor in the base table, using the table's index keys.
- All scrollable cursors and insensitive non-scrollable cursors require worktables to hold the cursor result set.
- When a worktable is used, the rows retrieved with a cursor fetch statement may not reflect the values in the actual base table rows.
- cursor select query is processed like a normal select query. This process, known as **cursor scans.**
- Adaptive Server requires that cursor scans use a unique index of a table, particularly for **isolation level 0 reads**.

Making cursors updatable:
You can update or delete a row returned by a cursor if the cursor is updatable.

Section 5- ANSI SQL - DML

- You can explicitly specify whether a cursor is updatable by using the read only or update keywords in the declare statement.
- Make sure the table being updated has a unique index. If it does not, Server rejects the declare cursor statement.
- All scrollable cursors and all insensitive cursors are read-only.

Determining which columns can be updated:
- If you do not specify a *column_name_list* with the for update clause, all the specified columns in the query are updatable.
- Adaptive Server considers an index containing an IDENTITY column to be unique, even if it is not so declared.

If you do not specify the for update clause	If you specify the for update clause
Adaptive Server chooses any unique index, although it can also use other indexes or table scans if no unique index exists for the specified table columns.	Adaptive Server must use a unique index defined for one or more of the columns to scan the base table. If no unique index exists, Adaptive Server returns an error message.
Adaptive Server allows you to update columns in the column_name_list that are not specified in the list of columns of the cursor's select_statement, but that are part of the tables specified in the select_statement.	you can update only the columns in that list.

If the cursor is declared with a for update clause, and table has only one unique index, you cannot include its column in the for update *column_name_list*; Adaptive Server uses it during the cursor scan. If the table has more than one unique index, you can include the index column in the for update *column_name_list*, so that Adaptive Server can use another unique index, which may not be in the *column_name_list*, to perform the cursor scan.

For example, the table used in the following declare cursor statement has one unique index, on the column c3, so that column should not be included in the for update list:

declare mycursor cursor
for select c1, c2, 3
from mytable
for update of c1, c2

However, if mytable has more than one unique index, for example, on columns c3 and c4, you must specify one unique index in the for update clause as follows:

declare mycursor cursor
for select c1, c2, 3
from mytable
for update of c1, c2, c3

Notice that you cannot include both c3 and c4 in the *column_name_list*. In general, Adaptive Server needs at least one unique index key, not on the list, to perform a cursor scan.

Allowing Adaptive Server to use the unique index in the cursor scan in this manner helps to prevent an update anomaly called the **Halloween problem**.
Another way to avoid the Halloween problem is to create tables with the unique auto_identity index database option set to on.

Updating cursor result set rows: You can use the where current of clause of the update statement to update the row at the current cursor position. Any update to the cursor result set also affects the base table row from which the cursor row is derived.
Example:
update employee set last_name = "Vyas",
where current of pubs_crsr
Note: After the update, the cursor position remains unchanged.

Deleting cursor result set rows: Using the where current of clause of the delete statement, you can delete the row at the current cursor position. When you delete a row from the cursor's result set, the row is deleted from the underlying database table. You can delete only one row at a time using the cursor.
Example:
Delete from employee set last_name = "Vyas",
where current of pubs_crsr

Note: After you delete a row from a cursor, Adaptive Server positions the cursor before the row following the deleted row in the cursor result set.

5.2 Identify important clauses of DML statements, such as where, having, order by, etc.
WHERE:
Sets the search conditions in a **select**, **insert**, **update**, or **delete** statement
If you use more than one search condition in a single statement, connect the conditions with **and** or **or**.

Few Examples:
Example 1
where advance * $2 > total_sales * price
Example 2 Finds all the rows in which the phone number does not begin with 415:
where phone not like '415%'
Example 3 Finds the rows for authors named Carson, Carsen, Karsen, and Karson:
where au_lname like "[CK]ars[eo]n"
Example 4 Finds the row of the sales_east table in which the IDENTITY column has a value of 4:
where sales_east.syb_identity = 4
Example 5
where advance < $5000 or advance is null
Example 6
where (type = "business" or type = "psychology") and advance > $5500
Example 7

where total_sales between 4095 and 12000
Example 8 Finds the rows in which the state is one of the three in the list:
where state in ('CA', 'IN', 'MD')

- The number of **and** and **or** conditions in a where clause is limited only by the amount of memory available to run the query.
- The pattern string included in the like predicate is limited only by the size of string that can be placed in a varchar.
- If a column is compared to a constant or variable in a where clause, Adaptive Server converts the constant or variable into the datatype of the column so that the optimizer can use the index for data retrieval. For example, float expressions are converted to int when compared to an int column. For example:
  where int_column = 2

GROUP BY AND HAVING:
Used in **select** statements to divide a table into groups and to return only groups that match conditions in the having clause. **group by** is typically used in conjunction with aggregates to specify how to group the unaggregated columns of a select query. **having** clauses are applied to these groups.

GROUP BY: specifies the groups into which the table is divided, and if aggregate functions are included in the select list, finds a summary value for each group. These summary values appear as columns in the results, one for each group. You can refer to these **summary columns** in the **having clause**.
You can use the **avg, count, count_big, max, min, and sum aggregate** functions in the select list before group by.

Note: there are two possible algorithms (implemened as operators) for doing group by: **GroupHashing** and **GroupSorted**. (In ASE 15.0 or later version of optimizer.)

GROUP BY all: **all** is a Transact-SQL extension that includes all groups in the results, even those excluded by a **where** clause. **Example:**
select type, avg(price) from titles where advance > 7000
group by all type

Type	
UNDECIDED	NULL
business	2.99
mod_cook	2.99
popular_comp	20
Psychology	NULL
trad_cook	14.99

"NULL" in the aggregate column indicates groups that would be excluded by the where clause. A having clause negates the meaning of all.

aggregate_free_expression: is an expression that includes no aggregates. A Transact-SQL extension allows grouping by an aggregate-free expression as well as by a column name. You cannot group by **column heading** or **alias**.
Example:
select Price=avg(price), Pay=avg(advance),Total=price * $1.15
from titles
group by price * $1.15

HAVING: Sets conditions for the group by clause, similar to the way in which **where** sets conditions for the select clause.
having search conditions can include aggregate expressions; otherwise, having search conditions are identical to where search conditions. This is an example of a having clause with aggregates:
select pub_id, total = sum(total_sales)
from titles
where total_sales is not null
group by pub_id
having count(*)>5

Few Examples:
Example 1 Calculates the average advance and the sum of the sales for each type of book:
select type, avg(advance), sum(total_sales)
from titles
group by type
Example 2 Groups the results by type, then by pub_id within each type:
select type, pub_id, avg(advance), sum(total_sales)
from titles
group by type, pub_id
Example 3 Calculates results for all groups, but displays only groups whose type begins with "p":
select type, avg(price)
from titles
group by type
having type like 'p%'
Example 4 Calculates results for all groups, but displays results for groups matching the multiple conditions in the having clause:
select pub_id, sum(advance), avg(price)
from titles
group by pub_id
having sum(advance) > $15000
and avg(price) < $10
and pub_id > "0700"

Example 5 Calculates the total sales for each group (publisher) after joining the titles and publishers tables:
select p.pub_id, sum(t.total_sales)
from publishers p, titles t
where p.pub_id = t.pub_id
group by p.pub_id

Example 6 Displays the titles that have an advance of more than $1000 and a price that is more than the average price of all titles:
select title_id, advance, price
from titles
where advance > 1000
having price > avg(price)

- The maximum number of group by columns (or expressions) is not explicitly limited. The only limit of group by results is that the width of the group by columns plus the aggregate results be no greater than 64K.
- Null values in the group by column are put into a **single** group.
- You cannot name **text, unitext, or image** columns in group by and having clauses.
- The having clause can include columns or expressions that are not in the select list and not in the group by clause.
- The group by clause can include columns or expressions that are not in the select list.
- You **cannot** use a group by clause in the select statement of an **updatable cursor**.
- Aggregate functions can be used only in the select list or in a having clause. They cannot be used in a where or group by clause.

Aggregate functions are of two types:

aggregates type	description
scalar	Aggregates applied to all the qualifying rows in a table (producing a single value for the whole table per function)
vector	Aggregates applied to a group of rows in a specified column or expression (producing a value for each group per function)

ORDER BY: Returns query results in the specified columns in sorted order.
Syntax:
[*Start of* select *statement*]
[order by {[*table_name.*| *view_name.*]*column_name*
| *select_list_number* | *expression*} [asc | desc]
[,{[*table_name.*| *view_name.*] *column_name*
select_list_number|*expression*} [asc
|desc]]...]
[*End of* select *statement*]
Note: ASC (ascending) is default sort order.
Example: Selects the titles whose price is greater than $19.99 and lists them with the titles in alphabetical order:

select title, type, price
from titles
where price > $19.99
order by title

- You can sort by a column heading, a column name, an expression, an alias name (if specified in the select list), or a number representing the position of the item in the select list (*select_list_number*).
- If you sort by *select_list_number*, the columns to which the order by clause refers must be included in the select list, and the select list cannot be * (asterisk).

Restrictions:
- The maximum number of columns allowed in an order by clause is **31**.
- You cannot use order by on text, unitext, or image datatype columns.
- **Subqueries** and **view** definitions cannot include an order by clause (or a **compute** clause or the keyword **into**). Conversely, you cannot use a subquery in an order by list.
- You cannot update the result set of a server- or language- type cursor if it contains an order by clause in its select statement.

Collating sequences:
- With order by, null values **precede** all others.
- The sort order (collating sequence) on your Adaptive Server determines how your data is sorted. The sort order choices are **binary, dictionary, case-insensitive, case-insensitive with preference**, and **case- and accent-insensitive**. Sort orders that are specific to national languages may also be provided.
    - *sp_helpsort reports the sort order installed on Adaptive Server.*

Sort rules:
- The values in the columns named in the order by clause are compared
- If two rows have equivalent column values, the binary value of the entire rows is compared byte by byte. This comparison is performed on the row in the order in which the columns are stored internally, not the order of the columns as they are named in the query or in the original create table clause. In brief, data is stored with all the fixed-length columns, in order, followed by all the variable-length columns, in order.
- If rows are equal, row IDs are compared.

Descending scans:
- Use of the keyword desc in an order by clause allows the query optimizer to choose a strategy that eliminates the need for a worktable and a sort step to return results in descending order.

5.3 Identify the performance and tuning aspects of DML statements, such as direct and deferred updates, etc.

Adaptive Server handles updates in different ways, depending on the changes being made to the data and the indexes used to locate the rows. The two major types of updates are **deferred updates** and **direct updates**.

Adaptive Server performs direct updates whenever possible.

Direct updates:
Adaptive Server performs direct updates in a single pass:
- It locates the affected index and data rows.
- It writes the log records for the changes to the transaction log.
- It makes the changes to the data pages and any affected index pages.

Advantage of Direct update over the Deferred update:
- Direct updates require less overhead than deferred updates.
- Generally faster, as they limit the number of log scans, reduce logging.
- Save traversal of index B-trees (reducing lock contention), and save I/O because Adaptive Server does not have to refetch pages to perform modifications based on log records.

There are three techniques for performing direct updates:
- **In-place updates**
- **Cheap direct updates**
- **Expensive direct updates**

In-place updates: When Adaptive Server performs an in-place update, subsequent rows on the page are not moved; the row IDs remain the same and the pointers in the row offset table are not changed.

An in-place update is the **fastest** type of update because it makes a **single** change to the data page. It changes all affected index entries by **deleting the old index rows and inserting the new index row.** In-place updates affect only indexes whose **keys are changed by the update**, since the page and row locations are not changed.

Cheap direct updates: If Adaptive Server cannot perform an update in place, it tries to perform a **cheap direct update. hanging the row and rewriting it at the same offset on the page.** Subsequent rows on the page are moved up or down so that the data remains contiguous on the page, but the **row IDs remain** the same. The pointers in the **row offset table** change to reflect the new locations.

Cheap direct updates are almost as fast as in-place updates. They require the same amount of I/O, but slightly **more processing**. Two changes are made to the data page (**the row and the offset table**). Any changed index keys are updated by deleting old values and inserting new values. Cheap direct updates affect only indexes whose **keys are changed by the update**, since the page and row ID are not changed.

Expensive direct updates: If the **data does not fit on the same page**, Adaptive Server performs an expensive direct update, if possible. An expensive direct update **deletes the data row, including all index entries, and then inserts the modified row and index entries.**

Adaptive Server uses a **table scan** or **an index** to find the row in its original location and then deletes the row. If the table has a clustered index, Adaptive Server uses the index to determine the new location for the row; otherwise, Adaptive Server inserts the new row at the end of the heap.

These updates must meet following requirements:

In-place updates	Cheap direct updates	Expensive direct updates
The row being changed cannot change its length.	The length of the data in the row is changed, but the row still fits on the same data page, or the row length is not changed, but there is a trigger on the table or the table is replicated.	The length of a data row is changed so that the row no longer fits on the same data page, and the row is moved to a different page, or the update affects key columns for the clustered index.
The column being updated cannot be the key, or part of the key, of a clustered index on an allpages-locked table. Because the rows in a clustered index on an allpages-locked table are stored in key order, a change to the key almost always means that the row location is changed.	The column being updated cannot be the key, or part of the key, of a clustered index. Because Adaptive Server stores the rows of a clustered index in key order, a change to the key almost always means that the row location is changed.	The index used to find the row is not changed by the update.
One or more indexes must be unique or must allow duplicates.	One or more indexes must be unique or must allow duplicates.	
The affected columns are not used for referential integrity.	The affected columns are not used for referential integrity.	The affected columns are not used for referential integrity.
There cannot be a trigger on the column.		
The table cannot be replicated (via Replication Server).		

Deferred updates:
Adaptive Server uses deferred updates when direct update conditions are not met. A deferred update is the **slowest** type of update. In a deferred update, Adaptive Server:
- Locates the affected data rows, writing the log records for deferred delete and insert of the data pages as rows are located.
- Reads the log records for the transaction and performs the deletes on the data pages and any affected index rows.
- Reads the log records a second time, and performs all inserts on the data pages, and inserts any affected index rows.

When deferred updates are required:
- Updates that use self-joins.
- Updates to columns used for self-referential integrity.
- Updates to a table referenced in a correlated subquery.
- The update moves a row to **a new page** while the table is being accessed via a **table scan or a clustered index**.
- Duplicate rows are not allowed in the table, and there is no unique index to prevent them.
- The index used to find the data row is not unique, and the row is moved because the update changes the clustered index key or because the new row does not fit on the page.

Disadvantage of Deferred updates over Direct updates:
- Deferred updates incur more overhead than direct updates because they require Adaptive Server to reread the transaction log to make the final changes to the data and indexes. This involves additional traversal of the index trees.

For example, if there is a clustered index on title, this query performs a deferred update:
update titles set emp_name = "Abhisek" where
emp_name = "Abhishek"

Deferred index inserts: Adaptive Server performs deferred index updates when the update affects the index used to access the table or when the update affects columns in a unique index. In this type of update, Adaptive Server:
- Deletes the index entries in direct mode.
- Updates the data page in direct mode, writing the deferred insert records for the index.
- Reads the log records for the transaction and inserts the new values in the index in deferred mode.

Deferred index update mode ensures that a row is found only **once** during **the index scan** and that the query does not prematurely violate a **uniqueness constraint**.

Note: During deferred update of a data row, there can be a significant time interval between the delete of the index row and the insert of the new index row. During this interval, there is no index row corresponding to the data row. If a process scans the index during this interval at isolation level 0, it will not return the old or new value of the data row.

Restrictions on update modes through joins: Updates and deletes that involve joins can be performed in direct, deferred_varcol, or deferred_index mode when the table being updated is the outermost table in the join order, or when it is preceded in the join order by tables where only a single row qualifies.

Note: The update mode that is used for the join query depends on whether the updated table is the outermost query in the join order—if it is not the outermost table, the update is performed **in deferred mode**.
Note: The update that uses a subquery is always performed as a **direct, deferred_varcol**, or **deferred_index** update.
Note: Triggers that join user tables with the deleted or inserted tables are run in **deferred mode**.

5.4 Identify techniques to promote the most efficient update method

Optimizing updates:

showplan messages provide information about whether an update is performed in direct mode or deferred mode. There are times when the optimizer cannot know whether a direct update or a deferred update will be performed, so two showplan messages are provided:

message type	description
deferred_varcol	message shows that the update may change the length of the row because a variable-length column is being updated. If the updated row fits on the page, the update is performed in direct mode; if the update does not fit on the page, the update is performed in deferred mode.
deferred_index	message indicates that the changes to the data pages and the deletes to the index pages are performed in direct mode, but the inserts to the index pages are performed in deferred mode

Designing for direct updates:

When you design and code your applications, be aware of the differences that can cause deferred updates. Follow these guidelines to help avoid deferred updates:
- Create at least one **unique index** on the table to encourage more direct updates.
- Whenever possible, use **nonkey** columns in the where clause when updating a different key.
- If you do not use null values in your columns, declare them as **not null** in your create table statement.

Effects of indexing on update mode:

Index	Var-length key	Fixed-length column	Var-length column
No index	N/A	direct	deferred_varcol
Clustered, unique	direct	direct	direct
Clustered, not unique	deferred	deferred	deferred
Clustered, not unique, with a unique index on another column	deferred	direct	deferred_varcol
Nonclustered, unique	deferred_varcol	direct	direct
Nonclustered, not unique	deferred_varcol	direct	deferred_varcol

- If the length of varchar or varbinary is close to the maximum length, use char or binary instead. Each variable-length column adds row overhead and increases the possibility of deferred updates.
- Using **max_rows_per_page** to reduce the number of rows allowed on a page increases direct updates, because an update that increases the length of a variable-length column may still fit on the same page.

Using *sp_sysmon* while tuning updates:

You can use **showplan** to determine whether an update is deferred or direct, but showplan does not give you detailed information about the type of deferred or direct update.

Run sp_sysmon as you tune updates, and look for reduced numbers of **deferred updates, reduced locking, and reduced I/O**.

5.5 Understand computed columns:

Computed columns were introduced in Sybase ASE 15 to provide easier data manipulation and faster data access.

Computed columns are columns that are defined by an **expression**. This expression can be built by combining **regular columns** in the same row and may contain **functions, arithmetic operators, case expressions, global variables, Java objects, and path names**.

Example:

create table parts_table
  (part_no int,
  name char(30),
  list_price money,
  quantity int,
  *total_cost **compute** quantity*list_price*
)

In the above example, total_cost is a computed column defined by an arithmetic operation between the columns list_price and quantity. The **datatype** of total_cost is automatically inferred from the **computed column expression**. Each system datatype has a datatype hierarchy, which is stored in the **systypes** system table. The datatype hierarchy determines the results of computations using values of different datatypes. The result value is assigned the datatype that has the **lowest hierarchy**. In this example, total_cost is a product of the money and int datatypes. Int has a hierarchy of 15 and money has a hierarchy of 11. Therefore, the datatype of the result is money.

Syntax: Create table
create table [database.[owner].] table_name
  (column_name{datatype
  | {compute | as} computed_column_expression
  [materialized | not materialized] }

Syntax: Alter Table
alter table
  add column_name {datatype | [{ [compute | as}
  computed_column_expression
  }...
  | modify column_name {datatype [null | not null]
  {materialized | not materialized} [null |not null] | {compute | as
  computed_column_expression
  [materialized | not materialized]}...

Materialization and **deterministic** characteristics are important concepts to understand behavior of the computed columns.

Materialization:

Materialized columns: are **preevaluated** and stored in the table when base columns are inserted or updated. The values associated with the computed columns are stored in both the data row and the index row.

Note: A materialized column is reevaluated only when one of its base columns is updated.

Example: Assuming getdate() is 15 Mar 2012, getdate() also would be same.
create table employee_detail
  (emp_id int, join_date as getdate() materialized,   last_update_date datetime)

insert into employee_detail (emp_id, last_update_date)
            values (1,   getdate()   )

Assume we are running below query on 16 Mar 2012. (After one day of insert)
select * from employee_detail

emp_id	join_date	last_update_date
1	15/03/2012 9:31:54.036 AM	15/03/2012 9:31:54.036 AM

employee_detail

Its displaying join_date as '15/03/2012 9:31:54:036 AM', that means it is giving same data value for join_date column, as we inserted in this column on 15 mar 2012. See how it works in not materialized in later section.

virtual columns(not materialized): If a column is virtual, or not materialized, its result value must be evaluated each time the column is accessed. This means that if the virtual computed column expression is based on, or calls, a nondeterministic expression, it may return different values each time you access it. You may also encounter run-time exceptions, such as domain errors, when you access virtual computed columns. The concept of nonmaterialized columns is similar to "views," where the definition of the view is evaluated each time the view is called.

Note: A nonmaterialized, or virtual, computed column becomes a materialized computed column once it is used as an index key.

Example: Assuming getdate() is 15 Mar 2012..
create table employee_detail_notmaterialized
  (emp_id int, join_date as getdate()not materialized,   last_update_date datetime)

insert into employee_detail_notmaterialized (emp_id, last_update_date)
            values (1,   getdate()   )

Assume we are running below query on 16 Mar 2012. (After one day of insert) *select * from employee_detail_notmaterialized*

employee detail notmaterialized

emp_id	join_date	last_update_date
1	16/03/2012 9:31:54.036 AM	15/03/2012 9:31:54.036 AM

Its displaying join_date as '16/03/2012 9:31:54:036 AM', that means it is giving current value of getdate() for join_date column.

A **computed column** is defined as **materialized** or **nonmaterialized** during the **create table** or **alter table process** using the keyword **materialized** or **not materialized** after the column name. **Note: The default is not materialized.**

Deterministic Property:

A deterministic algorithm will always produce the same output for a given set of inputs. Expressions and functions using deterministic algorithms exhibit a deterministic property. On the other hand, nondeterministic expressions may return different results each time they are evaluated, even when they are called with the same set of input values.

A good example of a nondeterministic function is the getdate() function. It always returns the current date, which is different each time the function is executed. Any expression built on a nondeterministic function will also be nondeterministic. For example, age (getdate() minus date of birth) will also be nondeterministic. Also, if a function's return value depends on factors other than input values, the function is probably nondeterministic. A nondeterministic function need not always return a different value for the same set of inputs. It just cannot guarantee the same result each time.

Relationship between Deterministic Property and Materialization:
Deterministic and Materialized Computed Columns: Deterministic materialized computed columns always have the same values; however, often they are reevaluated.
Deterministic and Nonmaterialized Computed Columns: Nonmaterialized columns can be either deterministic or nondeterministic. A deterministic nonmaterialized column always produces repeatable results, even though the column is evaluated each time it is referenced.
Nondeterministic and Materialized Computed Columns: Nondeterministic and materialized computed columns result in repeatable data. They are not reevaluated when referenced in a query. Instead, Adaptive Server uses the preevaluated values.
Nondeterministic and Nonmaterialized Computed Columns: Nonmaterialized columns that are nondeterministic do not guarantee repeatable results.

Benefits of Using Computed Columns:
Provide Shorthand and Indexing for an Expression:
Computed columns allow you to create a shorthand term for an expression. For example, "Age" can be used for "getdate –DateOfBirth." The computed columns can be indexed as long as the

resulting datatype can be in an index. The datatypes that cannot be indexed include text, image, Java class, and bit.

Composing and Decomposing Datatypes:
Computed columns can be used to compose and decompose complex datatypes. You can use computed columns either to make a complex datatype from simpler elements (compose), or to extract one or more elements from a complex datatype (decompose). Complex datatypes are usually composed of individual elements or fragments. You can define automatic decomposition or composition of complex datatypes when you define the table.

User-defined Sort Order:
Computed columns can be used to transform data into different formats — to customize data presentations for data retrieval. This is called **user-defined sort order**.
You can use computed columns to present your query result in a case-insensitive format, or you can use system sort orders other than the default sort order. To transform data into a different format, use either the built-in function sortkey or a user-defined sort order function.
For example, you can add a computed column called name_in_myorder with a user-defined function Xform_to_myorder():
alter table parts_table add name_in_myorder compute
  Xform_to_myorder(name)materialized

The following query then returns the result in the customized format:
select name, part_no, listPrice from parts_table order by
  name_in_myorder

This approach allows you to materialize the transformed and ordered data and create indexes on it. You can do the same thing using data manipulation language (DML), specifying the user-defined function in the select statement:
select name, part_no, listPrice from parts_table
  order by Xform_to_myorder(name)

However, using the computed column approach allows you to materialize the transformed and ordered data. Because materialized columns can be indexed, the query will have improved performance.

Rules and Properties of Computed Columns
- The datatype of a computed column is automatically inferred from its computed_column_expression.
- You can define triggers only on **materialized** computed columns; they are not allowed in virtual computed columns.
- Computed columns cannot have default constraints.
- Computed_column_expression can only reference columns in the same table.
- You cannot use a virtual computed column in any constraints.

- You can use a materialized computed column as a key column in an index or as part of a unique or primary constraint. However, this can only be done if the computed column value is a deterministic expression and if the resultant datatype is allowed in index columns.
- You can constrain nullability only for materialized computed columns. If you do not specify nullability, all computed columns are **nullable by default**; **virtual computed columns are always nullable.**
- If a user-defined function in a computed column definition is dropped or becomes invalid, any operations that call that function fail.
- You cannot change a regular column into a computed column, or a computed column into a regular column.
- You cannot drop or modify the base column referenced by a computed column.
- When you add a new computed column without specifying nullability, the default option is nullable.
- When adding a new materialized computed column, the computed_column_expression is evaluated for each existing row in the table, and the result is stored in the table.
- You can modify the entire definition of an existing computed column. This is a quick way to drop the computed column and add a new one with the same name. When doing this, keep in mind that a modified column behaves like a new computed column. The defaults are **nonmaterialized** and **nullable** if these options are not specified.
- You can add new computed columns and add or modify their base columns at the same time.
- When you change a not-null, materialized computed column into a virtual column, you must specify null in the modify clause.
- You cannot change a materialized computed column into a virtual column if it has been used as an index key; you must first drop the index.
- When you modify a nonmaterialized computed column to materialized, the computed_column_expression is evaluated for each existing row in the table. The result is stored in the table.
- If you modify computed columns that are index keys, the index is rebuilt.
- You cannot drop a computed column if it is used as an index key.
- You can modify the materialization property of an existing computed column without changing other properties, such as the expression that defines it.

Summary

We discussed about DML (Data Manipulation Language) in this section.

- Data manipulation language (DML) commands query and manipulate data. Following are DML commands:

    Select, Insert, Update, Delete

- A **cursor** accesses the results of a SQL select statement one or more rows at a time.
- Two attributes specify the cursor's behavior:
    - Sensitivity
    - Scrollability
- WHERE clause: Sets the search conditions in a **select**, **insert**, **update**, or **delete** statement
- The two major types of updates are **deferred updates** and **direct updates**.
- There are three techniques for performing direct updates:
    - In-place updates
    - Cheap direct updates
    - Expensive direct updates
- **showplan** messages provide information about whether an update is performed in direct mode or deferred mode.
- Computed columns are columns that are defined by an **expression**. This expression can be built by combining **regular columns** in the same row and may contain **functions, arithmetic operators, case expressions, global variables, Java objects, and path names.**
- Types of computed columns:
    - Materialized columns
    - Virtual columns(not materialized)
- The default is computed column type is Virtual (not materialized).

Practice Test

1. Which of the following are NOT DML commands [Choose 2]?
    A. SELECT
    B. TRUNCATE
    C. DELETE
    D. UPDATE
    E. INSERT
    F. DROP

2. Which of the following components of a 'select' statement will ALWAYS require a sort?
    A. Distinct
    B. Having
    C. Order by
    D. Union
    E. Union all

3. Which of the following are techniques of direct updates [Choose 3]?
    A. Cheap direct updates
    B. In-place updates
    C. Active direct updates
    D. Expensive direct updates
    E. Performance direct updates

4. What must an expression used in a function based index contain?
    A. Base column
    B. Aggregate function
    C. Computed column
    D. Subquery

5. Which of the following is TRUE about materialized computed columns?
    A. Require a function based index
    B. Can be based on columns in multiple tables
    C. Physically store the computed value in the table
    D. Generate the computed value when the column is queried

6. Which of the following statements is NOT TRUE regarding computed columns?
    A. Regular columns can be converted into computed columns.
    B. Computed columns are either deterministic or non-deterministic.
    C. If a computed column that is part of an index is modified, the index is rebuilt.
    D. Computed columns permit the use of expressions as column definitions.

Section 6 - Query Access Methods

6.1 Define range queries, point queries, and covered queries

Range Query:
Range queries are queries which are having between one value to another value
(eg 20 to 30)
Assume that you need to improve the performance of the following query:
select title from titles where price between $20.00 and $30.00
Some basic statistics on the table are:
- The table has 1,000,000 rows, and uses allpages locking.
- There are 10 rows per page; pages are 75 percent full, so the table has approximately 135,000 pages.
- 190,000 (19%) of the titles are priced between $20 and $30.
-

With no index, the query would scan all 135,000 pages.

With a clustered index on *price*, the query would find the first $20 book and begin reading sequentially until it gets to the last $30 book. With pages about 75 percent full, the average number of rows per page is 7.5. To read 190,000 matching rows, the query would read approximately 25,300 pages, plus 3 or 4 index pages.

With a nonclustered index on *price* and random distribution of *price* values, using the index to find the rows for this query requires reading about 19 percent of the leaf level of the index, about 1,500 pages.

If the price values are randomly distributed, the number of data pages that must be read is likely to be high, perhaps as many data pages as there are qualifying rows, 190,000. Since a table scan requires only 135,000 pages, you would not want to use this nonclustered.

Another choice is a nonclustered index on *price, title*. The query can perform a matching index scan, using the index to find the first page with a price of $20, and then scanning forward on the leaf level until it finds a price of more than $30. This index requires about 35,700 leaf pages, so to scan the matching leaf pages requires reading about 19 percent of the pages of this index, or about 6,800 reads.

For this query, the covering nonclustered index on *price, title* is best

Point Query:
Point queries are queries which are having absolute value.

Covered Query:
Covered queries and covering indexes are different, yet closely related. A query is covered if all the columns it uses come from one or more indexes. These columns include the columns you want the query to return as well as columns in any JOIN, WHERE, HAVING, and ORDER BY clause. A covered query typically is considered advantageous because data access through indexes can be more efficient. However, the high-speed access that this kind of query facilitates can become costly when you update the table because you must maintain the indexes.

A covering index: which is used in covered queries—can provide some or all of the indexed columns that a covered query uses. If a covering index is also a composite index (i.e., it indexes more than one column in its base table or view), it might contain columns that aren't used in the covered query but are used instead in other queries that have overlapping columns.

6.2 Explain how ASE accesses data in selects, inserts, deletes, and updates

If you create a table on Adaptive Server, but do not create a clustered index, the table is stored as a *heap*.

Select operations: When you issue a select query on a heap, and there is no useful nonclustered index, Adaptive Server must scan every data page in the table to find every row that satisfies the conditions in the query. There may be one row, many rows, or no rows that match.

On Allpages-locked heap tables: For allpages-locked tables, Adaptive Server reads the first column in sysindexes for the table, reads the first page into cache, and follows the next page pointers until it finds the last page of the table.

On Data-only locked heap tables: Since the pages of data-only-locked tables are not linked in a page chain,
a select query on a heap table uses the **table's OAM** and the allocation pages to locate all the rows in the table. The OAM page points to the allocation pages, which point to the extents and pages for the table.

Insert Operations:

On Allpages-locked heap table: When you insert data into an allpages-locked heap table, the data row is always added to the last page of the table. If there is no clustered index on a table, and the table is not partitioned, the **sysindexes.root** entry for the heap table stores a pointer to the last page of the heap to locate the page where the data needs to be inserted.
If the last page is full, a new page is allocated in the current extent and linked onto the chain. If the extent is full, Adaptive Server looks for empty pages on other extents being used by the table. If no pages are available, a new extent is allocated to the table.

Conflicts during heap inserts: One of the severe performance limits on heap tables that use allpages locking is that the page must be locked when the row is added, and that lock is held until the transaction completes. If many users are trying to insert into an allpages-locked heap table at the same time, each insert must wait for the preceding transaction to complete. This problem of last-page conflicts on heaps is true for:
- Single row inserts using insert
- Multiple row inserts using select into or insert…select, or several insert statements in a batch
- Bulk copy into the table

Some workarounds for last-page conflicts on heaps include:
- Switching to datapages or datarows locking
- Creating a clustered index that directs the inserts to different pages
- Partitioning the table, which creates multiple insert points for the table, giving you multiple "last pages" in an allpages-locked table
- Keeping transactions short
- Avoiding network activity and user interaction whenever possible, once a transaction acquires locks

On Data-only-locked heap table:
When users insert data into a data-only-locked heap table, Adaptive Server tracks page numbers where the inserts have recently occurred, and keeps the page number as a hint for future tasks that need space. Subsequent inserts to the table are directed to one of these pages. If the page is full, Adaptive Server allocates a new page and replaces the old hint with the new page number. Blocking while many users are simultaneously inserting data is much less likely to occur during inserts to data-only-locked heap tables. When blocking occurs, Adaptive Server allocates a small number of empty pages and directs new inserts to those pages using these newly allocated pages as hints.

For datarows-locked tables, blocking occurs only while the actual changes to the data page are being written; although row locks are held for the duration of the transaction, other rows can be inserted on the page. The row-level locks allow multiple transaction to hold locks on the page. There may be slight blocking on data-only-locked tables, because Adaptive Server allows a small amount of blocking after many pages have just been allocated, so that the newly allocated pages are filled before additional pages are allocated.

If conflicts occur during heap inserts:
Conflicts during inserts to heap tables are greatly reduced for data-onlylocked tables, but can still take place. If these conflicts slow inserts, some workarounds can be used, including:
- Switching to datarows locking, if the table uses datapages locking
- Using a clustered index to spread data inserts
- Partitioning the table, which provides additional hints and allows new pages to be allocated on each partition when blocking takes place

Delete Operations:
When you delete rows from a heap table, and there is no useful index, Adaptive Server scans the data rows in the table to find the rows to delete. It has no way of knowing how many rows match the conditions in the query without examining every row.

On Allpages-locked heap table: When a data row is deleted from a page in an allpages-locked table, the rows that follow it on the page move up so that the data on the page remains contiguous.

On Data-only-locked heap table: When you delete rows from a data-only-locked heap table, a table scan is required if there is no useful index. The OAM and allocation pages are used to locate the pages. The space on the page is not recovered immediately. Rows in data-onlylocked tables must maintain fixed row IDs, and need to be reinserted in the same place if the transaction is rolled back.

After a delete transaction completes, one of the following processes shifts rows on the page to make the space usage contiguous:
- The housekeeper process
- An insert that needs to find space on the page
- The reorg reclaim_space command

Deleting the last row on a page: If you delete the last row on a page, the page is deallocated. If other pages on the extent are still in use by the table, the page can be used again by the table when a page is needed. If all other pages on the extent are empty, the entire extent is deallocated. It can be allocated to other objects in the database. **The first data page for a table or an index is never deallocated.**

Update Operations:
Like other operations on heaps, an update that has no useful index on the columns in the where clause performs a table scan to locate the rows that need to be changed.

On Allpages-locked heap tables: Updates on allpages-locked heap tables can be performed in several ways:
- If the length of the row does not change, the updated row replaces the existing row, and no data moves on the page.
- If the length of the row changes, and there is enough free space on the page, the row remains in the same place on the page, but other rows move up or down to keep the rows contiguous on the page. The row offset pointers at the end of the page are adjusted to point to the changed row locations.
- If the row does not fit on the page, the row is deleted from its current page, and the "new" row is inserted on the last page of the table. This type of update can cause a conflict on the last page of the heap, just as inserts do. If there are any nonclustered indexes on the table, all index references to the row need to be updated.

On Data-only-locked heap tables: One of the requirements for data-only-locked tables is that the row ID of a data row never changes (except during intentional rebuilds of the table). Therefore, updates to data-only-locked tables can be performed by the first two methods described above, as long as the row fits on the page.

But when a row in a data-only-locked table is updated so that it no longer fits on the page, a process called **row forwarding** performs the following steps:
- The row is inserted onto a different page, and
- A pointer to the row ID on the new page is stored in the original location for the row.

Indexes do not need to be modified when rows are forwarded. All indexes still point to the original row ID.

If the row needs to be forwarded a second time, the original location is updated to point to the new page—the forwarded row is never more than one hop away from its original location.

Row forwarding increases concurrency during update operations because indexes do not have to be updated. It can slow data retrieval, however, because a task needs to read the page at the original location and then read the page where the forwarded data is stored.

Note: Forwarded rows can be cleared from a table using the reorg command.

6.3 Define I/O for a select using a non-clustered index

When you select a row using a nonclustered index, the search starts at the root level. sysindexes.root stores the page number for the root page of the nonclustered index.
Eg:- select * from employee where lname ='Green'
The above query requires the following I/O:
- One read for the root level page
- One read for the intermediate level page
- One read for the leaf-level page
- One read for the data page

If your applications use a particular nonclustered index frequently, the root and intermediate pages will probably be in cache, so only one or two physical disk I/Os need to be performed.

6.4 Define performance benefits of using indexes

- Avoid table scans when accessing data
- Target specific data pages that contain specific values in a point query
- Establish upper and lower bounds for reading data in a range query
- Avoid data page access completely, when an index covers a query
- Use ordered data to avoid sorts or to favor **merge joins** over **nestedloop** joins

In addition, you can create indexes to enforce the uniqueness of data and to randomize the storage location of inserts.

6.5 Define bulk copy and BCP commands

Transact-SQL commands cannot transfer data in bulk. For this reason, you must use bcp for any large transfers.
Adaptive Server can accept data in any **character** or **binary** format, as long as the data file describes either the length of the fields or the **terminators**, the characters that separate columns. The structures in the tables involved in the transfer need not be identical, because when bcp:
- Imports *from* a file, it appends data to an existing database table.
- Exports *to* a file, it overwrites the previous contents of the file.

When the transfer is complete, bcp informs you of the:
- Number of rows of data successfully copied
- Number of rows (if any) that it could not copy

- Total time the copy took
- Average amount of time, in milliseconds, that it took to copy one row
- Number of rows copied per second.

Example:
Starting copy...
1000 rows sent to SQL Server.
2000 rows sent to SQL Server.
3000 rows sent to SQL Server.
.
.
95133 rows copied.
Clock Time (ms.): total = 6257 Avg = 0 (15204.25 rows per sec.)

If bcp runs successfully, you see a return status of 0. The return status generally reflects errors from the operating system level and correspond to the ones listed in the *errno.h* file in the */usr/include/sys/* directory.

Basic requirements You must supply the following information to transfer data successfully to and from Adaptive Server:
- Name of the database and table or view
- Name of the operating system file
- Direction of the transfer (in or out)

Note: You can also use bcp to modify the **storage type**, **storage length**, and **terminator** for each column if you want to do so.

bcp in works in one of two modes:

Slow bcp: logs each row insert that it makes, used for tables that have one or more indexes or triggers.

Fast bcp: logs only page allocations, copying data into tables without indexes or triggers at the fastest speed possible.

Note: Fast bcp might enhance performance; however, slow bcp gives you greater data recoverability.

Before you can use bcp in, you must prepare the command and the data for transfer:
- To use either fast or slow bcp, set select into/bulkcopy/pllsort to true. For example, to turn on this option for the pubs2 database, you would enter:
  sp_dboption pubs2, "select into/bulkcopy/pllsort", true
- To use fast bcp, remove indexes and triggers on the target table.
- If you are running Open Client version 11.1 or later and are using an external Sybase configuration file, you must add the following to enable bcp:
  [BCP]
- You must set the SYBASE environment variable to the location of the current version of Adaptive Server before you can use bcp.
- To use a previous version of bcp, you must set the CS_BEHAVIOR property in the [bcp] section of the *ocs.cfg* file:

```
[bcp]
CS_BEHAVIOR = CS_BEHAVIOR_100
```
If CS_BEHAVIOR is not set to CS_BEHAVIOR_100, you can use functionality for bcp 11.1 and later.

Copying data to a file:
Example: *table1* in database *testdb* to file1
bcp testdb..table1 out file1
Example: To copy the data from different partitions of a table to one file. (Partitions are ptn1, ptn2 and ptn3)
bcp testdb.. table1 partition ptn1, ptn2, ptn3 out file2
Example: To a single file for each partition (Partitions are ptn1, ptn2 and ptn3)
bcp testdb.. table1 partition ptn1, ptn2 out ptn1.dat,ptn2.dat
or
bcp testdb.. table1 partition ptn1, ptn2 out

Using fast or slow *bcp*
The existence of indexes and triggers on tables affects transfer speed. When you use bcp on such tables, bcp automatically uses its slow mode, which logs data inserts in the transaction log. These logged inserts can cause the transaction log to become very large.
To control this data excess and ensure that the database is fully recoverable in the event of a failure, you can back up the log with dump transaction.

Note: bcp does not fire any **trigger** that exists on the target table.

Fast bcp logs only the page allocations. For copying data in, bcp is fastest if your database table has no indexes or triggers.

***bcp* in and locks**
When you copy in to a table using bcp, and particularly when you copy in to a table using parallel bcp, the copy process acquires the following locks:
- An exclusive intent lock on the table
- An exclusive page lock on each data page or data row
- An exclusive lock on index pages, if any indexes exist

6.6 Define logging & minimally-logged operations

When you create and populate temporary tables in *tempdb*, use the **select into** command, rather than **create table** and **insert...select**, whenever possible. The **select into/bulkcopy** database option is turned on by default in *tempdb* to enable this behavior.

select into operations are faster because they are only minimally logged. Only the allocation of data pages is tracked, not the actual changes for each data row. Each data insert in an **insert...select** query is fully logged, resulting in more overhead.

Transaction logging performed by SQL Server cannot be turned off, to ensure the recoverability of all transactions performed on SQL Server. Any SQL statement or set of statements that modifies data is a transaction and is logged. You can, however, limit the amount of logging performed for some specific operations, such as bulk copying data into a database using bulk copy (bcp) in the fast mode, performing a select/into query, or truncating the log. See the Tools and Connectivity Troubleshooting Guide and the SQL Server Reference Manual for more information on bcp. These minimally logged operations cause the transaction log to get out of sync with the data in a database, which makes the transaction log useless for media recovery.

Once a non-logged operation has been performed, the transaction log cannot be dumped to a device, but it can still be truncated. You must do a dump database to create a new point of synchronization between the database and the transaction log to allow the log to be dumped to device.

REORG REBUILD is a **minimally logged operation**. That means the physical object changes are logged (OAM; AllocUnits; AllocPages) but not the data changes. The command is already very slow, if data changes were logged, it would be even slower. The log space requirement is very small, you definitely do not need more log space.

The following DML operations are either nonlogged or minimally logged:
- TRUNCATE TABLE
- SELECT INTO

The TRUNCATE TABLE statement cannot be used on tables that are referenced by a FOREIGN KEY constraint, unless the FOREIGN KEY constraint is self-referencing. The TRUNCATE TABLE statement cannot be used on a table that is a part of an indexed view. You cannot use the TRUNCATE TABLE statement on tables that are published by transactional or merge replication. The TRUNCATE TABLE statement will not activate triggers, as *triggers rely on transaction logs*

The TRUNCATE TABLE statement uses much less transaction log space. The DELETE statement logs information about every row that is affected in the transaction log. When deleting from a table with millions of rows, this is both time- and disk-space-consuming.

The DELETE statement holds a lock on each individual row it is deleting. The TRUNCATE TABLE statement locks only the table and each data page. This offers better performance, as locking is one of the most time-consuming SQL Server activities.

The DELETE statement will leave empty data pages for the table and its indexes. If you wish to shrink the database by deleting data in a large table, the DELETE statement may prove counterproductive. The TRUNCATE TABLE statement, on the other hand, is guaranteed to.

Summary

In this section, you read about Query Access Methods.

- **Range Query** : Range queries are queries which are having between one value to another value (eg 20 to 30).
- **Point Query:** Point queries are queries which are having absolute value
- **Covered Query:** A query is covered if all the columns it uses come from one or more indexes. These columns include the columns you want the query to return as well as columns in any JOIN, WHERE, HAVING, and ORDER BY clause
- If you create a table on Adaptive Server, but do not create a clustered index, the table is stored as a *heap*.
- When you select a row using a nonclustered index, the search starts at the root level.
- You must use bcp for any large transfers.
- There are two types of BCP
    - Slow bcp: logs each row insert that it makes
    - Fast bcp : logs only page allocations

- The following DML operations are either nonlogged or minimally logged:
    - TRUNCATE TABLE
    - SELECT INTO

Practice Test

1. Point queries are queries which are having?
    A. between one values to another values
    B. absolute value
    C. Non matching values
    D. None of the above

2. Which of the following would be best used in a heavy DSS workload environment?
    A. Primarily DOL tables with few indexes
    B. Primarily DOL tables with numerous indexes
    C. Primarily APL tables with few indexes
    D. Primarily APL tables with numerous indexes

3. If you create a table on Adaptive Server, but do not create a clustered index, the table is stored as a
    A. temp table
    B. system table
    C. heap
    D. index table

4. Which of the following is a NOT performance benefit of using indexes?
    A. Avoid table scans when accessing data
    B. Target specific data pages that contain specific values in a point query
    C. Establish upper and lower bounds for reading data in a range query
    D. Avoid data page access completely, when an index covers a query
    E. Use ordered data to avoid sorts or to favor nestedloop over merge joins joins

5. Which of the following statements are true about Fast bcp? [Choose 2]
    A. logs each row insert that it makes
    B. logs only page allocations
    C. used for tables that have one or more indexes or triggers
    D. copying data into tables without indexes or triggers at the fastest speed possible

6. Which of the following commands are NOT True? [Choose 2]
    A. The DELETE statement holds a lock on each individual row it is deleting
    B. The TRUNCATE TABLE statement locks only the table and each data page.
    C. The DELETE statement locks only the table and each data page.
    D. The TRUNCATE TABLE statement holds a lock on each individual row it is deleting

Section 7 - Query Optimization

7.1 Define the 'Or Strategy' and showplan, plus options

OR strategy:

An OR strategy uses a set of index scans to limit the scan with each of the OR terms, then passes the resulting RIDs through a **UnionDistinct** operator to get, with a **RidJoin** from the table, the tuples corresponding to the unique RIDs.

Note: The **rid join** operator is a binary operator that joins two data streams, based on row IDs generated for the same source table. Each data row in a SQL table is associated with a unique row ID or RID.

Example of OR clause:

where column_name1 = <value>
or column_name1 = <value>

***in (values_list)* converts to *or* processing:**
Preprocessing converts in lists to or clauses, so this query:
    select title_id, price
    from titles
    where title_id in ("PS1372", "PS2091","PS2106")
becomes:
    select title_id, price
    from titles
    where title_id = "PS1372"
    or title_id = "PS2091"
    or title_id = "PS2106"

For example, there can be rows for which both of these conditions are true:
select title_id
from titles
where pub_id = "P076" or type > "business"
If there is an index on pub_id, and another on type, the OR strategy can be used.

Dynamic index (OR strategy):
If there is a possibility that one or more of the or clauses could match values in the same row, the query is resolved using the ***OR strategy***, also known as using a ***dynamic index***.
If the query uses the OR strategy because the query could return duplicate rows, the appropriate indexes are used to retrieve the row IDs for rows that satisfy each or clause. **The row IDs for each or clause are stored in a worktable**.
Since the worktable contains only row IDs, it is called a "dynamic index." Adaptive Server then sorts the worktable to remove the duplicate row IDs. The row IDs are used to retrieve the rows from the base tables. The total cost of the query includes:

- The sum of the index accesses, that is, for each or clause, the cost of using the index to access the row IDs on the leaf pages of the index (or on the data pages, for a clustered index on an allpages-locked table)
- The cost of reading the worktable and performing the sort
- The cost of using the row IDs to access the data pages

Note: The worktable does not contain the actual data rows from the table, but rather it contains the row IDs for the matching rows. The row IDs are simply a combination of the **page number** and **row number** on that page for each of the rows.

Multiple matching index scans (special OR strategy):
Adaptive Server uses multiple matching index scans when the or clauses are on the same table, and there is no possibility that the or clauses will return duplicate rows. For example, this query cannot return any duplicate rows:

```
select title
from titles
where title_id in ("T6650", "T95065", "T11365")
```

This query can be resolved using multiple matching index scans, using the index on title_id. The total cost of the query is the sum of the multiple index accesses performed. If the index on title_id has 3 levels, each or clause requires 3 index reads, plus one data page read, so the total cost for each clause is 4 logical and 4 physical I/Os, and the total query cost is estimated to be 12 logical and 12 physical I/Os.

The optimizer determines which index to use for each or clause or value in the in (values_list) clause by costing each clause or value separately. If each column named in a clause is indexed, a different index can be used for each clause or value.

Note: showplan displays the message **"Using N Matching Index Scans"** when the special OR strategy is used.

Note: The *OR Strategy* (multiple matching index scans) is only considered for equality predicates.

It is disqualified for range predicates even if meeting other conditions. As an example, when a select statement contains the following:
where bar between 1 and 5
or bar between 10 and 15
This will not be considered for the *OR Strategy*.

Table scans for Or queries: A query with or clauses or an in (values_list) uses a table scan if either of these conditions is true:
- The cost of all the index accesses is greater than the cost of a table scan, or
- At least one of the columns is not indexed, so the only way to resolve the query conditions is to perform a table scan.

Showplan:
Sybase ASE Server includes a very intelligent cost-based query optimizer which, given an ad-hoc query, can quickly determine the best access method for retrieving the data, including the order in which to join tables and whether or not to use indexes that may be on those tables. By using a cost-based query optimizer, the System Administrator or end user is released from having to determine the most efficient way of structuring the query to get optimal performance -- instead, the optimizer looks at all possible join orders, and the cost of using each index, and picks the plan with the least cost in terms of page I/O's.

Detailed information on the final access method that the optimizer chooses can be displayed for the user by executing the Transact-SQL "SET SHOWPLAN ON" command. This command will show each step that the optimizer uses in joining tables and which, if any, indexes it chooses to be the least-cost method of accessing the data. This can be extremely beneficial when analyzing certain queries to determine if the indexes that have been defined on a table are actually being considered by the optimizer as useful in getting to the data. This document will define and explain each of the output messages from SHOWPLAN, and give example queries and the output from SHOWPLAN to illustrate the point. The format will be consistent throughout: a heading which corresponds to the exact text of a SHOWPLAN statement, followed by a description of what it means, a sample query which generates that particular message, and the full output from executing the query with the SHOWPLAN option on. Wherever possible, the queries will use the existing tables and indexes, unaltered, from the SQL Server "Pubs" sample database.

STEP n
This statement will be included in the SHOWPLAN output for every query, where n is an integer, beginning with "STEP 1". For some queries, SQL Server cannot effectively retrieve the results in a single step, and must break the query plan into several steps. For example, if a query includes a GROUP BY clause, the query will need to be broken into at least two steps: one step to select the qualifying rows from the table, and another step to group them. The following query demonstrates a singlestep query.

Query: SELECT au_lname, au_fname
FROM Authors
WHERE city = "Oakland"

SHOWPLAN: STEP 1
The type of query is SELECT
FROM TABLE
authors
Nested iteration
Table Scan

The type of query is SELECT (into a worktable)
This SHOWPLAN statement indicates that SQL Server needs to insert some of the query results into an intermediate worktable, and later in the query processing will then select the values out

of that table. This is most often seen with a query which involves a GROUP BY clause, as the results are first put into a work table, and then the qualifying rows in the work table are grouped based on the given column in the GROUP BY clause. The following query returns a list of all cities and indicates the number of authors that live in each city. The query plan is composed of two steps: the first step selects the rows into a worktable, and the second step retrieves the grouped rows from the worktable:

Query: SELECT city, total_authors = count(*)
FROM Authors
GROUP BY city

SHOWPLAN: STEP 1
The type of query is SELECT (into a worktable)
GROUP BY
Vector Aggregate
FROM TABLE
authors
Nested iteration
Table Scan
TO TABLE
Worktable

STEP 2
The type of query is SELECT
FROM TABLE
Worktable
Nested iteration
Table Scan

The type of query is

This statement describes the type of query for each step. For most user queries, the value for will be SELECT, INSERT, UPDATE, or DELETE. If SHOWPLAN is turned on while other commands are issued, the will reflect the command that was issued. The following examples show various outputs for different queries/commands:

Query 1: CREATE TABLE Mytab (col1 int)
SHOWPLAN 1: STEP 1
The type of query is TABCREATE

Query 2: INSERT Publishers
VALUES ("9904", "NewPubs", "Seattle", "WA")

SHOWPLAN 2: STEP 1
The type of query is INSERT
The update mode is direct
Table Scan
TO TABLE
publishers

The update mode is deferred
There are two methods or "modes" that SQL Server can use to perform update operations such as INSERT, DELETE, UPDATE, and SELECT INTO. These methods are called deferred update and direct update. When the deferred method is used, the changes are applied to all rows of the table by making log records in the transaction log to reflect the old and new value of the column(s) being modified (in the case of UPDATE operations), or the values which will be inserted or deleted (in the case of INSERT and DELETE, respectively). When all of the log records have been constructed, the changes are then applied to the data pages. This method generates more log records than a direct update (discussed later), but it has the advantage of allowing the execution of commands which may cascade changes throughout a table. For example, consider a table which has a column "col1" with a unique index on it, and data values numbered consecutively from 1 to 100 in that column. Assume an UPDATE statement is executed to increase the value in each row by 1:

Query 1: UPDATE Mytable
SET col1 = col1 + 1

SHOWPLAN 1: STEP 1
The type of query is UPDATE
The update mode is deferred
FROM TABLE
Mytable
Nested iteration
Table Scan
TO TABLE
Mytable

Consider the consequences of starting at the first row in the table, and updating each row, through the end of the table. Updating the first row (which has an initial value of 1) to 2 would cause an error, as the unique index would be violated since there is already a value of 2 in the table; likewise, updating the second row (which has an initial value of 2) to 3 would also cause a unique key violation, as would all rows through the end of the table, except for the last row. By using deferred updates, this problem is easily avoided. The log records are first constructed to show what the new values for each row will be, the existing rows are deleted, and the new values inserted.

Just as with UPDATE commands, INSERT commands may also be deferred for very similar reasons.

Consider the following query (there is no clustered index or unique index on the "roysched" table):

Query 2: INSERT roysched SELECT * FROM roysched

SHOWPLAN 2: STEP 1
The type of query is INSERT
The update mode is deferred
FROM TABLE
roysched
Nested iteration
Table Scan
TO TABLE
roysched

Since there is no clustered index on the table, the new rows will be added to the end of the table. The query processor needs to be able to differentiate between the existing rows that are currently in the table (prior to the INSERT command) and the rows which will be inserted, so as to not get into a continuous loop of selecting a row, inserting it at the end of the table, selecting that row that it just inserted, and re-inserting it again. By using the deferred method of inserting, the log records can be first be constructed to show all of the currently-existing values in the table, then SQL Server will re-read those log records to insert them into the table.
The update mode is direct
Whenever possible, SQL Server will attempt to use the direct method of applying updates to tables, since it is faster and requires fewer log records to be generated than the deferred method. Depending on the type of command, one or more criteria must be met in order for SQL Server to perform the update using the direct method. Those criteria are:

* INSERT: For the direct update method to be used for INSERT operations, the table into which the rows are being inserted cannot be a table which is being read from in the same command. The second query example in the previous section demonstrates this, where the rows are being inserted into the same table in which they are being selected from. In addition, if rows are being inserted into the target table, and one or more of the target table's columns appear in the WHERE clause of the query then the deferred method, rather than the direct method, will be used.
* SELECT INTO: When a table is being populated with data by means of a SELECT INTO command, the direct method will always be used to insert the new rows.
* DELETE: For the direct update method to be used for DELETE operations, the query optimizer must be able to determine that either 0 or 1 rows qualify for the delete. The only means for it to verify this is to check that there is a unique index on the table, which is qualified in the WHERE clause of the DELETE command, and the target table is not joined with any other table(s).
* UPDATE: For the direct update method to be used for UPDATE operations, the same criteria apply as for DELETE: a unique index must exist such that the query optimizer can determine that no more than 1 row qualifies for the update, and the only table in the UPDATE command is the

Section 7 - Query Optimization 155

target table to update. In addition, all columns that are being updated must be datatypes that are fixedlength, rather than variable-length. Note that any column that allows NULLs is internally stored by SQL Server as a variable-length datatype column.

Query 1: DELETE
FROM authors
WHERE au_id = "172-32-1176"

SHOWPLAN 1: STEP 1
The type of query is DELETE
The update mode is direct
FROM TABLE
authors
Nested iteration
Using Clustered Index
TO TABLE
authors

Query 2: UPDATE titles
SET type = "popular_comp"
WHERE title_id = "BU2075"

SHOWPLAN 2: STEP 1
The type of query is UPDATE
The update mode is direct
FROM TABLE
titles
Nested iteration
Using Clustered Index
TO TABLE
titles

Query 3: UPDATE titles
SET price = $5.99
WHERE title_id = "BU2075"

SHOWPLAN 3: STEP 1
The type of query is UPDATE
The update mode is deferred
FROM TABLE
titles
Nested iteration
Using Clustered Index
TO TABLE

titles

Note that the only difference between the second and third example queries is the column of the table which is being updated. In the second query, the direct update method is used, whereas in the third query, the deferred method is used. This difference is due to the datatype of the column being updated: the titles.type column is defined as "char(12) NOT NULL", while the titles.price column is defined as "money NULL". Since the titles.price column is not a fixed-length datatype, the direct method cannot be used.

GROUP BY

This statement appears in the SHOWPLAN output for any query that contains a GROUP BY clause. Queries that contain a GROUP BY clause will always be at least two-step queries: one step to select the qualifying rows into a worktable and group them, and another step to return the rows from the worktable. The following example illustrates this:

Query: SELECT type, AVG(advance),
SUM(ytd_sales)
FROM titles
GROUP BY type

SHOWPLAN: STEP 1
The type of query is SELECT (into a
worktable)
GROUP BY
Vector Aggregate
FROM TABLE
titles
Nested iteration
Table Scan
TO TABLE
Worktable

STEP 2
The type of query is SELECT
FROM TABLE
Worktable
Nested iteration
Table Scan

Scalar Aggregate

Transact-SQL includes the aggregate functions:

* AVG()
* COUNT()
* COUNT(*)
* MAX()

* MIN()
* SUM()

Whenever an aggregate function is used in a SELECT statement that does not include a GROUP BY clause, it produces a single value, regardless of whether it is operating on all of the rows in a table or on a subset of the rows defined by a WHERE clause. When an aggregate function produces a single value, the function is called a "scalar aggregate", and is listed as such by SHOWPLAN. The following example shows the use of scalar aggregate functions:

Query: SELECT AVG(advance), SUM(ytd_sales)
FROM titles
WHERE type = "business"

SHOWPLAN: STEP 1
The type of query is SELECT
Scalar Aggregate
FROM TABLE
titles
Nested iteration
Table Scan

STEP 2
The type of query is SELECT
Table Scan

Notice that SHOWPLAN considers this a two-step query, which is very similar to the SHOWPLAN from the GROUP BY query listed earlier. Since the query contains a scalar aggregate, which will return a single value, SQL Server keeps internally a "variable" to store the result of the aggregate function. It can be thought of as a temporary storage space to keep a running total of the aggregate function as the qualifying rows from the table are evaluated. After all rows have been evaluated from the table (Step 1), the final value from the "variable" is then selected (Step 2) to return the scalar aggregate result.

Vector Aggregate

When a GROUP BY clause is used in a query which also includes an aggregate function, the aggregate function produces a value for each group. These values are called "vector aggregates". The "Vector Aggregate" statement from SHOWPLAN indicates that the query includes a vector aggregate. Below is an example query and SHOWPLAN which includes a vector aggregate:

Query: SELECT title_id, AVG(qty)
FROM sales
GROUP BY title_id

SHOWPLAN: STEP 1

The type of query is SELECT (into a worktable)
GROUP BY
Vector Aggregate
FROM TABLE
sales
Nested iteration
Table Scan
TO TABLE
Worktable

STEP 2
The type of query is SELECT
FROM TABLE
Worktable
Nested iteration
Table Scan

FROM TABLE
This SHOWPLAN step indicates the table that the query is reading from. In most queries, the "FROM TABLE" will be followed on the next line by the name of the table which is being selected from. In other cases, it may indicate that it is selecting from a worktable (discussed later). The main importance of examining the table names after the "FROM TABLE" output is to determine the order in which the query optimizer is joining the tables. The order of the tables listed after the "FROM TABLE" statements in the SHOWPLAN output indicate the same order that the tables were joined; this order may be (and often times is) different than the order that they are listed in the FROM clause of the query, or the order that they appear in the WHERE clause of the query. This is because the query optimizer examines all different join orders for the tables involved, and picks the join order that will require the least amount of I/O's.

Query: SELECT authors.au_id, au_fname, au_lname
FROM authors, titleauthor, titles
WHERE authors.au_id = titleauthor.au_id
AND titleauthor.title_id = titles.title_id
AND titles.type = "psychology"

SHOWPLAN: STEP 1
The type of query is SELECT
FROM TABLE
titles
Nested iteration
Table Scan
FROM TABLE
titleauthor

Nested iteration
Table Scan
FROM TABLE
authors
Nested iteration
Table Scan

This query illustrates the order in which the SQL Server query optimizer chooses to join the tables, which is not the order that they were listed in the FROM clause or the WHERE clause. By examining the order of the "FROM TABLE" statements, it can be seen that the qualifying rows from the titles table are first located (using the search clause). Those rows are then joined with the titleauthor table (using the join clause), and finally the titleauthor table is joined with the authors table to retrieve the desired columns (using the join clause).

TO TABLE

When a command is issued which makes or attempts to make a modification to one or more rows of a table, such as INSERT, DELETE, UPDATE, or SELECT INTO, the "TO TABLE" statement will show the target table which is being modified. For some operations which require an intermediate step which inserts rows into a worktable (discussed later), the "TO TABLE" will indicate that the results are going to the "Worktable" table, rather than a user table. The following examples illustrate the use of the "TO TABLE" statement:

Query 1: INSERT sales
VALUES ("8042", "QA973", "7/15/92", 7,
"Net 30", "PC1035")

SHOWPLAN 1: STEP 1
The type of query is INSERT
The update mode is direct
Table Scan
TO TABLE
sales

Query 2: UPDATE publishers
SET city = "Los Angeles"
WHERE pub_id = "1389"

SHOWPLAN 2: STEP 1
The type of query is UPDATE
The update mode is deferred
FROM TABLE
publishers
Nested iteration
Using Clustered Index
TO TABLE

publishers

Notice that the SHOWPLAN for the second query indicates that the publishers table is used both as the "FROM TABLE" as well as the "TO TABLE". In the case of UPDATE operations, the optimizer needs to read the table which contains the row(s) to be updated, resulting in the "FROM TABLE" statement, and then needs to modify the row(s), resulting in the "TO TABLE" statement.

Worktable

For some types of queries, such as those that require the results to be ordered or displayed in groups, the SQL Server query optimizer may determine that it is necessary to create its own temporary worktable. The worktable is used to hold the intermediate results of the query, at which time the result rows can be ordered or grouped, and then the final results selected from that worktable. When all results have been returned, the worktable is automatically dropped. The worktables are always created in the Tempdb database, so it is possible that the system administrator may have to increase the size of Tempdb to accomodate that queries which require very large worktables. Since the query optimizer creates these worktables for its own internal use, the names of the worktables will not be listed in the tempdb..sysobjects table.

Worktables will always need to be used when a query contains a GROUP BY clause. For queries involving ORDER BY, it is possible that the ordering can be done without the use of the worktable. If there is a clustered index on the column(s) in the ORDER BY clause, the optimizer knows that the rows are already stored in sorted order, so a sort in a worktable is not necessary (although there are exceptions to this, depending on the sort order which is installed on the server). Since the data is not stored in sorted order for nonclustered indexes, the worktable will not be necessary if the cheapest access plan is by using the nonclustered index. However, if the optimizer determines that scanning the entire table will require fewer I/Os than using the nonclustered index, then a worktable will need to be created for the ordering of the results. The following examples illustrate the use of worktables:

Query 1: SELECT type, AVG(advance), SUM(ytd_sales)
FROM titles
GROUP BY type

SHOWPLAN 1: STEP 1
The type of query is SELECT (into a
worktable)
GROUP BY
Vector Aggregate
FROM TABLE
titles
Nested iteration
Table Scan
TO TABLE
Worktable

STEP 2
The type of query is SELECT
FROM TABLE
Worktable
Nested iteration
Table Scan

Query 2: SELECT *
FROM authors
ORDER BY au_lname, au_fname

SHOWPLAN 2: STEP 1
The type of query is INSERT
The update mode is direct
Worktable created for ORDER BY
FROM TABLE
authors
Nested iteration
Table Scan
TO TABLE
Worktable

STEP 2
The type of query is SELECT
This step involves sorting
FROM TABLE
Worktable
Using GETSORTED
Table Scan

Query 3: SELECT *
FROM authors
ORDER BY au_id

SHOWPLAN 3: STEP 1
The type of query is SELECT
FROM TABLE
authors
Nested iteration
Table Scan

In the third example above, notice that no worktable was created for the ORDER BY clause. This is because there is a unique clustered index on the authors.au_id column, so the data is already stored in sorted order based on the au_id value, and an additional sort for the ORDER BY is not

necessary. In the second example, there is a composite nonclustered index on the columns au_lname and au_fname. However, since the optimizer chose not to use the index, and due to the sort order on the SQL Server, a worktable needed to be created to accomodate the sort.
Worktable created for SELECT_INTO
SQL Server's SELECT INTO operation performs two functions: it first creates a table with the exact same structure as the table being selected from, and then it insert all rows which meet the WHERE conditions (if a WHERE clause is used) of the table being selected from. The "Worktable created for SELECT_INTO" statement is slightly misleading, in that the "worktable" that it refers to is actually the new physical table that is created. Unlike other worktables, it is not dropped when the query finishes executing. In addition, the worktable is not created in Tempdb, unless the user specifies Tempdb as the target database for the new table.

Query: SELECT *
INTO seattle_stores
FROM stores
WHERE city = "seattle"

SHOWPLAN: STEP 1
The type of query is TABCREATE

STEP 2
The type of query is INSERT
The update mode is direct
Worktable created for SELECT_INTO
FROM TABLE
stores
Nested iteration
Table Scan
TO TABLE
Worktable

Worktable created for DISTINCT
When a query is issued which includes the DISTINCT keyword, all duplicate rows are excluded from the results so that only unique rows are returned. To accomplish this, SQL Server first creates a worktable to store all of the results of the query, including duplicates, just as though the DISTINCT keyword was not included. It then sorts the rows in the worktable, and is able to easily discard the duplicate rows. Finally, the rows from the worktable are returned, which insures that no duplicate rows will appear in the output.

Query: SELECT DISTINCT city
FROM authors

SHOWPLAN: STEP 1
The type of query is INSERT

The update mode is direct
Worktable created for DISTINCT
FROM TABLE
authors
FROM TABLE
authors
Nested iteration
Table Scan
TO TABLE
Worktable

STEP 2
The type of query is SELECT
This step involves sorting
FROM TABLE
Worktable
Using GETSORTED
Table Scan

Worktable created for ORDER BY
As discussed previously, queries which include an ORDER BY clause will often require the use of a temporary worktable. When the optimizer cannot use an available index for the ordering, it creates a worktable for use in sorting the result rows prior to returning them. Below is an example which shows the worktable being created for the ORDER BY clause:

Query: SELECT *
FROM authors
ORDER BY city

SHOWPLAN: STEP 1
The type of query is INSERT
The update mode is direct
Worktable created for ORDER BY
FROM TABLE
authors
FROM TABLE
authors
Nested iteration
Table Scan
TO TABLE
Worktable

STEP 2
The type of query is SELECT

This step involves sorting
FROM TABLE
Worktable
Using GETSORTED
Table Scan

Worktable created for REFORMATTING
When joining tables, SQL Server may in some cases choose to use a "reformatting strategy" to join the tables and return the qualifying rows. This strategy is only considered as a last resort, when the tables are large and neither table in the join has a useful index to use. The reformatting strategy inserts the rows from the smaller of the two tables into a worktable. Then, a clustered index is created on the worktable, and the clustered index is then used in the join to retrieve the qualifying rows from each table. The main cost in using the reformatting strategy is the time and I/Os necessary to build the clustered index on the worktable; however, that cost is still cheaper than joining the tables with no index. If user queries are using the reformatting strategy, it is generally a good idea to examine the tables involved and create indexes on the columns of the tables which are being joined. The following example illustrates the reformatting strategy. Since none of the tables in the Pubs database are large enough for the optimizer to consider using this strategy, two new tables are used. Each table has 5 columns defined as "char(200)". Tab1 has 500 rows and Tab2 has 250 rows.

Query: SELECT Tab1.col1
FROM Tab1, Tab2
WHERE Tab1.col1 = Tab2.col1

SHOWPLAN: STEP 1
The type of query is INSERT
The update mode is direct
Worktable created for REFORMATTING
FROM TABLE
Tab2
Nested iteration
Table Scan
TO TABLE
Worktable

STEP 2
The type of query is SELECT
FROM TABLE
Tab1
Nested iteration
Table Scan
FROM TABLE
Worktable

Nested iteration
Using Clustered Index

This step involves sorting
This SHOWPLAN statement indicates that the query must sort the intermediate results before returning them to the user. Queries that specify DISTINCT will require an intermediate sort, as well as queries that have an ORDER BY clause which cannot use an available index. As stated earlier, the results are put into a worktable, and the worktable is then sorted. The example on the following page demontrates a query which requires a sort:

Query: SELECT DISTINCT state
FROM stores

SHOWPLAN: STEP 1
The type of query is INSERT
The update mode is direct
Worktable created for DISTINCT
FROM TABLE
stores
FROM TABLE
stores
Nested iteration
Table Scan
TO TABLE
Worktable

STEP 2
The type of query is SELECT
This step involves sorting
FROM TABLE
Worktable
Using GETSORTED
Table Scan

Using GETSORTED
This statement indicates one of the ways in which the result rows can be returned from a table. In the case of "Using GETSORTED", the rows will be returned in sorted order. However, not all queries which return rows in sorted order will have this step. In the case of a query which has an ORDER BY clause, and an index with the proper sort sequence exists on those columns being ordered, an intermediate sort may not be necessary, and the rows can simply be returned in order by using the available index. The "Using GETSORTED" method is used when SQL Server must first create a temporary worktable to sort the result rows, and then return them in the proper sorted order. The following example shows a query which requires a worktable to be created and the rows returned in sorted order:

Query: SELECT au_id, au_lname, au_fname, city
FROM authors
ORDER BY city

SHOWPLAN: STEP 1
The type of query is INSERT
The update mode is direct
Worktable created for ORDER BY
FROM TABLE
authors
FROM TABLE
authors
Nested iteration
Table Scan
TO TABLE
Worktable
STEP 2
The type of query is SELECT
This step involves sorting
FROM TABLE
Worktable
Using GETSORTED
Table Scan

Nested iteration
The "Nested iteration" is the default technique used to join tables and/or return rows from a table. It simply indicates that the optimizer is using one or more sets of loops to go through a table and retrieve a row, qualify the row based on the search criteria given in the WHERE clause, return the row to the front-end, and loop again to get the next row. The method in which it gets the rows (such as using an available index) is discussed later. The following example shows the optimizer doing nested iterations through each of the tables in the join:

Query: SELECT title_id, title
FROM titles, publishers
WHERE titles.pub_id = publishers.pub_id
AND publishers.pub_id = '1389'

SHOWPLAN: STEP 1
The type of query is SELECT
FROM TABLE
publishers
Nested iteration
Using Clustered Index

Section 7 - Query Optimization

FROM TABLE
titles
Nested iteration
Table Scan

EXISTS TABLE : nested iteration
This SHOWPLAN step is very similar to the previous one of "Nested iteration". The difference, however, is that this step indicates a nested iteration on a table which is part of an existence test in a query. There are several ways an existence test can be written in Transact-SQL, such as "EXISTS", "IN", or "=ANY". Prior to SQL Server version 4.2, queries which contained an IN clause followed by a subquery were treated as table joins. Beginning with version 4.2, these queries are now treated the same as if they were written with an EXISTS clause. The following examples demonstrate the SHOWPLAN output with queries which test for existence of values:

Query 1: SELECT au_lname, au_fname
FROM authors
WHERE EXISTS
(SELECT *
FROM publishers
WHERE authors.city = publishers.city)

SHOWPLAN 1: STEP 1
The type of query is SELECT
FROM TABLE
authors
Nested iteration
Table Scan
FROM TABLE
publishers
EXISTS TABLE : nested iteration
Table Scan

Query 2: SELECT title
FROM titles
WHERE pub_id IN
(SELECT pub_id
FROM publishers
WHERE city LIKE "B%")

SHOWPLAN 2: STEP 1
The type of query is SELECT
FROM TABLE
titles
Nested iteration

Table Scan
FROM TABLE
publishers
EXISTS TABLE : nested iteration
Table Scan

Table Scan
This SHOWPLAN statement indicates which method was used to retrieve the physical result rows from the given table. When the "table scan" method is used, the execution begins with the first row in the table; each row is then retrieved and compared with the conditions in the WHERE clause, and returned to the front-end if it meets the given criteria. Regardless of how many rows qualify, every row in the table must be looked at, so for very large tables, a table scan can be very costly in terms of page I/Os. If a table has one or more indexes on it, the query optimizer may still choose to do a table scan instead of using one of the available indexes if the optimizer determines that the indexes are too costly or are not useful for the given query. The following query shows a typical table scan:

Query: SELECT au_lname, au_fname
FROM authors

SHOWPLAN: STEP 1
The type of query is SELECT
FROM TABLE
authors
Nested iteration
Table Scan

Using Clustered Index
This SHOWPLAN statement indicates that the query optimizer chose to use the clustered index on a table to retrieve the rows. Unlike a table scan, using an index to retrieve rows does not require the optimizer to examine every row in the table (unless the WHERE clause applies to all rows). For queries which return a small percentage of the rows from a large table, the savings in terms of I/Os of using an index versus doing a table scan can be very significant. The following query shows the clustered index being used to retrieve the rows from the table:

Query: SELECT title_id, title
FROM titles
WHERE title_id LIKE "PS2%"

SHOWPLAN: STEP 1
The type of query is SELECT
FROM TABLE
titles
Nested iteration

Using Clustered Index

Index :
Like the previous statement with the clustered index, this statement indicates that the optimizer chose to use an index to retrieve the rows instead of doing a table scan. The

Query: SELECT *
FROM master..sysobjects
WHERE name = "mytable"
AND uid = 5

SHOWPLAN: STEP 1
The type of query is SELECT
FROM TABLE
master..sysobjects
Nested iteration
Index : ncsysobjects

Using Dynamic Index
This SHOWPLAN statement indicates that the query optimizer has chosen to build its own index during the execution of the query, for use in its "OR strategy". Since queries involving OR clauses are generally not very efficient in terms of being able to quickly access the data, the SQL Server optimizer may choose to use the OR strategy. When the OR strategy is used, the optimizer makes several passes through the table -- one pass for each argument to each OR clause. The results of each pass are added to a single worktable, and the worktable is then sorted to remove any duplicate rows. The worktable does not contain the actual data rows from the table, but rather it contains the row IDs for the matching rows. The row IDs are simply a combination of the page number and row number on that page for each of the rows. When the duplicates have been eliminated, the optimizer considers the worktable of row IDs to be, essentially, its own index ("Dynamic Index") pointing to the table's data rows. It can then simply scan through the worktable, get each row ID, and return the data row from the table that has that row ID.

The OR strategy is not limited only to queries that contain OR clauses. When an IN clause is used to list a group of possible values, SQL Server interprets that the same way as though the query had a separate equality clause for each of the values in the IN clause. To illustrate the OR strategy and the use of the Dynamic Index, the queries will be based on a table with 10,000 unique data rows, a unique nonclustered index on column "col1", and a unique nonclustered index on column "col2".

Query 1: SELECT *
FROM Mytable
WHERE col1 = 355
OR col2 = 732

SHOWPLAN 1: STEP 1
The type of query is SELECT
FROM TABLE
Mytable
Nested iteration
Index : col1_idx
FROM TABLE
Mytable
Nested iteration
Index : col2_idx
FROM TABLE
Mytable
Nested iteration
Using Dynamic Index

Query 2: SELECT *
FROM Mytable
WHERE col1 IN (700, 1503, 311)

SHOWPLAN 2: STEP 1
The type of query is SELECT
FROM TABLE
Mytable
Nested iteration
Index : col1_idx
FROM TABLE
Mytable
Nested iteration
Index : col1_idx
FROM TABLE
Mytable
Nested iteration
Index : col1_idx
FROM TABLE
Mytable
Nested iteration
Using Dynamic Index

SQL Server does not always resort to using the OR strategy for every query that contains OR clauses. The following conditions must be met before it will choose to use the OR strategy:

* All columns in the OR clause must belong to the same table.
* If any portion of the OR clause requires a table scan (due to lack of index or poor selectivity of a

given index), then a table scan will be used for the entire query, rather than the OR strategy.
* The decision to use the OR strategy is made after all indexes and costs are evaluated. If any other access plan is less costly (in terms of page I/Os), SQL Server will choose to use the plan with the least cost. In the examples above, if a straight table scan would result in less page I/Os than using the OR strategy, then the queries would be processed as a table scan instead of using the Dynamic Index.

7.2 Identify optimization 'set' command tools

Adaptive Server provides the following diagnostic and informational tools to help you understand query optimization and improve the performance of your queries:

set statistics io: set statistics io reports information about physical and logical I/O and the number of times a table was accessed. *set statistics io* output follows the query results and provides actual I/O performed by the query.
Syntax:
set statistics {io, simulate, subquerycache, time} [on | off]
Example:
set statistics io on

set showplan on: displays the steps performed for each query in a batch. It is often used with set noexec on, especially for queries that return large numbers of rows.
Syntax:
set showplan on
To stop displaying query plans
set showplan off

> **Note:** You can use showplan in conjunction with other set commands.
> **Note:** When you want to display showplans for a stored procedure, but not execute them, use the **set fmtonly** command.
> **Note:** Do not use set noexec with stored procedures - compilation and execution will not occur and you will not get the necessary output

set statistics subquerycache on: displays the number of cache hits and misses and the number of rows in the cache for each subquery.
Example:
select type, title_id
from titles
where price > all
(select price
from titles
where advance < 15000)
Statement: 1 Subquery: 1 cache size: 75 hits: 4925

misses: 75

set statistics time on: displays the time it takes to parse and compile each command.

Advanced Optimizing Tools can use to enforce index choice, join order, and other query optimization choices. These tools include:
set forceplan: forces the query to use the tables in the order specified in the from clause.

set table count: increases the number of tables that the optimizer considers at one time while determining join order.

set prefetch*:* toggles prefetch for query tuning experimentation.
By default, a query uses large I/O whenever a large I/O pool is configured and the query processor determines that large I/O would reduce the query cost.
To disable large I/O during a session, use:
set prefetch off
To reenable large I/O, use:
set prefetch on

set sort_merge: allows/disallows sort-merge joins.

set parallel_degree*:* specifies the degree of parallelism for a query.

sp_cachestrategy: sets status bits to enable or disable prefetch and fetch-and-discard cache strategies.

derived_stat:
Returns derived statistics for the specified object and index.

Syntax:
derived_stat(object_name | object_id,
*   index_name | index_id,*
*   [partition_name | partition_id,]*
*   "statistic")*

Returns:
- data page cluster ratio or dpcr
- The data page cluster ratio for the object/index pair
- index page cluster ratio or ipcr
- The index page cluster ratio for the object/index pair
- data row cluster ratio or drcr
- The data row cluster ratio for the object/index pair
- large io efficiency or lgio
- The large I/O efficiency for the object/index pair

Section 7 - Query Optimization

- space utilization or sput
- The space utilization for the object/index pair

Example 1:
Selects the space utilization for the titleidind index of the titles table:
select derived_stat("titles", "titleidind", "space utilization")

Example 2:
Selects the data page cluster ratio for index ID 2 of the titles table. Note that you can use either "dpcr" or "data page cluster ratio":
select derived_stat("titles", 2, "dpcr")

Usage:
- derived_stat returns a double precision value.
- The values returned by derived_stat match the values presented by the optdiag utility.
- If the specified object or index does not exist, derived_stat returns NULL.
- Specifying an invalid statistic type results in an error message.
- Using the optional partition_name or partition_id reports the target partition; otherwise, derived_stat reports for the   entire object.

If you provide:
Four arguments – derived_stat uses the third argument as the partition, and returns derived statistics on the fourth argument.
Three arguments – derived_stat assumes you did not specifiy a partition, and returns derived statistic on the third argument.

7.3 Use of Abstract Plans

An abstract plan describes the execution plan for a query using a language created for that purpose. This language contains operators to specify the choices and actions that can be generated by the optimizer. For example, to specify an index scan on the titles table, using the index title_id_ix, the abstract plan says:
(i_scan title_id_ix titles)
To use this abstract plan with a query, you can modify the query text and add a PLAN clause:
select * from titles where title_id = "On Liberty"
plan "(i_scan title_id_ix titles)"

Adaptive Server can generate an abstract plan for a query, and save the text and its associated abstract plan in the **sysqueryplans** system table. Using a **rapid hashing method**, incoming SQL queries can be compared to saved **query text**, and if a match is found, the corresponding saved abstract plan is used to execute the query.
The main purpose of abstract plans is to provide a means to capture query plans before and after major system changes.

Other uses are:
- Searching for specific types of plans, such as table scans or reformatting
- Searching for plans that use particular indexes
- Specifying full or partial plans for poorly-performing queries
- Saving plans for queries with long optimization times

A full set of system procedures allows System Administrators and Database Owners to administer plans and plan groups. Individual users can view, drop, and copy the plans for the queries that they have run.
For managing an abstract plan group:
sp_add_qpgroup, sp_drop_qpgroup, sp_help_qpgroup, sp_rename_qpgroup
Finding abstract plans
sp_find_qplan
Managing individual abstract plans
sp_help_qplan, sp_copy_qplan , sp_drop_qplan , sp_cmp_qplans , sp_set_qplan
Managing all plans in a group
sp_copy_all_qplans , sp_cmp_all_qplans, sp_drop_all_qplans
Importing and exporting groups of plans
sp_export_qpgroup, sp_import_qpgroup

When you first install Adaptive Server, there are two abstract plan groups:
- **ap_stdout:** used by default for capturing plans
- **ap_stdin:** used by default for plan association

How abstract plans are associated with queries:
When an abstract plan is saved, all white space (tabs, multiple spaces, and returns, except for returns that terminate a --style comment) in the query is trimmed to a single space, and a hash-key value is computed for the white-space trimmed SQL statement. The trimmed SQL statement and the hash key are stored in sysqueryplans along with the abstract plan, a unique plan ID, the user's ID, and the ID of the current abstract plan group.
When abstract plan association is enabled, the hash key for incoming SQL statements is computed, and this value is used to search for the matching query and abstract plan in the current association group, with the corresponding user ID. The full association key of an abstract plan consists of:
- The user ID of the current user
- The group ID of the current association group
- The full query text

Once a matching hash key is found, the full text of the saved query is compared to the query to be executed, and used if it matches. The association key combination of user ID, group ID and query text means that for a given user, there cannot be two queries in the same abstract plan group that have the same query text, but different query plans.

Section 7 - Query Optimization

At the session level, any user can enable and disable capture and use of abstract plans with the set plan dump and set plan load commands. The set plan replace command determines whether existing plans are overwritten by changed plans.

> **Note:** Enabling and disabling abstract plan modes takes effect at the end of the batch in which the command is included (similar to showplan). Therefore, change the mode in a separate batch before you run your queries:

set plan dump on
go
/*queries to run*/
go

Any set plan commands used in a stored procedure do not affect the procedure (except those statements affected by deferred compilation) in which they are included, but remain in effect after the procedure completes.

To save the plans to the default group **ap_stdout:**
set plan dump on
To start capturing plans in a specific abstract plan group
set plan dump <abstract_plan_group_name> on
Note: sp_add_qpgroup creates abstract plan groups
If you are currently saving plans to a group, you must turn off the plan dump mode, and re-enable it for the new group, as shown here:
set plan dump on /*save to the default group*/
go
/*some queries to be captured */
go
set plan dump off
go
set plan dump dev_plans on
go
/*additional queries*/
go

To start the association mode using the default group ap_stdin:
set plan load on
To enable association mode using another abstract plan group:
set plan load < abstract_plan_group_name > on

Only one abstract plan group can be active for plan association at one time. If plan association is active for a group, you must deactivate the current group and start association for the new group, as shown here:
set plan load test_plans on
go

```
/*some queries*/
go
set plan load off
go
set plan load dev_plans on
go
```

While plan capture mode is active, you can choose whether to have plans for the same query replace existing plans by enabling or disabling set plan replace. This command activates plan replacement mode:
set plan replace on
You do not specify a group name with set plan replace; it affects the current active capture group. To disable plan replacement:
set plan replace off

Note: When you are capturing plans, and a query has the same query text as an already-saved plan, the existing plan is not replaced unless **replace mode is enabled.**

Note: You can have both plan dump and plan load mode active simultaneously, with or without replace mode active

set plan exists check option:
The exists check mode can be used during query plan association to speed performance when users require abstract plans for fewer than 20 queries from an abstract plan group. If a small number of queries require plans to improve their optimization, enabling exists check mode speeds execution of all queries that do not have abstract plans, because they do not check for plans in sysqueryplans.
When set plan load and set exists check are both enabled, the hash keys for up to 20 queries in the load group are cached for the user. If the load group contains more than 20 queries, exists check mode is disabled. Each incoming query is hashed; if its hash key is not stored in the abstract plan cache, then there is no plan for the query and no search is made. This speeds the compilation of all queries that do not have saved plans.
syntax :
set plan exists check {on | off}
You must enable load mode before you enable plan hash-key caching. A System Administrator can configure server-wide plan hash-key caching with the configuration parameter abstract plan cache. To enable serverwide plan caching, use:
sp_configure "abstract plan cache", 1

Using *showplan*:
When showplan is turned on, and abstract plan association mode has been enabled with set plan load, showplan prints the plan ID of the matching abstract plan at the beginning of the showplan output for the statement:
QUERY PLAN FOR STATEMENT 1 (at line 1).

Optimized using an Abstract Plan (ID : 832005995).
If you run queries using the plan clause added to a SQL statement, showplan displays:
Optimized using the Abstract Plan in the PLAN clause.

Using *noexec*:
You can use noexec mode to capture abstract plans without actually executing the queries. If noexec mode is in effect, queries are optimized and abstract plans are saved, but no query results are returned.

Using *fmtonly*:
A similar behavior can be obtained for capturing plans in stored procedures without actually executing the stored procedures, using fmtonly set.
sp_add_qpgroup pubs_dev
go
set plan dump pubs_dev on
go
set fmtonly on
go
exec stored_proc(...)
go

Using *forceplan*:
If set forceplan on is in effect, and query association is also enabled for the session, forceplan is ignored if a full abstract plan is used to optimize the query. If a partial plan does not completely specify the join order:
- First, the tables in the abstract plan are ordered, as specified.
- The remaining tables are ordered as specified in the from clause.
- The two lists of tables are merged.

Server-wide abstract plan capture and association modes:
To enables dumping to the default abstract plans capture group, ap_stdout.
    sp_configure "abstract plan dump", 1
To enables loading from the default abstract plans loading group, ap_stdin.
    sp_configure "abstract plan load", 1
To enables plan replacement, when plan dump mode is also enabled.
    sp_configure "abstract plan replace", 1
To enables caching of abstract plan hash IDs, when abstract plan load is enabled.
    sp_configure "abstract plan cache", 1

Note: By default, these configuration parameters are set to 0, which means that capture and association modes are off. To enable a mode, set the configuration value to 1:
Note: Enabling any of the server-wide abstract plan modes is dynamic; you do not have to reboot the server.

Note: Server-wide capture and association allows the System Administrator to capture all plans for all users on a server. You cannot override the serverwide modes at the session level.

Creating plans using SQL:
Using *create plan*:
This example creates an abstract plan:
> create plan
> "select avg(price) from titles"
> "(scalar_agg
> (i_scan type_price_ix titles)
>)"

The plan is saved in the current active plan group. You can also specify the group name:
> create plan
> "select avg(price) from titles"
> "(scalar_agg
> (i_scan type_price_ix titles)
>)"
> into dev_plans

If you want to see the plan ID that is used for a plan you create, create plan can return the ID as a variable. You must declare the variable first. This example returns the plan ID:
> create plan
> "select avg(price) from titles"
> "(scalar_agg
> (i_scan type_price_ix titles)
>)"
> into dev_plans
> and set @id
> select @id

Using the *plan* clause: You can use the plan clause with the following SQL statements to specify the plan to use to execute the query:
- select   • insert...select • delete   • update   • if   • while • return

Example:
> select avg(price) from titles
> plan
> "(scalar_agg
> (i_scan type_price_ix titles
>)"

7.4 Determine if the optimizer selected serial or parallel access

Worker process model:
Adaptive Server uses a **coordinating process** and multiple **worker processes** to execute queries in parallel. A query that runs in parallel with eight worker processes is much like eight serial queries accessing one-eighth of the table, with the coordinating process supervising the interaction and managing the process of returning results to the client. Each worker process uses approximately the same amount of memory as a user connection. Each worker process runs as a task that must be scheduled on an engine, scans data pages, queues disk I/Os, and performs in many ways like any other task on the server. One major difference is that in last phase of query processing, the coordinating process manages merging the results and returning them to the client, coordinating with worker processes.

1. The client submits a query.
2. The client task assigned to execute the query becomes the coordinating process for parallel query execution.
3. The coordinating process requests four worker processes from the pool of worker processes. The coordinating process together with the worker processes is called a **family**.
4. The worker processes execute the query in parallel
5. The coordinating process returns the results produced by all the worker processes

Note: During query processing, the tasks are tracked in the system tables by a family ID (fid). Each worker process for a family has the same family ID and its own unique server process ID (spid). System procedures such as sp_who and sp_lock display both the fid and the spid for parallel queries.

Parallel query execution:
The total amount of work performed by the query running in parallel is greater than the amount of work performed by the query running in serial, but the response time is shorter.

Returning results from parallel queries: Results from parallel queries are returned through one of three merge
strategies, or as the final step in a sort. Parallel queries that do not have a final sort step use one of these merge types:
- Queries that contain a vector (grouped) aggregate use worktables to store temporary results; the coordinating process merges the results into one worktable and returns results to the client.
- Queries that contain a scalar (ungrouped) aggregate use internal variables, and the coordinating process performs the final computations to return the results to the client.
- Queries that do not contain aggregates and that do not use clauses that do not require a final sort can return results to the client as the tables are being scanned. Each worker process stores results in a result buffer and uses address locks to coordinate transferring the results to the network buffers for the task.

More than one merge type can be used when queries require several steps for multiple worktables.

Note: Since parallel queries use multiple processes to scan data pages, queries that do not use aggregates and do not include a final sort step may return results in different order than serial queries and may return different results for queries with **set rowcount** in effect and for queries that select into a local variable.

Types of parallel data access:
Adaptive Server accesses data in parallel in different ways, depending configuration parameter settings, table partitioning, and the availability of indexes. The optimizer may choose a mix of serial and parallel methods for queries that involve multiple tables or multiple steps. Parallel methods include:
- Hash-based table scans
- Hash-based nonclustered index scans
- Partition-based scans, either full table scans or scans positioned with a clustered index
- Range-based scans during merge joins

Hash-based table scans: Hash-based table scans increase the **logical I/O** for the scan, since each worker process must access each page to hash on the **page ID**. For **dataonly-locked tables**, hash-based table scans hash either on the **extent ID** or the **allocation page ID**, so that only a single worker process scans a page, and logical I/O does not increase.

With only one engine, the query still benefits from parallel access because one worker process can execute while others wait for I/O. If there are multiple engines, some of the worker processes could be running simultaneously.

Note: Hash-based table scans are used only for the **outer query** in a join.

Partition-based scans: scans a table that has different partitions on different physical disks. If multiple engines are available, the worker processes can run simultaneously. This configuration can yield high parallel performance by providing I/O parallelism.

Hash-based index scans: Hash-based index scans can be performed using nonclustered indexes or clustered indexes on **dataonly- locked** tables. Each worker process navigates higher levels of the index and reads the leaf-level pages of the index. Each worker process then hashes on either the **data page ID** or the **key value** to determine which data pages or data rows to process. Reading every leaf page produces negligible overhead.

Note: A parallel query's **degree of parallelism** is the **number of worker processes** used to execute the query.

This number depends on several factors, including:
- The values to which of the parallel configuration parameters or the session-level limits,
- The number of partitions on a table (for partition-based scans)
- The level of parallelism suggested by the optimizer
- The number of worker processes that are available at the time the query executes.

Section 7 - Query Optimization

You can establish limits on the degree of parallelism:
- Server-wide – using sp_configure with parameters
  Example:
  sp_configure "number of worker processes", 50
- For a session – using set with the parameters
  Example:
  set parallel_degree 5
  To remove the session limit, use:
  set parallel_degree 0
  or
  set scan_parallel_degree 0
  To run subsequent queries in serial mode, use:
  set parallel_degree 1
  or
  set scan_parallel_degree 1
- In a select query – using the parallel clause
  Example:
  select ...
  from *tablename* [([index *index_name*]
  [parallel [*degree_of_parallelism* | 1]]
  [prefetch *size*] [lru|mru])] ,
  tablename [([index *index_name*]
  [parallel [*degree_of_parallelism* | 1]
  [prefetch *size*] [lru|mru])] ...
  Example:
  select * from huge_table (parallel 1)

Configuration parameters for controlling parallelism:

Parameters	Explanation	Comment
number of worker processes	The maximum number of worker processes available for all parallel queries. Each worker process requires approximately as much memory as a user connection.	Restart of server required
max parallel degree	The number of worker processes that can be used by a single query. It must be **equal to or less than** number of worker processes and **equal to or greater than** max scan parallel degree. **number of worker processes >= max parallel degree >= max scan parallel degree**	Dynamic, no restart required
max scan parallel degree	The maximum number of worker processes that can be used for a **hash scan**. It must **be equal to or less than** number of worker processes and max parallel degree. **number of worker processes >= max scan parallel degree <= max parallel degree**	Dynamic, no restart required

set options for parallel execution tuning:

Parameters	Explanation
parallel_degree	Sets the maximum number of worker processes for a query in a session, stored procedure, or trigger. Overrides the max parallel degree configuration parameter, but must be less than or equal to the value of max parallel degree.
scan_parallel_degree	Sets the maximum number of worker processes for a hash-based scan during a specific session, stored procedure, or trigger. Overrides the max scan parallel degree configuration parameter but must be less than or equal to the value of max scan parallel degree.

Note: If a minimal number of worker processes are required but unavailable, the query aborts with this error message:
Insufficient number of worker processes to execute the parallel query. Increase the value of the configuration parameter 'number of worker processes'

Parallel query optimization is the process of analyzing a query and choosing the best combination of parallel and serial access methods to yield the fastest response time for the query.
Serial query optimization: selects the query plan that is the least costly to execute. Since only one process executes the query, choosing the least costly plan yields the fastest response time *and* requires the least amount of total work from the server.
Parallel query optimization: The goal of executing queries in parallel is to get the fastest response time, even if it involves more total work from the server. During parallel query optimization, the optimizer uses cost-based comparisons similar to those used in serial optimization to select a final query plan.

Serial query optimization improves performance by minimizing the use of server resources, but parallel query optimization improves performance for individual queries by fully utilizing available resources to get the fastest response time.

Parallel access methods: Parallel access methods fall into these general categories:
Partition-based access methods: Use two or more worker processes to access separate partitions of a table. Partition-based methods yield the fastest response times because they can distribute the work in accessing a table over both CPUs and physical disks. At the CPU level, worker processes can be queued to separate engines to increase processing performance. At the physical disk level, worker processes can perform I/O independently of one another, if the table's partitions are distributed over separate physical devices and controllers.

Hash-based access methods: provide parallel access to partitioned tables, using either table scans or index scans. Hash-based strategies employ multiple worker processes to work on a single chain of data pages or a set of index pages. I/O is not distributed over physical devices or controllers, but worker processes can still be queued to multiple engines to distribute processing and improve response times.

Range-based access methods: provide parallel access during **merge joins** on partitioned tables and unpartitioned tables, including worktables created for sorting and merging, and via indexes. The partitioning on the tables is not considered when choosing the **degree of parallelism**, so it is not distributed over physical devices or controllers. Worker processes can be queued to multiple engines to distribute processing and improve response times.

Note: Commands that insert, delete, or update data, and commands executed from within **cursors** are never considered for parallel query optimization.

Queries that benefit from parallel processing:
- select statements that scan large numbers of pages but return relatively few rows, such as table scans or clustered index scans with grouped or ungrouped aggregates
- Table scans or clustered index scans that scan a large number of pages, but have where clauses that return only a small percentage of rows.
- select statements that include union, order by, or distinct, since these query operations can make use of **parallel sorting** or **parallel hashing**.
- select statements where a reformatting strategy is chosen by the optimizer , since these can populate worktables in parallel and can make use of parallel sorting.
- join queries.

Parallel sorting: Any Transact-SQL command that requires data row sorting can benefit from parallel sorting techniques. These commands are:
- Create index commands and the alter table…add constraint commands that build indexes, unique and primary key
- Queries that use the order by clause
- Queries that use distinct
- Queries that perform merge joins requiring sorts
- Queries that use union (except union all)
- Queries that use the **reformatting strategy**

In addition, any cursors that use the above commands can benefit from parallel sorting.

Parallel sorting strategy:
Like the Adaptive Server optimizer, the Adaptive Server parallel sort manager analyzes the available worker processes, the input table, and other resources to determine the number of worker processes to use for the sort.

After determining the number of worker processes to use, Adaptive Server executes the parallel sort. The process of executing a parallel sort is the same for create index commands and queries that require sorts. Adaptive Server executes a parallel sort by:

1. Creating a distribution map. For a merge join with statistics on a join column, **histogram statistics** are used for the distribution map. In other cases, the **input table** is sampled to build the map.

2. Reading the table data and dynamically partitioning the key values into a set of **sort buffers**, as determined by the distribution map.
3. Sorting each individual range of key values and creating subindexes.
4. Merging the sorted subindexes into the final result set.

Partition skew:
Partition skew plays an important part in determining whether a parallel partitioned scan can be used. Adaptive Server partition skew is defined as the ratio of the size of the **largest partition** to the **average size of a partition**.
Consider a table with four partitions of sizes 10, 20, 35, and 80 pages.
The size of the average partition is (20 + 20 + 35 + 85)/4 = 40 pages.
The biggest partition has 85 pages so partition skew is calculated as 85/40 = 2.125.
In partitioned scans, the cost of doing a parallel scan is as expensive as doing the scan on the largest partition. Instead, a hash-based partition may turn out to be fast, as each worker process may hash on a page number or an allocation unit and scan its portion of the data. The penalty paid in terms of loss of performance by skewed partitions is not always at the scan level, but rather as more complex operators like several join operations are built over the data. The margin of error increases exponentially in such cases.

Partition skew can be easily found by running sp_help on a table:

Alternatively, skew can be calculated by querying the **systabstats system catalog**, where the number of pages in each partition is listed.

Partition elimination:
One of the advantages of semantic partitioning is that the query processor may be able to take advantage of this and be able to disqualify partitions at compile time. This is possible for **range, hash, and list** partitions. With hash partitions, only **equality predicates** can be used, whereas for range and list partitions **equality and in-equality predicates** can be used to eliminate partitions.

7.5 Define Procedure Cache & explain how stored procedures are processed

Procedure cache:
Adaptive Server maintains an **MRU/LRU (most recently used/least recently used)** chain of stored procedure query plans. As users execute stored procedures, Adaptive Server looks in the procedure cache for a query plan to use. If a query plan is available, it is placed on the MRU end of the chain, and execution begins.
If no plan is in memory, or if all copies are in use, the query tree for the procedure is read from the sysprocedures table. It is then optimized, using the parameters provided to the procedure, and put on the MRU end of the chain, and execution begins. Plans at the LRU end of the page chain that are not in use are aged out of the cache.
The memory allocated for the procedure cache holds the optimized query plans (and occasionally trees) for all batches, including any triggers.
If more than one user uses a procedure or trigger simultaneously, there will be multiple copies of it in cache. If the procedure cache is too small, a user trying to execute stored procedures or

queries that fire triggers receives an error message and must resubmit the query. Space becomes available when unused plans age out of the cache.

When you first install Adaptive Server, the default procedure cache size is **3271 memory pages**. The optimum value for the procedure cache varies from application to application, and it may also vary as usage patterns change.

When you start Adaptive Server, the error log states how much procedure cache is available.
proc buffers: Represents the maximum number of compiled procedural objects that can reside in the procedure cache at one time.
proc headers: Represents the number of pages dedicated to the procedure cache. Each object in cache requires at least 1 page.
Monitoring procedure cache performance: *sp_sysmon* reports on stored procedure executions and the number of times that stored procedures need to be read from disk.
Procedure cache errors: If there is not enough memory to load another query tree or plan or the maximum number of compiled objects is already in use, Adaptive Server reports Error 701.
Procedure cache sizing: On a production server, you want to minimize the procedure reads from disk. When a user needs to execute a procedure, Adaptive Server should be able to find an unused tree or plan in the procedure cache for the most common procedures. The percentage of times the server finds an available plan in cache is called the **cache hit ratio**. Keeping a high cache hit ratio for procedures in cache improves performance.
Formulas:
Procedure cache size = (Max # of concurrent users) * (Size of largest plan) *   1.25

Minimum procedure cache size needed = (# of main procedures) *(Average plan size)
Estimating stored procedure size: To get a rough estimate of the size of a single stored procedure, view, or trigger, use:
  select(count(*) / 8) +1
  from sysprocedures
  where id = object_id("procedure_name")

7.6 Identify factors for setting Prefetch at the Query-Level

Prefetch:
Specifies the I/O size to use for the scan of a stored table.
Syntax :
(prop table_name
(prefetch size)
)
select * from t1
(prop t1
(prefetch 16)

)
16K I/O size is used for the scan of t1.
- The specified I/O size is used in the resultant query plan if a pool of that size exists in the cache used by the table.
- Partial plans can specify scan properties without specifying other portions of the query plan.
- If large I/O specifications in a saved plan do not match current pool configuration or other options:
    - If the plan specifies 16K I/O, and the 16K pool does not exist, the next largest available I/O size is used.
    - If session or server-level options have made large I/O unavailable for the query (set prefetch for the session, or sp_cachestrategy for the table), 2K I/O is used.
- If you save plans that specify only 2K I/O for the scan properties, and later create large I/O pools, enable replace mode to save the new plans if you want these plans to use larger I/O sizes.

7.7 Identify Query Degradation

In some cases, when a server is upgraded to a newer version, QP metrics may be useful for comparing performance. To identify queries that may have some degradation, use the following process:
1. Back up the QP metrics from the old server into a backup group:
sp_metrics 'backup', '@gid'
2. Enable QP metrics on the new server:
sp_configure "enable metrics capture", 1
3. Compare QP metrics output from the old and new servers to identify any queries that may have regression problems.

Tables with clustered indexes that experience many inserts, updates, and deletes over time tend to lead to data pages that are approximately 70 to 75% full. This can lead to performance degradation in several ways

If queries with high performance requirements use clustered indexes to return large numbers of rows in index order, you may see performance degradation if you change these tables to use data-only locking. Clustered indexes on data-only-locked tables are structurally the same as nonclustered indexes.

The configuration parameter 'allocate max shared memory' can be turned on during boot-time and run-time to allocate all the shared memory up to 'max memory' with the least number of shared memory segments. Large number of shared memory segments has the disadvantage of some performance degradation on certain platforms.

Section 7 - Query Optimization

7.8 Identify tasks for which internal working tables are created in tempdb or in memory

Worktables are automatically created in tempdb by Adaptive Server for merge joins, sorts, and other internal server processes. These tables:
- Are never shared
- Disappear as soon as the command completes

Queries that require worktables
Parallel queries that require worktables create partitioned worktables and populate them in parallel. For queries that require sorts, the parallel sort manager determines whether to use a serial or parallel sort.

union **queries:**
The optimizer considers parallel access methods for each part of a union query separately. Each select in a union is optimized separately, so one query can use a parallel plan, another a serial plan, and a third a parallel plan with a different number of worker processes. If a union query requires a worktable, then the worktable may also be partitioned and populated in parallel by worker processes.
If a union query is to return no duplicate rows, then a parallel sort may be performed on the internal worktable to remove duplicate rows.

Queries with aggregates:
Adaptive Server considers parallel access methods for queries that return aggregate results in the same way it does for other queries. For queries that use the group by clause to return a grouped aggregate result, Adaptive Server also creates multiple worktables with clustered indexes—one worktable for each worker process that executes the query. Each worker process stores partial aggregate results in its designated worktable. As worker processes finish computing their partial results, they merge those results into a common worktable. After all worker processes have merged their partial results, the common worktable contains the final grouped aggregate result set for the query.

select into **statements:**
select into creates a new table to store the query's result set. Adaptive Server optimizes the base query portion of a select into command in the same way it does a standard query, considering both parallel and serial access methods. A select into statement that is executed in parallel:
1. Creates the new table using columns specified in the select into statement.
2. Creates n partitions in the new table, where n is the degree of parallelism that the optimizer chose for the query as a whole.
3. Populates the new table with query results, using n worker processes.
4. Unpartitions the new table.

Performing a select into statement in parallel requires additional steps than the equivalent serial query plan. Therefore, the execution of a parallel select into statement takes place using four discrete transactions, rather than the two transactions of a serial select into statement.

7.9 Design queries to take maximum advantage of optimizer features

Some of the key features in the query optimizer include support for:
New optimization techniques and query execution operator supports that enhance query performance, such as:
- On-the-fly grouping and ordering operator support using in-memory sorting and hashing for queries with group by and order by clauses
- hash and MergeJoin operator support for efficient join operations
- index union and index intersection strategies for queries with predicates on different indexes

7.10   Identify guidelines to minimize join related performance problems

The query optimizer deals with join predicates the same way it deals with search arguments, in that it uses statistics, number of rows in the table, index heights, and the cluster ratios for the index and data pages to determine which index and join method provides the cheapest access. In addition, the query optimizer also uses join density estimates derived from join histograms that give accurate estimates of qualifying joining rows and the rows to be scanned in the outer and inner tables. The query optimizer also must decide on the optimal join ordering that will yield the most efficient query plan. The next sections describe the key techniques used in processing joins.

Join density and join histograms: The query optimizer uses a cost model for joins that use **table-normalized histograms** of the joining attributes. This technique gives an exact value for the skewed values (that is, frequency count) and uses the range cell densities from each histogram to estimate the cell counts of corresponding range cells.

The join density is dynamically computed from the "join histogram," which considers the joining of histograms from both sides of the join operator. The first histogram join occurs typically between two base tables when both attributes have histograms. Every histogram join creates a new histogram on the corresponding attribute of the parent join's projection.

The outcome of the join histogram technique is accurate join selectivity estimates, even if data distributions of the joining columns are skewed, resulting in superior join orders and performance.

Joins with mixed datatypes: A basic requirement is the ability to build keys for index lookups whenever possible, without regard to mixed datatypes of any of the join predicates versus the index key. The query optimizer will use the column value from the outer table to position the index scan on the inner table, even when the lookup value from the outer table has a different datatype than the respective index attribute of the inner table.

Join ordering: One of the key tasks of the query optimizer is to generate a query plan for join queries so that the order of the relations in the joins processed during query execution is optimal. This involves elaborate plan search strategies that can consume significant time and memory.

7.11 Identify factors of Subquery Optimization

SUBQURY OPTIMIZATION: subqueries use the following optimizations to improve performance:
- Flattening: converting the subquery to a join
- Materializing: storing the subquery results in a worktable
- Short circuiting: placing the subquery last in the execution order
- Caching subquery results: recording the results of executions

Flattening *in*, *any*, and *exists* subqueries:
Adaptive Server can flatten some quantified predicate subqueries to a join. Quantified predicate subqueries are introduced with in, any, or exists. Each result row in the outer query is returned once, and only once, if the subquery condition evaluates to TRUE.

Exceptions to flattening
A subquery introduced with in, any, or exists cannot be flattened if one of the following is true:
- The subquery is correlated and contains one or more aggregates.
- The subquery is in the select list or in the set clause of an update statement.
- The subquery is connected to the outer query with or.
- The subquery is part of an isnull predicate.
- The subquery is the outermost subquery in a case expression.
- If the subquery computes a scalar aggregate, materialization rather than flattening is used.

Flattening methods:
Adaptive Server uses one of these flattening methods to resolve a quantified predicate subquery using a join:
- A regular join – if the uniqueness conditions in the subquery mean that it returns a unique set of values, the subquery can be flattened to use a regular join.
- An existence join, also known as a semi-join – instead of scanning a table to return all matching values, an existence join returns TRUE when it finds the first matching value and then stops processing. If no matching value is found, it returns FALSE. When subqueries are flattened to use existence joins, the showplan output shows output for a join, with the message "EXISTS TABLE: nested iteration" as the join type for the table in the subquery.
- A unique reformat – the subquery result set is selected into a worktable, sorted to remove duplicates, and a clustered index is built on the worktable. The clustered index is used to perform a regular join.
- A duplicate elimination sort optimization – the subquery is flattened into a regular join that selects the results into a worktable, then the worktable is sorted to remove duplicate rows

Flattening expression subqueries:
Expression subqueries are included in a query's select list or that are introduced by >, >=, <, <=, =, or !=. Adaptive Server converts, or flattens, expression subqueries to **equijoins** if:
- The subquery joins on unique columns or returns unique columns, and
- There is a unique index on the columns.

Materializing subquery results:
In some cases, a subquery is processed in two steps: the results from the inner query are *materialized*, or stored in a temporary worktable or internal variable, before the outer query is executed. The subquery is executed in one step, and the results of this execution are stored and then used in a second step. Adaptive Server materializes these types of subqueries:
• Noncorrelated expression subqueries
• Quantified predicate subqueries containing aggregates where the having clause includes the correlation condition

Optimizing subqueries:
When queries containing subqueries are not flattened or materialized:
- The outer query and each unflattened subquery are optimized one at a time.
- The innermost subqueries (the most deeply nested) are optimized first.
- The estimated buffer cache usage for each subquery is propagated outward to help evaluate the I/O cost and strategy of the outer queries.

Summary

You read about query optimization in Sybase ASE 15 in this section.

- OR strategy: If there is a possibility that one or more of the or clauses could match values in the same row, the query is resolved using the **OR strategy**, also known as using a **dynamic index**.

- Multiple matching index scans (special OR strategy): Adaptive Server uses multiple matching index scans when the or clauses are on the same table, and there is no possibility that the or clauses will return duplicate rows.

- Detailed information on the final access method that the optimizer chooses can be displayed for the user by executing the Transact-SQL "SET SHOWPLAN ON" command.

- Adaptive Server can generate an abstract plan for a query, and save the text and its associated abstract plan in the sysqueryplans system table.

- Adaptive Server uses a **coordinating process** and multiple **worker processes** to execute queries in parallel.

- **Parallel query execution:** The total amount of work performed by the query running in parallel is greater than the amount of work performed by the query running in serial, but the response time is shorter.

- Procedure cache: Adaptive Server maintains an **MRU/LRU (most recently used/least recently used)** chain of stored procedure query plans.

- Formulas:

    *Procedure cache size = (Max # of concurrent users) * (Size of largest plan) * 1.25*

    *Minimum procedure cache size needed = (# of main procedures) *(Average plan size)*

- **Prefetch:** Specifies the I/O size to use for the scan of a stored table.

- Worktables are automatically created in tempdb by Adaptive Server for merge joins, sorts, and other internal server processes. These tables:
    - Are never shared
    - Disappear as soon as the command completes

- The query optimizer uses a cost model for joins that use **table-normalized histograms** of the joining attributes.

- Subqueries use the following optimizations to improve performance:
    - Flattening: converting the subquery to a join
    - Materializing: storing the subquery results in a worktable
    - Short circuiting: placing the subquery last in the execution order
    - Caching subquery results: recording the results of executions

Practice Test

1. The ___ operator is a binary operator that joins two data streams, based on row IDs generated for the same source table
   A. DistinctUnion operator
   B. UnionDistinct operator
   C. RidJoin operator
   D. Union operator

2. Which of the following set command reports information about physical and logical I/O and the number of times a table was accessed?
   A. set statistics io
   B. set statistics time
   C. set statistics subquerycache
   D. set statistics simulate

3. Adaptive Server can generate an abstract plan for a query, and save the text and its associated abstract plan in?
   A. syscomments system table
   B. sysqueryplans system table
   C. In a user table
   D. sysstatistics system table

4. Which of the following is not a parallel method?
   A. Hash-based table scan
   B. Hash-based nonclustered index scan
   C. Partition-based scan, either full table scans or scans positioned with a clustered index
   D. Merge table scan
   E. Range-based scan during merge joins

5. A parallel query's degree of parallelism is the?
   A. Number of family processes used to execute the query
   B. Number of worker processes used to execute the query
   C. Number of tables used to execute the query
   D. Number of disks used to execute the query

6. How to calculate *Minimum procedure cache size needed?*
   A. Minimum procedure cache size needed = (# of total procedures) *(Average plan size)
   B. Minimum procedure cache size needed = (# of main procedures) *(Average plan size)
   C. Minimum procedure cache size needed = (Max # of concurrent users) * (Size of largest plan) * 1.25
   D. Minimum procedure cache size needed = (# of main procedures) *(largest plan size)

Section 8 - Stored Procedures and Triggers

8.1 Write and tune stored procedures and triggers

Stored Procedures: is a collection of SQL statements and optional control-of-flow statements stored under a name.
Syntax: Basic syntax
create procedure *procedure_name*
as *SQL_statements*
Example:
create procedure employee_proc
as select emp_id, name from employee

Note: You can create a procedure in the current database only and you can include more than one SQL_statement in a procedure.

You can execute procedure in any of following ways:
- employee_proc
- execute employee_proc
- exec employee_proc

The first syntax (without exec or execute keyword) is acceptable as long as the statement is the only one or the first one in a batch.

Create procedure *with recompile* (optional): A new plan is created each time the procedure is executed. If we do not include with recompile in create procedure, Adaptive Server stores the execution plan that it created and uses same all the time (usually its satisfactory).
Syntax:
create procedure *procedure_name* with recompile
as *SQL_statements*
Example:
create procedure employee_proc with recompile
as select emp_id, name from employee

Execute *with recompile*(optional): To compile a new plan, which is used for subsequent executions.
Example:
exec proc_emp_dob with recompile

Note: Using execute procedure *with recompile* many times can adversely affect the procedure cache performance. Since a new plan is generated every time you use *with recompile*, a useful performance plan may age out of the cache if there is insufficient space for new plans.

> **Note: If you use select * in your create procedure statement, the procedure, even if you use the with recompile option to execute, does not pick up any new columns added to the table. You must drop the procedure and re-create it.**

Remote procedure call (To execute procedure on remote server):
Syntax:
execute *server_name.[database_name].[owner].procedure_name*

> **Note:** The database name is optional only if the stored procedure is located in your **default database**. The owner name is optional only if the Database Owner ("dbo") owns the procedure or if you own it. You must have **permission** to execute the procedure.
> **Note:** Stored procedures are database objects, and their names must follow the rules for identifiers.
> **Note:** The procedures stored in the sybsystemprocs database whose names begin with "sp_" are known as **system procedure**s, because they insert, update, delete, and report on data in the system tables.

Stored procedures can:
- Take parameters
- Call other procedures
- Return a status value to a calling procedure or batch to indicate success or failure and the reason for failure
- Return values of parameters to a calling procedure or batch
- Be executed on remote Adaptive Servers

The first time you run a procedure, Adaptive Server's query processor analyzes it and prepares an execution plan that is ultimately stored in a **system table**. Subsequently, the procedure is executed according to the stored plan. Since most of the query processing work has already been performed, stored procedures execute almost instantly. Procedure's name is stored in sysobjects table and its text in syscomments table.

To display source text of a procedure use sp_helptext <proc_name> command (sp_helptext is a system procedure).
Example: sp_helptext enmployee_proc

Permissions: Permission to issue create procedure defaults to the Database Owner, who can transfer it to other users.
Stored procedures can serve as security mechanisms, since a user can be granted permission to execute a stored procedure, even if she or he does not have permissions on the tables or views referenced in it or permission to execute specific commands.
Example: User can be granted execute permission on procedure *employee_proc,* even user doesn't have permission on tables references (*employee* table) in the procedure.
How to protect source text of a stored procedure:

- By restricting select permission on the text column of the syscomments table to the creator of the procedure and the System Administrator.
- Hide the source text using sp_hidetext (system procedure).

Parameters: is an argument to a stored procedure. You can optionally declare one or more parameters in a create procedure statement. Parameter names must be preceded by an @ sign. Parameter names are local to the procedure that creates them; the same parameter names can be used in other procedures. Parameter names, including the @ sign, can be a maximum of 255 bytes long.

Parameters must be given a **system datatype (except text, unitext, or image)** or a user-defined datatype.

Example: Passing employee id to get full name of an employee
create proc proc_emp_name @p_emp_id int as
select f_name + ' ' l_name
from employee where id = @p_emp_id

You can pass parameter in above created above procedure in following ways:
execute employee_proc @p_emp_id = 1
execute employee_proc 1

Note: You can use more than one parameter (The maximum number of arguments for stored procedures is 2048.)

Note: If you supply parameters in the form *@parameter = value*, you can supply parameters in any order. You can also omit a parameter for which a default has been supplied. If you supply one value in the form *@parameter = value*, then supply all subsequent parameters this way.

Adaptive Server ignores the extra parameters. For example "name" is extra parameter in example and it will still execute the proc.
execute employee_proc 1, "name"

You can assign default parameters in Create Procedure statement:
This value, which can be any constant, is used as the argument to the procedure if the user does not supply one.
Example: 0 is default value for parameter @a
create procedure proc_1 @a int = 0
as select @a
If user run command **exec proc_1 @a=3** it will return value 3
If user run command **exec proc_1** (Without passing any value to parameter @a, it will return 0 (default value))

NULL as the default parameter: you can declare null as the default value for individual parameters
Example:
create procedure proc_emp_name @p_emp_id int = NULL as

```
if @p_emp_id is null
   print "Please pass p_emp_id"
else
select f_name + ' ' l_name
from employee where id = @p_emp_id
```

Wildcard characters in the default parameter: The default can include the wildcard characters (%, _, [] , and [^]) if the procedure uses the parameter with the like keyword.

```
create procedure proc_emp_dob @p_emp_fname char(30) = "Abhi%" as
select f_name + l_name name, dob
from employee where f_name like @p_emp_fname
```

Procedure Groups: The optional semicolon and integer number after the name of the procedure in the create procedure and execute statements allow you to group procedures of the same name.

Example:
```
create procedure proc_emp_dob;1 @p_emp_fname char(30) = "Abhi%" as
select f_name + l_name name, dob
from employee where f_name like @p_emp_fname

create procedure proc_emp_dob;2 @p_emp_fname char(30) = "Mike%" as
select f_name + l_name name, dob
from employee where f_name like @p_emp_fname
```

In above examples, you can see procedure name is same for both the procedure but order is different i.e. 1 and 2 and definition is also different as procedure proc_emp_dob;1 will give result set for "Abhi%" (by default) and procedure proc_emp_dob;2 will give result set for "Mike%"(by default). You can execute these procedures as
```
execute exec proc_emp_dob;1
execute exec proc_emp_dob;2
```

If you execute it as *execute proc_emp_dob*, **it will execute procedure** proc_emp_dob; as default procedure.

You can not drop individual group of a procedure. Following command will drop entire group
drop proc proc_emp_dbo

Nesting procedures within procedures: Nesting occurs when one stored procedure or trigger calls another. The nesting
level is incremented when the called procedure or trigger begins execution and is decremented when the called procedure or trigger completes execution. The nesting level is also incremented by one when a cached statement is created.
- Maximum levels of nesting is 16
- The current nesting level is stored in the *@@nestlevel* global variable

- You can call another procedure by name or by a variable name in place of the actual procedure name.

Temporary tables in stored procedures: You can create and use temporary tables in a stored procedure, but the temporary table exists only for the duration of the stored procedure that creates it. When the procedure completes, Adaptive Server automatically drops the temporary table. A single procedure can:
- Create a temporary table
- Insert, update, or delete data
- Run queries on the temporary table
- Call other procedures that reference the temporary table

Note: The maximum size for expressions, variables, and arguments passed to stored procedures is 16384 (16K) bytes, for any page size. This can be either character or binary data. You can insert variables and literals up to this maximum size into text columns without using the writetext command.

Note: You can use some of the set command options inside a stored procedure. The set option remains in effect during the execution of the procedure and most options revert to the former setting at the close of the procedure. Only the dateformat, datefirst, language, and role options do not revert to their former settings.

Returning information:

Return type	Description
Return status	indicates whether or not the stored procedure completed successfully.
proc role function	checks whether the procedure was executed by a user with sa_role, sso_role, or ss_oper privileges.
Return parameters	report the parameter values back to the caller, who can then use conditional statements to check the returned value.

Return status:
Example:
declare @p_status int
execute @p_status = proc_1 @a=3
select @p_status

Note: ASE reserves value 0 (for success) and values from -1 through -99 to indicate failures.

Number 0 and -1 to -14 are currently used in ASE as shown in below table. (-15 to -99 are reserved for future use).

Return type	Description
0	Procedure executed without error
-1	Missing object
-2	Datatype error
-3	Process was chosen as deadlock victim

-4	Permission error
-5	Syntax error
-6	Miscellaneous user error
-7	Resource error, such as out of space
-8	Nonfatal internal problem
-9	System limit was reached
-10	Fatal internal inconsistency
-11	Fatal internal inconsistency
-12	Table or index is corrupt
-13	Database is corrupt
-14	Hardware error

Note: If more than one error occurs during execution, the status with the highest absolute value is returned.

Note: You can generate your own return values (user generated return values) in stored procedures by adding a parameter to the return statement. You can use any integer outside the 0 through -99 range.

Example:
create proc emp_check
as
if exists (select * from employee)
return 1
else
return 2

proc_role function: The proc_role function allows you to check roles when the procedure is executed. It returns 1 if the user possesses the specified role. The role names are **sa_role**, **sso_role**, and **oper_role**.

Example:
create proc emp_proc
as
if (proc_role("sa_role") = 0)
begin
print "You do not have the right role."
return -1
end
else
print "You have a proc role."
return 0

Return parameters: When both a create procedure statement and an execute statement include the output option with a parameter name, the procedure returns a value to the caller. The caller can be a SQL batch or another stored procedure.

Example: Create and execute proc with output variable.
create procedure test_proc
@a int, @b int, @output int output

as
select @output = @a * @b

declare @output int
exec test_proc 5, 6, @output output

Note: A stored procedure can return several values; each must be defined as an output variable in the stored procedure and in the calling statements. The output keyword can be abbreviated to out.

Restrictions:
- You cannot combine create procedure statements with other statements in the same batch.
- You cannot create view, default, rule, trigger, procedure in side create procedure command.
- Within a stored procedure, you cannot create an object, drop it, and then create a new object with the same name.
  Example:

  create procedure test_proc_2
  as
  begin
  create table t4 (col1 int)
  drop table t4
  create table t4 (col1 int)
  end
- Adaptive Server creates the objects defined in a stored procedure when the procedure is executed, not when it is compiled.
- The maximum number of parameters in a stored procedure is 255.
- The maximum number of local and global variables in a procedure is limited only by available memory.

Rename a stored procedure by using sp_rename:
Example: sp_rename, proc_name, new_procname

Note: You must drop and re-create a procedure if you rename any of the objects it references.
Note: sp_depends to get a report of the objects referenced by a procedure.

Drop procedure: Syntax:
drop proc[edure] [owner.]procedure_name
[, [owner.]procedure_name] ...
Example:
drop proc test_proc

8.2 Define query plans and the procedure cache

Procedure cache:
Stored procedures query plans are stored in the procedure cache.
Adaptive Server maintains an MRU/LRU (most recently used/least recently used) chain of stored procedure query plans. As users execute stored procedures, Adaptive Server looks in the procedure cache for a query plan to use. If a query plan is available, it is placed on the MRU end of the chain, and execution begins.
If no plan is in memory, or if all copies are in use, the query tree for the procedure is read from the sysprocedures table. It is then optimized, using the parameters provided to the procedure, and put on the MRU end of the
chain, and execution begins. Plans at the LRU end of the page chain that are not in use are aged out of the cache.
The memory allocated for the procedure cache holds the optimized query plans (and occasionally trees) for all batches, including any triggers.
If more than one user uses a procedure or trigger simultaneously, there will be multiple copies of it in cache. If the procedure cache is too small, a user trying to execute stored procedures or queries that fire triggers receives an
error message and must resubmit the query. Space becomes available when unused plans age out of the cache.

> **Note:** An increase in procedure cache size causes a corresponding decrease in data cache size.
> **Note:** When you first install Adaptive Server, the default procedure cache size is 3271 memory pages.

Getting information about the procedure cache size:
When SQL Server is started, the error log states how much procedure cache is available.

```
          Maximum number of procedures in cache
          Number of proc buffers allocated: 6632.
          Number of blocks left for proc headers: 7507.
                  Procedure cache size, in pages
```

proc buffers: Represents the maximum number of compiled procedural objects that can reside in the procedure cache at one time. In this example, no more than 6632 compiled objects can reside in the procedure cache simultaneously.
proc headers: Represents the number of pages dedicated to the procedure cache. Each object in cache requires at least 1 page. In this example, 7507 pages are dedicated to the procedure cache. Each object in cache requires at least one page.
Monitoring procedure cache performance: sp_sysmon reports on stored procedure executions and the number of
times that stored procedures need to be read from disk.
Procedure cache errors: If there is not enough memory to load another query tree or plan or the maximum number of compiled objects is already in use, Adaptive Server reports **Error 701**.
Procedure cache sizing: On a production server, you want to minimize the procedure reads from disk. When a user needs to execute a procedure, Adaptive Server should be able to find an unused tree or plan in the procedure cache for the most common procedures. The percentage of

times the server finds an available plan in cache is called the **cache hit ratio**. Keeping a high cache hit ratio for procedures in cache improves performance.
Formulas for sizing the procedure cache:

Procedure cache size = (Max # of concurrent users) * (Size of largest plan) * 1.25
Minimum procedure cache size needed = (# of main procedures) * (Average plan size)
If you have nested stored procedures (for example, A, B and C)—procedure A calls procedure B, which calls procedure C—all of them need to be in the cache at the same time. Add the sizes for nested procedures, and use the largest sum in place of "Size of largest plan" in the above formula.

The minimum procedure cache size is the smallest amount of memory that allows at least one copy of each frequently used compiled object to reside in cache. However, the procedure cache can also be used as additional memory at execution time, such as when an ad hoc query uses the distinct keyword which uses the internal lmlink function that will dynamically allocate memory from the procedure cache. Then the create index will also use the procedure cache memory and can generate the 701 error though no stored procedure is involved.

Estimating stored procedure size
To get a rough estimate of the size of a single stored procedure, view, or trigger, use:
select(count(*) / 8) +1
from sysprocedures
where id = object_id("procedure_name")
For example, to find the size of the titleid_proc in pubs2:
select(count(*) / 8) +1
from sysprocedures
where id = object_id("titleid_proc")

3

8.3 Define triggers and their usage

Trigger : A trigger is a stored procedure that instructs the system to take one or more actions when a specific change is attempted. Trigger is often used for enforcing integrity constraints. A trigger executes automatically when a user attempts a specified data modification statement on a specified table.

A trigger is specific to one or more of the data modification operations (**update, insert, and delete**), and is executed once for each SQL statement.

A trigger "fires" only after the data modification statement has completed and Adaptive Server has checked for any datatype, rule, or integrity constraint violation. The trigger and the statement that fires it are treated as a **single transaction** that can be rolled back from within the trigger. If Adaptive Server detects a severe error, the entire transaction is rolled back.

Syntax:
create trigger [*owner .*]*trigger_name* on [*owner .*]*table_name*
for {insert , update , delete}
as *SQL_statements*

if update clause:
create trigger [*owner .*]*trigger_name* on [*owner .*]*table_name*
for {insert , update}
as
[if update (*column_name*)
[{and | or} update (*column_name*)]...]
SQL_statements
[if update (*column_name*)
[{and | or} update (*column_name*)]...
SQL_statements]...

Example:
create trigger t1
on titles
for insert, update, delete
as
print "Now modify the titleauthor table the same way."

> **Note:** Use **sp_rename** to rename a trigger and Use **sp_depends** to see a report on the tables and views referred to in a trigger. Use sp_help to get a report on a trigger. Use **sp_helptext** to display source text of a trigger
>
> **Note:** As database objects, triggers are listed in sysobjects by name.
> *select * from sysobjects where type = "TR"*
>
> **Note:** The source text for each trigger is stored in syscomments. Execution plans for triggers are stored in sysprocedures.

Adaptive Server uses two special tables in trigger statements:

deleted table: stores copies of the affected rows during delete and update statements. During the execution of a delete or update statement, rows are removed from the trigger table and transferred to the deleted table.

Inserted table: stores copies of the affected rows during insert and update statements. During an insert or an update, new rows are added to the inserted and trigger tables at the same time.

These are temporary tables used in trigger tests.

> **Note:** An **update** is, effectively, a delete followed by an insert; the old rows are copied to the deleted table first; then the new rows are copied to the trigger table and to the inserted table.

You can create three types of trigger in ASE: **Insert Trigger, Delete Trigger, Update Trigger**
Insert Trigger: Example: Following insert trigger checks if id which is getting inserted in *emp_detail* table is already exist in employee (Assume its master table).
create trigger Trg_empdetail_insert
on emp_detail
for insert
as
if (select count(*) from employee, inserted where employee.id = inserted.id) !=@@rowcount
begin
rollback transaction
print "No, the id does not exist in employee table."
end
else
print "Added! "

UpdateTrigger: Following trigger insert old row (which got updated in *employee* table) in *employee_audit* table (for audit purpose).
create trigger Trg_emp_update
on employee
for update
as
insert into employee_audit(id,f_name, l_name, dob,usr_updated_by,update_date)
select id, f_name, l_name, dob, suser_name(), getdate() from deleted

Delete Trigger: Following trigger insert deleted row in *employee_audit* table (for audit purpose).
create trigger Trg_emp_delete
on employee
for delete
as
insert into employee_audit(id,f_name, l_name, dob,usr_updated_by,update_date)
select id, f_name, l_name, dob, suser_name(), getdate() from deleted

Note: We can achieve Cascading delete from delete trigger.

Diable /EnableTrigger: To disable trigger you can user below command
Syntax:
alter table [*database_name*.[*owner_name*].]*table_name*
{enable | disable } trigger [*trigger_name*]
Example:
alter table employee
disable trigger Trg_Stop_update_fname

To disable all the trigger on a table: don't specify a trigger name
Syntax:
alter table employee
disable trigger

Rollback triggers:
Syntax:
rollback trigger
[with raiserror_statement]
Or
rollback transaction
[with raiserror_statement]
You can roll back triggers using either the **rollback trigger** statement or the **rollback transaction** statement (if the trigger is fired as part of a transaction). However, rollback trigger rolls back only the effect of the trigger and the statement that caused the trigger to fire; rollback transaction rolls back the entire transaction.

Example:
begin tran
insert into publishers (pub_id) values ("9999")
insert into publishers (pub_id) values ("9998")
commit tran

If the second insert statement causes a trigger on publishers to issue a rollback trigger, only that insert is affected; the first insert is not rolled back. If that trigger issues a rollback transaction instead, both insert statements are rolled back as part of the transaction.

Example: rollback trigger
create trigger forinsertrig2
on salesdetail
for insert
as
if (select count(*) from titles, inserted
where titles.title_id = inserted.title_id) !=
@@rowcount
rollback trigger with raiserror 25003

*"Trigger rollback: salesdetail row not added
because a title_id does not exist in titles."*

When the rollback trigger is executed, Adaptive Server aborts the currently executing command and halts execution of the rest of the trigger. If the trigger that issues the rollback trigger is nested within other triggers, Adaptive Server rolls back all the work done in these triggers up to and including the update that caused the first trigger to fire.

Example: rollback transaction
*create trigger Trg_empdetail_insert
on emp_detail
for insert
as
if (select count(*) from employee, inserted where employee.id = inserted.id) !=@@rowcount
begin
rollback transaction
print "No, the id does not exist in employee table."
end
else
print "Added! "*

if update clause in trigger: if update clause tests for an insert or update to a specified column (not for delete). For updates, *if update* clause evaluates to true when the column name is included in the set clause of an update statement, even if the update does not change the value of the column.
Note: You can specify more than one column, and you can use more than one if update clause in a create trigger statement.
Example: Following trigger prevents updates to f_name column of employee table
*create trigger Trg_Stop_update_fname
on employee
for update
as
if update (f_name)
begin
rollback transaction
print "We do not allow changes on column f_name"
end
if you execute below script, it will not update column 'f_name' and will print message "We do not allow changes on column f_name"
update employee set f_name ='test' where id = 1*

Bleow update will update column without printing any message
update employee set l_name ='test' where id = 1

The if update(*column_name*) clause is true for an insert statement whenever the column is
assigned a value in the select list or in the values clause. An *explicit* null or a default assigns a
value to a column, and thus activates the trigger. An *implicit* null does not.
Example: Explicit NULL: insert test values (NULL, 1)
Example: Implicit NULL: insert test (col2) values (1)

Nesting triggers: If nested triggers are enabled, a trigger that changes a table on which there is
another trigger fires the second trigger, which can in turn fire a third trigger, and so forth. If any
trigger in the chain sets off an infinite loop, the nesting level is exceeded and the trigger aborts.
To turn on nesting triggers
EXEC sp_configure 'nested triggers', 1
To turn off nesting triggers
EXEC sp_configure 'nested triggers', 0

Note: max level of nesting is 16. @@nestlevel global variable stores the current nesting level.

Note: When you put triggers into a transaction, a failure at any level of a set of nested triggers
cancels the transaction and rolls back all data modifications. A **rollback transaction** in a trigger at
any nesting level rolls back the effects of each trigger and cancels the entire transaction. A
rollback trigger affects only the nested triggers and the data modification statement that caused
the initial trigger to fire.

self-recursion Trigger: By default, a trigger does not call itself recursively. That is, an update
trigger does not call itself in response to a second update to the same table within the trigger.
However, you can turn on the self_recursion option of the set command to allow triggers to call
themselves recursively. The allow nested triggers configuration variable must also be enabled for
self-recursion to occur.

To turn on:
EXEC sp_dboption '<name of db>', 'recursive triggers', 'true'
To turn off:
EXEC sp_dboption '<name of db>', 'recursive triggers', 'false'

Permission: A trigger is defined on a particular table. Only the owner of the table has create
trigger and drop trigger permissions for the table.

Drop Trigger:
Syntax:
drop trigger [*owner.*]*trigger_name*
[, [*owner.*]*trigger_name*]...
Example:
Drop trigger Trg_Stop_update_fname

Note: When you drop a table, Adaptive Server drops any triggers associated with it.

Use of Trigger:
- Triggers can reduce network traffic.
- Triggers can cascade changes through related tables in the database.
- Triggers can disallow, or roll back, changes that would violate referential integrity, canceling the attempted data modification transaction.
- Triggers can enforce restrictions that are much more complex than those that are defined with rules.
- Triggers can perform simple "what if" analyses. For example, a trigger can compare the state of a table before and after a data modification and take action based on that comparison.

Actions that do not cause triggers to fire:
- A truncate table command is not caught by a delete trigger. Although a truncate table statement is, in effect, like a delete without a where clause (it removes all rows), changes to the data rows are not logged, and so cannot fire a trigger.
- The writetext command, whether logged or unlogged, does not cause a trigger to fire.

Trigger restrictions:
- A table can have a maximum of three triggers: one update trigger, one insert trigger, and one delete trigger.
- Each trigger can apply to only one table. However, a single trigger can apply to all three user actions: update, insert, and delete.
- You cannot create a trigger on a view or on a temporary table, though triggers can reference views or temporary tables.
- The writetext statement does not activate insert or update triggers.k
- Although a truncate table statement is, in effect, like a delete without a where clause, because it removes all rows, it cannot fire a trigger, because individual row deletions are not logged.
- You cannot create a trigger or build an index or a view on a temporary object (@object)
- You cannot create triggers on system tables. If you try to create a trigger on a system table, Adaptive Server returns an error message and cancels the trigger.
- You cannot use triggers that select from a text column or an image column of the inserted or deleted table.
- If Component Integration Services is enabled, triggers have limited usefulness on proxy tables because you cannot examine the rows being inserted, updated, or deleted (via the inserted and deleted tables). You can create a trigger on a proxy table, and it can be invoked. However, deleted or inserted data is not written to the transaction log for proxy tables because the insert is passed to the remote server. Hence, the inserted and deleted tables, which are actually views to the transaction log, contain no data for proxy tables.

SQL statements that are not allowed in triggers: Since triggers execute as part of a transaction, the following statements are not allowed in a trigger:
- All create commands, including create database, create table, create index, create procedure, create default, create rule, create trigger, and create view
- All drop commands
- alter table and alter database
- truncate table
- grant and revoke
- update statistics
- reconfigure
- load database and load transaction
- disk init, disk mirror, disk refit, disk reinit, disk remirror, disk unmirror
- select into

Summary

You read about Stored Procedures and Triggers **in this section.**

- Stored Procedures is a collection of SQL statements and optional control-of-flow statements stored under a name.
- **Parameters:** is an argument to a stored procedure. You can optionally declare one or more parameters in a create procedure statement.
- You can create and use temporary tables in a stored procedure, but the temporary table exists only for the duration of the stored procedure that creates it. When the procedure completes, Adaptive Server automatically drops the temporary table.
- You can not create view, default, rule, trigger, procedure in side create procedure command.
- The proc_role function allows you to check roles when the procedure is executed.
- Stored procedures query plans are stored in the procedure cache.
- An increase in procedure cache size causes a corresponding decrease in data cache size.
- Trigger is a stored procedure that instructs the system to take one or more actions when a specific change is attempted. Trigger is often used for enforcing integrity constraints.
- You can create three types of trigger in ASE.
    - Insert trigger
    - Delete trigger
    - Update trigger
- Adaptive Server uses two special tables in trigger statements:
    - Deleted
    - Inserted
- You can roll back triggers using either the **rollback trigger** statement or the **rollback transaction** statement (if the trigger is fired as part of a transaction). However, rollback trigger rolls back only the effect of the trigger and the statement that caused the trigger to fire; rollback transaction rolls back the entire transaction.

Practice Test

1. Which of the following statement is correct to execute a stored procedure *employee_proc*?
    A. employee_proc
    B. execute employee_proc
    C. exec employee_proc
    D. All of the above

2. The maximum number of arguments for stored procedures is?
    A. 2048
    B. 255
    C. 30
    D. 1

3. Which of the following statement are TRUE about stored procedures? [Choose 3]
    A. You can assign default parameters in Create Procedure statement.
    B. Adaptive Server ignores the extra parameters passed in stored procedure.
    C. You can not use wildcard characters in the stored procedure parameter
    D. you can declare null as the default value for individual parameters of stored procedure.
    E. You can drop individual group of a procedure

4. When do triggers fire?
    A. Before the log records are written
    B. Only if the key column(s) are affected
    C. Once for each row affected by the data modification
    D. Once regardless of the number of rows affected

5. Which of the following command is correct to disable all the triggers on a table?
    A. ALTER TABLE <table_name> DISABLE ALL TRIGGER
    B. ALTER TABLE <table_name> DISABLE TRIGGER
    C. ALTER TABLE <table_name> DISABLE TRIGGERS
    D. None of the above

6. Which of the following commands trun on self-recursion for triggers?
    A. EXEC sp_dboption '<name of db>', 'recursive triggers', 1
    B. EXEC sp_dboption '<name of db>', 'recursive triggers', true
    C. EXEC sp_dboption '<name of db>', 'triggers 'recursive ', true
    D. EXEC sp_dboption '<name of db>', ' self recursion ', true

Section 9 - Transact-SQL Statements

9.1 Use of Sybase-specific Transact-SQL commands, such as functions, programming commands such as if and while, local and global variables

Adaptive Server can also process multiple statements submitted as a batch, either interactively or from a file.
Example:
select count(*) from titles
select count(*) from authors
go

Transact-SQL provides special keywords called control-of-flow language that allow the user to control the flow of execution of statements. The Transact-SQL control-of-flow language transforms standard SQL into a very high-level programming language.
Adaptive Server compiles a batch before **executing** it. During compilation, Adaptive Server makes **no permission checks** on objects, such as tables and views, that are referenced by the batch. Permission checks occur when Adaptive Server **executes the batch**.

Programming Commands:
if...else:
The keyword if, with or without its companion else, introduces a condition that determines whether the next statement is executed. The Transact-SQL statement executes if the condition is satisfied, that is, if it returns TRUE. The else keyword introduces an alternate Transact-SQL statement that executes when the if condition returns FALSE.
Syntax:
if
boolean_expression
statement
[else
[if *boolean_expression*]
statement]
Note: *boolean_expression* can include a column name, a constant, any combination of column names and constants connected by arithmetic or bitwise operators, or a subquery, as long as the subquery returns a single value. If ... else frequently used in stored procedures and triggers for testing of existence of some parameter. for each if...else construct, there can be one select statement for the if and one for the else. To include more than one select statement, use the begin...end keywords.
Example:
if not exists (SELECT * FROM syscolumns where id = object_id('employee') and name = 'status')
begin
  alter table employee add status int null
  print 'Added column status in employee Table'
end
else

```
  print 'There is already a column name status exist'
go
```

case:
Instead of using a series of if statements, case expression allows you to use a series of conditions that return the appropriate values when the conditions are met. Case expression is ANSI-SQL-compliant.
Note: case expression includes the keywords case, when, then, coalesce, and nullif. **coalesce and nullif are an abbreviated form of case expression.**
Example:
```
select emp_name,
     case when status = 1 then 'Active'
         when status = 0 then 'Inactive'
         else
         'Status Missing'
     end 'Status'
from employee
```
Resultset:

emp_name	Status
Mike	Active
Salman	Inactive
Abhisek	Active

Example: Case expression to avoid division by zero error.
```
select title_id, total_sales, advance, "Cost Per Book" =
case
when advance != 0
then convert(char, total_sales/advance)
else "No Books Sold"
end
from titles
```

Example: case expression requires at least one non-null result
```
select price,
case
when title_id like "%" then NULL
when pub_id like "%" then NULL
end
from titles
```
returns the error message: All result expressions in a CASE expression must not be NULL

Example: Using case expression, you can test for conditions that determine the result set.
```
select stor_id, title_id, qty, "Book Sales Catagory" =
case when qty < 1000 then "Low Sales Book"
when qty >= 1000 and qty <= 3000 then "Medium Sales Book"
when qty > 3000 then "High Sales Book"
end
from salesdetail group by title_id
```

Example: case and value comparisons
```
select title, pub_id, "Publisher" =
case pub_id
when "0736" then "New Age Books"
when "0877" then "Binnet & Hardley"
when "1389" then "Algodata Infosystems"
else "Other Publisher"
end
from titles order by pub_id
```

coalesce: coalesce examines a series of values (*value1*, *value2*, ..., *valuen*) and returns the first non-null value. The syntax of coalesce is:
coalesce(*value1*, *value2*, ..., *valuen*)
Example:
```
select stor_id, discount, "Quantity" =
coalesce(lowqty, highqty)
from discounts
```

nullif: compares two values; if the values are equal, nullif returns a null value. If the two values are not equal, nullif returns the value of the first value. This is useful for finding any missing, unknown, or inapplicable information that is stored in an encoded form.
Example:
```
select title, "type"= nullif(type, "UNDECIDED")
from titles
```

begin...end:
The begin and end keywords enclose a series of statements so that they are treated as a unit by control-of-flow constructs like if...else. A series of statements enclosed by begin and end is called a **statement block**.
Syntax:
```
begin
statement block
end
```
Example:
```
if not exists (     SELECT * FROM syscolumns where id = object_id('employee') and name = 'status')
begin
  alter table employee add status int  null
  print 'Added column status in employee Table'
end
```
Note: begin...end blocks can nest within other begin...end blocks.

while* and *break...continue:
while sets a condition for the repeated execution of a statement or statement block. The statements are executed repeatedly as long as the specified condition is true.
Syntax:

while *boolean_expression*
statement
Example: select and update statements are repeated, as long as the average tran_amount remains less than 2000.
```
while (select avg(tran_amount) from emp_transactions) < 2000
begin
select * from emp_transactions
update emp_transactions set tran_amount = tran_amount * 2
end
```

break and continue control the operation of the statements inside a while loop.
- break causes an exit from the while loop. Any statements that appear after the end keyword that marks the end of the loop are executed.
- continue causes the while loop to restart, skipping any statements after continue but inside the loop.

Syntax:
while *boolean expression*
begin
statement
[*statement*]...
break
[*statement*]...
continue
[*statement*]...
End

Example: In the following example, if the average list price of a product is less than $300, the WHILE loop doubles the prices and then selects the maximum price. If the maximum price is less than or equal to $500, the WHILE loop restarts and doubles the prices again. This loop continues doubling the prices until the maximum price is greater than $500, and then exits the WHILE loop and prints a message.
```
WHILE (SELECT AVG(ListPrice) FROM Production.Product) < $300
BEGIN
  UPDATE Production.Product
    SET ListPrice = ListPrice * 2
  SELECT MAX(ListPrice) FROM Production.Product
  IF (SELECT MAX(ListPrice) FROM Production.Product) > $500
    BREAK
  ELSE
    CONTINUE
END
PRINT 'Too much for the market to bear';
```
Note: If two or more while loops are nested, break exits to the next outermost loop. First, all the statements after the end of the inner loop execute. Then, the outer loop restarts.

goto: The **goto** keyword causes unconditional branching to a user-defined **label**. goto and labels can be used in stored procedures and batches

Syntax:
label:
goto *label*
Example:
declare @count smallint
select @count = 1
restart:
print "yes"
select @count = @count + 1
while @count <=4
goto restart
ResultSet:
(1 row affected)
yes
(1 row affected)
yes
(1 row affected)
yes
(1 row affected)
yes
(1 row affected)

return: The return keyword exits from a batch or procedure unconditionally. It can be used at any point in a batch or a procedure. When used in stored procedures, return can accept an optional argument to return a status to the caller. Statements after return are not executed.
Syntax:
return [*int_expression*]

print: The print keyword displays a user-defined message or the contents of a local variable on the user's screen. The message itself can be up to 255 bytes long.
Syntax:
print {*format_string* | *@local_variable* |
@@global_variable} [,*arg_list*]
Example:
if exists (SELECT * FROM syscolumns where id = object_id('employee') and name = 'status')
  print 'There is already a column name status exist'
Example:
declare @var_print char(30)
select @var_print = "This is test message"
print @var_print

raiserror:
raiserror both displays a user-defined error or local variable message on the user's screen and sets a system flag to record the fact that an error has occurred. As with print, the local variable must be declared within the same batch or procedure in which it is used. The message can be up to 255 characters long.

Syntax:
raiserror *error_number*
[{*format_string* | *@local_variable*}] [, *arg_list*]
[*extended_value* = *extended_value* [{,
extended_value = *extended_value*}...]]
Example:
raiserror 99999 "You must give a user name"

- The *error_number* is placed in the global variable *@@error*, which stores the error number most recently generated by Adaptive Server.
- Error numbers for user-defined error messages must be greater than 17,000.
- If the *error_number* is between 17,000 and 19,999, and *format_string* is missing or empty (" "), Adaptive Server retrieves error message text from the sysmessages table in the master database.
- The length of the *format_string* alone is limited to 255 bytes; the maximum output length of *format_string* plus all arguments is 512 bytes.
- Local variables used for raiserror messages must be char or varchar.
- The *format_string* or variable is optional; if you do not include one, Adaptive Server uses the message corresponding to the *error_number* from sysusermessages in the default language.
- The severity level of all user-defined error messages is 16, which indicates that the user has made a nonfatal mistake.

You can call messages from **sysusermessages** for use by either print or raiserror with sp_getmessage. Use sp_addmessage to create a set of messages.
set language us_english
go
sp_addmessage 25001, "There is already a remote user named '%1!' for remote server '%2!'."
go

Note: To drop a user-defined message, use sp_dropmessage. To change a message, drop it with sp_dropmessage and add it again with sp_addmessage.

waitfor:
The waitfor keyword specifies a specific time of day, a time interval, or an event at which the execution of a statement block, stored procedure, or transaction is to occur.
Syntax:
waitfor {delay "*time*" | time "*time*" | errorexit | processexit | mirrorexit}
Example: where delay *time* instructs Adaptive Server to wait until the specified period of time has passed. . (wait until 4:23 pm).
waitfor time "16:23"
Example: time *time* instructs Adaptive Server to wait until the specified time. (wait for 50 seconds).
waitfor delay "00:00:50"

errorexit instructs Adaptive Server to wait until a process terminates abnormally. *processexit* waits until a process terminates for any reason. mirrorexit waits until a read or write to a mirrored device fails.

Note: After you give the **waitfor** command, you cannot use your connection to Adaptive Server until the time or event that you specified occurs.

Comments: Use the comment notation to attach comments to statements, batches, and stored procedures.
Note: Comments are not executed.
Styles available for comment are:
slash-asterisk style: This style is useful for multiline comments.
 /* text of comment */
double-hyphen style: You can not use this style for multiline comment
-- text of comment
Note : There is no maximum length for comments.

Local variables:
Local variables are often used as counters for while loops or if...else blocks in a batch or stored procedure.
When they are used in stored procedures, they are declared for automatic, non-interactive use by the procedure when it executes.
Syntax:
declare @*variable_name datatype*
[, @*variable_name datatype*]...
The variable name must be preceded by the **@ sign** (@l_testvar) and conform to the rules for identifiers. Specify either a user-defined datatype or a system-supplied datatype other than text, image, or sysname.
Example: first method is more efficient.
declare @a int, @b char(20), @c float
or
declare @a int
declare @b char(20)
declare @c float

Note: When you declare a variable, it has the value NULL.

Assign values to local variables with a select statement:
Example:
select @a = 1, @b = 2, @c = 3
If the select statement that assigns values to a variable returns more than one value, the last value that is returned is assigned to the variable.

Example: Table *employee* has following rows

emp_id	emp_name	Status
101	Mike	Active
102	Salman	Inactive
103	Abhisek	Active

And if you run belo commands:
declare @p_emp_id int
select @p_emp_id = emp_id from employee
select @p_emp_id
It will print assign value 103(which is last value of select) in @p_emp_id.

Local variables with subqueries:
A subquery that assigns a value to the local variable *must* return only one value.
Example: Following will assign total count of *employee* table
declare @p_emp_id int
select @p_emp_id = (select count(*) from employee)
select @p_emp_id
Example: Following will give an error as subquery is returning more than 1 value (101, 102,103) from *employee* table.
declare @p_emp_id int
select @p_emp_id = (select emp_id from employee)
select @p_emp_id

Local variables are assigned the value NULL when they are declared, and may be assigned the null value by a select statement.
Example:
select @p_emp_id = null

Global Variables: Global variables are system-supplied, predefined variables. They are distinguished from local variables by the two @ signs preceding their names— for example, @@error. The two @ signs are considered part of the identifier used to define the global variable.

9.2 Describe 'scrollable cursors'
Please read following sections:
1.2 Identify aspects of insensitive/semi-sensitive scrollable cursors
5.1 Describe the data manipulation commands: select, insert, update, and delete, and the use of cursors

9.3 Identify guidelines for SARGs

The query optimizer uses I/O cost as the measure of query execution cost. The significant costs in query processing are:
- Physical I/O, when pages must be read from disk
- Logical I/O, when pages in cache are read for a query

If you think a particular query plan is unusual, you can used dbcc traceon(302) to determine why the optimizer made the decision. This output includes page number estimates.

After a query is **parsed** and **normalized**, but before the optimizer begins its analysis, the query is preprocessed to increase the number of clauses that can be optimized:

- Some search arguments are converted to equivalent arguments.
- Some expressions used as search arguments are preprocessed to generate a literal value that can be optimized.
- Search argument transitive closure is applied where possible.
- Join column transitive closure is applied where possible.
- For some queries that use or, additional search arguments can be generated to provide additional optimization paths.

Converting clauses to search argument equivalents: Preprocessing looks for some query clauses that it can convert to the form used for search arguments (SARGs).

Search argument equivalents:

Clause	Conversion
between	Converted to >= and <= clauses. For example, between 10 and 20 is converted to >= 10 and <= 20.
Like	If the first character in the pattern is a constant, like clauses can be converted to greater than or less than queries. For example, like "sm%" becomes >= "sm" and < "sn". If the first character is a wildcard, a clause such as like "%x" cannot use an index for access, but histogram alues can be used to estimate the number of matching rows.
in (values_list)	Converted to a list of or queries, that is, int_col in (1, 2, 3) becomes int_col= 1 or int_col = 2 or int_col = 3.

Many expressions are converted into literal search strings before query optimization. For example:

Example: Implicit conversion
If where clause has **numeric_col = 5** will be processed as **numeric_col = 5.0**
Example: Convert function
int_column = convert(int, "77") will be processed as int_column = 77
Example: Arithmetic
salary = 5000*12 will be processed as salary = 60000
Example: String function
shoe_width = replicate("E", 5) will be processed as shoe_width = "EEEEE"

Note: getdate() and most system functions such as object_id or object_name are not converted to literal values before optimizations and can not be optimized.

Search argument transitive closure: Preprocessing applies transitive closure to search arguments. For example, the
following query joins *titles* and *titleauthor* on *title_id* and includes a search argument on *titles.title_id*:

```
select au_lname, title
from titles t, titleauthor ta, authors a
where t.title_id = ta.title_id
and a.au_id = ta.au_id
and t.title_id = "T81002"
```
This query is optimized as if it also included the search argument on titleauthor.title_id:
```
select au_lname, title
from titles t, titleauthor ta, authors a
where t.title_id = ta.title_id
and a.au_id = ta.au_id
and t.title_id = "T81002"
and ta.title_id = "T81002"
```
With this additional clause, the optimizer can use **index statistics on titles.title_id** to estimate the number of matching rows in the titleauthor table. The more accurate cost estimates improve index and join order selection.

Join transitive closure: Preprocessing applies transitive closure to join columns for normal equijoins if join transitive closure is enabled at the server or session level. The following query specifies the equijoin of t1.c11 and t2.c21, and the equijoin of t2.c21 and t3.c31:
```
select *
from t1, t2, t3
where t1.c11 = t2.c21
and t2.c21 = t3.c31
and t3.c31 = 1
```
Without join transitive closure, the only join orders considered are (t1, t2, t3), (t2, t1, t3), (t2, t3, t1),and (t3, t2, t1). By adding the join on t1.c11 = t3.31, the optimizer expands the list of join orders with these possibilities: (t1, t3, t2) and (t3, t1, t2). Search argument transitive closure applies the condition specified by t3.c31 = 1 to the join columns of t1 and t2. Transitive closure is used only for normal equijoins, as shown above. Join transitive closure is not performed for:
- Non-equijoins; for example, t1.c1 > t2.c2
- Equijoins that include an expression; for example, t1.c1 = t2.c1 + 5
- Equijoins under an *or* clause
- **Outer joins**; for example t1.c11 *= t2.c2 or left join or right join
- Joins across subquery boundaries
- Joins used to check referential integrity or the with check option on views
- Columns of incompatible datatypes

Predicate transformation and factoring:
Predicate transformation and factoring improves the number of choices available to the optimizer. It adds clauses that can be optimized to a query by extracting clauses from blocks of predicates linked with or into clauses linked by and. These additional optimized clauses mean that there are more access paths available for query execution. The original or predicates are retained to ensure query correctness.

Guidelines for creating search arguments: Follow these guidelines when you write search arguments for your queries:

- Avoid functions, arithmetic operations, and other expressions on the column side of search clauses. When possible, move functions and other operations to the expression side of the clause.
  Example: permitted
  price   = 1000*2
  Example: not permitted
  price * 2 = 1000 /*expression on column side not permitted */
- Avoid incompatible datatypes for columns that will be joined and for variables and parameter used as search arguments.
- Use the leading column of a composite index as a search argument. The optimization of secondary keys provides less performance.
- Use all the search arguments you can to give the optimizer as much as possible to work with.
- If a query has more than 102 predicates for a table, put the most potentially useful clauses near the beginning of the query, since only the first 102 SARGs on each table are used during optimization. (All of the search conditions are used to qualify the rows.)
- Some queries using > (greater than) may perform better if you can rewrite them to use >= (greater than or equal to). For example, this query, with an index on int_col uses the index to find the first value where int_col equals 3, and then scans forward to find the first value that is greater than 3. If there are many rows where int_col equals 3, the server has to scan many pages to find the first row where int_col is greater than 3:
  select * from table1 where int_col > 3
  It is probably more efficient to write the query like this:
  select * from table1 where int_col >= 4
  This optimization is more difficult with character strings and floatingpoint data. You need to know your data.
- Check **showplan** output to see which keys and indexes are used.
- If you expect an index is not being used when you expect it to be, check dbcc traceon(302) output to see if the optimizer is considering the index.

Search arguments and useful indexes: It is important to distinguish between where and having clause predicates that can be used to optimize the query, and those that are used later during query processing to filter the rows to be returned. For example, if the authors table has on an index on au_lname and another on city, either index can be used to locate the matching rows for this query:

select au_lname, city, state
from authors
where city = "Washington"
and au_lname = "Catmull"

The optimizer uses statistics, including histograms, the number of rows in the table, the index heights, and the cluster ratios for the index and data pages to determine which index provides the cheapest access. The index that provides the cheapest access to the data pages is chosen and used to execute the query, and the other clause is applied to the data rows once they have been accessed.

Search argument syntax:
Search arguments (SARGs) are expressions in one of these forms:
<column> <operator> <expression>
<expression> <operator> <column>
<column> is null
Where:
- *column* is only a column name. If functions, expressions, or concatenation are added to the column name, an index on the column cannot be used.
- *operator* must be one of the following:
- =, >, <, >=, <=, !>, !<, <>, !=, is null
- *expression* is either a constant, or an expression that evaluates to a constant. The optimizer uses the index statistics differently, depending on whether the value of the expression is known at compile time:
    - If *expression* is a known constant or can be converted to a known constant during preprocessing, it can be compared to the **histogram** values stored for an **index** to return accurate row estimates.
    - If the value of *expression* is not known at **compile time**, the optimizer uses the **total density** to estimate the number of rows to be returned by the query. The value of variables set in a query batch or parameters set within a stored procedure cannot be known until execution time.
    - If the datatype of the expression is not compatible with the datatype of the column, an index cannot be used, and is not considered.

Nonequality operators: The nonequality operators, < > and !=, are special cases. The optimizer checks for covering nonclustered indexes if the column is indexed and uses a nonmatching index scan if an index covers the query. However, if the index does not cover the query, the table is accessed via a table scan.

Statistics for SARGS:
When you create an index, statistics are generated and stored in system tables. Some of the statistics relevant to determining the cost of search arguments and joins are:
• Statistics about the index: the number of pages and rows, the height of the index, the number of leaf pages, the average leaf row size.
• Statistics about the data in the column:
    • A histogram for the leading column of the index. Histograms are used to determine the selectivity of the SARG, that is, how many rows from the table match a given value.
    • Density values, measuring the density of keys in the index.
• Cluster ratios that measure the fragmentation of data storage and the effectiveness of large I/O.

Only a subset of these statistics (the number of leaf pages, for example) are maintained during query processing. Other statistics are updated only when you run update statistics or when you drop and re-create the index. You can display these statistics using optdiag

Histogram cells:

When you create an index, a histogram is created on the **first column** of the index. The histogram stores information about the **distribution of values in the column.**

The histogram for a column contains data in a **set of steps** or **cells**. You can specify the number of cells can when the index is created or when the update statistics command is run. For each cell, the histogram stores a column value and a weight for the cell.

Types of histograms:

Histograms Type	Description
A frequency cell	represents a value that has a high proportion of duplicates in the column. The weight of a frequency cell times the number of rows in the table equals the number of rows in the table that match the value for the cell. If a column does not have highly duplicated values, there are only range cells in the histogram.
Range cells	represent a range of values. Range cell weights and the range cell density are used for estimating the number of rows to be returned when search argument values falls within a range cell.

Density values:

Density is a measure of the average proportion of duplicate keys in the index.

It varies between 0 and 1. An index with N rows whose keys are unique has a density of $1/N$; an index whose keys are all duplicates of each other has a density of 1.

For indexes with multiple keys, density values are computed and stored for each prefix of keys in the index. That is, for an index on columns A, B, C, D, densities are stored for:

- A
- A, B
- A, B, C
- A, B, C, D

For each prefix subset, two density values are stored:
- Range cell density, used for search arguments
- Total density, used for joins

Range cell density represents the average number of duplicates of all values that are represented by range cells in the histogram. Total density represents the average number of duplicates for all values, those in both frequency and range cells. Total density is used to estimate the number of matching rows for joins and for search arguments whose value is not known when the query is optimized.

When the optimizer analyzes a SARG, it uses the **histogram values, densities, and the number of rows** in the table to estimate the number of rows that match the value specified in the SARG:

- If the SARG value matches a frequency cell, the estimated number of matching rows is equal to the weight of the frequency cell multiplied by the number of rows in the table. This query includes a data value with a high number of duplicates, so it matches a frequency cell:

    where authors.city = "New York"

    If the weight of the frequency cell is #.015606, and the authors table has 5000 rows, the optimizer estimates that the query returns 5000 * .015606 = 78 rows.

- If the SARG value falls within a range cell, the optimizer uses the **range cell density** to estimate the number of rows. For example, a query on a city value that falls in a range cell, with a range cell density of .000586 for the column, would estimate that 5000 * .000586 = 3 rows would be returned.
- For range queries, the optimizer adds the weights of all cells spanned by the range of values. When the beginning or end of the range falls in a range cell, the optimizer uses interpolation to estimate the number of rows from that cell that are included in the range.

Default values for search arguments: When statistics are not available for a search argument or when the value of a search argument is not known at optimization, the optimizer uses default values.

Operation Type	Operator	Density Approximation
Equality	=	Total density, if statistics are available for the column, or 10%
Open-ended range	<, <=, >, or >=	33%
Closed range	between	25%

The datatype hierarchy controls the use of indexes when search arguments or join columns have different datatypes. The following query prints the hierarchy values and datatype names:
select hierarchy, name from systypes order by 1
Note: If you have created user-defined datatypes, they are also listed in the query output, with the corresponding hierarchy values.

Basic units of costing: When the optimizer estimates costs for the query, the two factors it considers are the cost of physical I/O, reading pages from disk, and the cost of logical I/O, finding pages in the data cache. The optimizer assigns 18 as the cost of a physical I/O and 2 as the cost of a logical I/O. These are relative units of cost and do not represent time units such as milliseconds or clock ticks. These units are used in the formulas in this section, with the physical I/O costs first, then the logical I/O costs. The total cost of accessing a table can be expressed as:

$$\text{Cost} = \text{All physical IOs} * 18 + \text{All logical IOs} * 2$$

Summary

You read about **t**ransact-sql statements in this section.

- Adaptive Server can also process multiple statements submitted as a batch, either interactively or from a file

- Transact-SQL provides special keywords called control-of-flow language that allow the user to control the flow of execution of statements. The Transact-SQL control-of-flow language transforms standard SQL into a very high-level programming language.

- Global variables are system-supplied, predefined variables. They are distinguished from local variables by the two @ signs preceding their names— for example, *@@error*. The two @ signs are considered part of the identifier used to define the global variable.

- The query optimizer uses I/O cost as the measure of query execution cost. The significant costs in query processing are:
    - Physical I/O, when pages must be read from disk
    - Logical I/O, when pages in cache are read for a query

- **Search argument transitive closure:** Preprocessing applies transitive closure to search arguments

- **Join transitive closure:** Preprocessing applies transitive closure to join columns for normal equijoins if join transitive closure is enabled at the server or session level.

- When you create an index, a histogram is created on the **first column** of the index. The histogram stores information about the **distribution of values in the column.**

- When you create an index, statistics are generated and stored in system tables.

- **Cost = All physical IOs * 18 + All logical IOs * 2**

1. Which of the following can be including in CASE expression?

A. WHEN
B. CASE
C. THEN
D. coalesce
E. nullif
F. All of the above

2. Which of the following keyword control the operation of the statements inside a while loop? [Choose 2]
    A. break
    B. end
    C. continue
    D. start

3. Which of the following statements is NOT true about the case expression?
    A. It is a T-SQL extension.
    B. It can be used anywhere an expression can be used.
    C. At least one clause must return a non-null value.
    D. It can execute statements.
    E. It must return values of a compatible datatype.

4. If you think a particular query plan is unusual, you can use ___ to determine why the optimizer made the decision.
    A. errorlog file
    B. dbcc traceon(302)
    C. dbcc traceon(100)
    D. sysqueryplan

5. Which of the statements is true about Histogram?
    A. The histogram stores information about the distribution of values in the index.
    B. The histogram stores information about the distribution of index of the table.
    C. The histogram stores information about the distribution of values in the column.
    D. All of the above

6. Which of the following are types of Histogram? [Choose 2]
    A. Frequency cell
    B. Range cell
    C. Index cell
    D. density cell

Section 10 - Data Integrity and Constraints

10.1 Identify and define both the ANSI-standard constraints, such as check constraints and primary key constraints

Check Constraints:
You can declare a check constraint to limit the values users insert into a column in a table. Check constraints are useful for applications that check a limited, specific range of values. A check constraint specifies a *search_condition* that any value must pass before it is inserted into the table. A *search_condition* can include:
- A list of constant expressions introduced with in
- A range of constant expressions introduced with between
- A set of conditions introduced with like, which may contain wildcard characters

An expression can include arithmetic operations and Transact-SQL built-in functions. The *search_condition* cannot contain subqueries, a set function specification, or a target specification.

You can apply Column level and table level check constraint:
Column level: Can reference only the column on which the constraint is defined.
CREATE TABLE employee
(emp_id int ,
emp_name char(50),
emp_address varchar(255),
gender char(1) NULL CHECK (gender in ('M','F'))
)

Table level: Can reference any columns in the table.
CREATE TABLE employee
(emp_id int ,
emp_name char(50),
emp_address varchar(255),
gender char(1) NULL,
CONSTRAINT gender_ck CHECK (gender in ('M','F'))
)

The column definition overrides the check constraint because the following expression always evaluates to true:
col_name != null
If you declare a check constraint on a column that allows null values, you can insert NULL into the column, implicitly or explicitly, even though NULL is not included in the *search_condition*.
For example, suppose you define the following check constraint on a table column that allows null values:
check (pub_id in ("1389", "0736", "0877", "1622","1756"))
You can still insert NULL into that column.

Primary Key:
The primary key of a relational table uniquely identifies each record in the table. It can either be a normal attribute that is guaranteed to be unique.
Examples:
   CREATE TABLE employee
   (emp_id int PRIMARY KEY ,
    emp_name char(50),
    emp_addess varchar(255))

   CREATE TABLE employee
   (emp_id int CONSTRAINT pk_emp_id PRIMARY KEY ,
    emp_name char(50),
    emp_addess varchar(255))

   CREATE TABLE employee
   (emp_id int ,
    emp_name char(50),
    emp_addess varchar(255),
    CONSTRAINT pk_emp_id PRIMARY KEY (emp_id)
)

Note: Please see section **3.4 Identify qualities for Primary Key** for more detail

10.2   Describe traditional Sybase data integrity mechanisms such as rules and defaults

Defaults: The DEFAULT constraint is used to insert or update a default value into a column.
Syntax:
create default [owner.]default_name
as constant_expression

Default names must follow the rules for identifiers. You can create a default in the current database only. Within a database, default names must be unique for each user.
You can apply default for a column in following ways:
With CREATE table:
CREATE TABLE employee
(emp_id int ,
 emp_name char(50),
 emp_address varchar(255),
 join_date   datetime DEFAULT getdate()
)
Or
With ALTER table:
ALTER TABLE employee REPLACE join_date DEFAULT getdate()

CREATE default and Bind it to a column:
Syntax: CREATE DEFAULT <default_name> AS <default>
Example: *CREATE DEFAULT todays_date AS getdate()*

Bind created default to a column of a table as below
Syntax: sp_bindefault <default_name> , "<table_name>.<column_name>"
Example: *sp_bindefault todays_date , "employee.join_date"*

Note: getdate() is system function to get system date.
Note: To get the default, you must issue an insert or update command with a column list that does not include the column that has the default.

Restrictions:
- The default applies to new rows only. It does not retroactively change existing rows. Defaults take effect only when no entry is made. If you supply any value for the column, including NULL, the default has no effect.
- You cannot bind a default to a system datatype.
- You cannot bind a default to a timestamp column, because Adaptive Server generates values for timestamp columns.
- You cannot bind defaults to system tables.
- You can bind a default to an IDENTITY column or to a user-defined datatype with the IDENTITY property, but Adaptive Server ignores such defaults and assigns value that is greater than the last IDENTITY value assigned.
- If a default already exists on a column, you must remove it before binding a new default.

Unbinding a default means disconnecting it from a particular column or userdefined datatype. An unbound default is still stored in the database and is available for future use. Use sp_unbindefault to remove the binding between a default and a column or datatype.
Remove default from a column (if default is created in CREATE Table statement)
ALTER TABLE employee REPLACE join_date DEFAULT NULL
Note: In above statement you can define NOT NULL as well (it depends on column type .. if its NULL you have to REPLACE default as NULL, if its NOT NULL then you have to REPLACE default as NOT NULL)
Or
Remove default from a column (if default is created by 'CREATE DEFUALT' command and bind to column by 'sp_bindefault' command)
Syntax:
sp_unbindefault *objname*
Example:
sp_unbindefault "employee.join_date"

If you specify NOT NULL when you create a column and do not create a default for it, Adaptive Server produces an error message whenever anyone inserts a row and fails to make an entry in that column. When you drop a default for a NULL column, Adaptive Server inserts NULL in that position each time you add rows without entering any value for that column. When you drop a default for a NOT NULL column, you get an error message when rows are added, without a value entered for that column.

Dropping defaults:
You must unbind a default with **sp_unbindefault**, before you drop it otherwise it will give error.
Syntax:
drop default [owner.]default_name
[, [owner.]default_name] ...
Example:
Drop default join_date

RULES:
A rule lets you specify what users can or cannot enter into a particular column or any column with a user-defined datatype.
Syntax:
create rule [owner.]rule_name
as condition_expression
Example: To make sure entered empid is between 1 – 1000.
create rule empid_rule
as @p_emp_id between 1 and 1000
Example: To make sure entered employee's first name contains word 'ABHI'
create rule empname_rule
as @p_fname like '%ABHI%'

Note: You can create a rule in the current database only.
- The rule definition can contain any expression that is valid in a where clause, and can include arithmetic operators, comparison operators, like, in, between, and so on.
- The rule definition cannot reference any column or other database object directly.
- Built-in functions that do not reference database objects *can* be included.

Bind rules: use **sp_bindrule** to link the rule to a column or user-defined datatype.
sp_bindrule *rulename, objname* [, futureonly]

Note: *objname* can be column name or user datatype.
Note: Use the optional futureonly parameter only when binding a rule to a userdefined datatype.
Note: All columns of a specified user-defined datatype become associated with the specified rule unless you specify futureonly, which prevents existing columns of that user datatype from inheriting the rule. If the rule associated with a given user-defined datatype has previously been changed, Adaptive Server maintains the changed rule for existing columns of that userdefined datatype.

Example: rule bind to a column.

sp_bindrule empid_rule, "employee.id"
Now if you try to insert a row as below, it will give a error message and value won't be insert in the table because we are trying to insert value 1002, which is not between 1 – 1000 and its violating rule *empid_rule* bind to column *id*.
insert into employee values (1002, 'test name', 'test last name', getdate())

Note: Rules cannot be bound to columns and used during the same batch. sp_bindrule cannot be in the same batch as insert statements that invoke the rule.
Example: rules bind to user-defined datatypes. *U_id* is a user defined datatype
sp_bindrule empid_rule, 'T_id'

Note: You cannot bind a rule to a system datatype.

Note: Rules bound to columns always take precedence over rules bound to user datatypes. Binding a rule to a column replaces a rule bound to the user datatype of that column, but binding a rule to a datatype does not replace a rule bound to a column of that user datatype.

You cannot define a column to allow nulls, and then override this definition with a rule that prohibits null values. For example, if a column definition specifies NULL and the rule specifies the following, an implicit or explicit NULL does not violate the rule:
@val in (1,2,3)
The column definition overrides the rule, even a rule that specifies:
@val is not null

Unbind rules: There are two ways to unbind a rule:
- Use sp_unbindrule to remove the binding between a rule and a column or user-defined datatype.
  Example: unbind from a column
  sp_unbindrule "employee.id"
  Example: unbind from the user-defined datatype
  sp_unbindrule "T_id"
- Use sp_bindrule to bind a new rule to that column or datatype. The old one is automatically unbound.
  Example: Assume there is already a rule bind to column\
  sp_bindrule emp_newrule, "employee.id"

Note: An unbound rule's definition is still stored in the database and is available for future use.

If you use sp_unbindrule *objname* [, futureonly]
- prevents existing columns of that datatype from losing their binding with the rule, or
- The rule on a column of that user-defined datatype has been changed so that its current value is different from the rule being unbound.

Drop rule:
Syntax:
drop rule [*owner.*]*rule_name*
[, [*owner.*]*rule_name*] ...
Example:
Drop rule empid_rule

Note: Unbind the rule from all columns and user datatypes before you drop it.

Summary

You read about data integrity and constraints in this section.

- A check constraint specifies a *search_condition* that any value must pass before it is inserted into the table. Check constraints are useful for applications that check a limited, specific range of values.
- You can apply Column level and table level check constraint
- CHECK CONSTRAINT: If you declare a check constraint on a column that allows null values, you can insert NULL into the column, implicitly or explicitly, even though NULL is not included in the *search_condition*
- PRIMARY KEY: The primary key of a relational table uniquely identifies each record in the table. It can either be a normal attribute that is guaranteed to be unique.
- DEFAULT: The DEFAULT constraint is used to insert or update a default value into a column.
- Unbinding a default means disconnecting it from a particular column or userdefined datatype. An unbound default is still stored in the database and is available for future use. Use sp_unbindefault to remove the binding between a default and a column or datatype.
- RULE: A rule lets you specify what users can or cannot enter into a particular column or any column with a user-defined datatype.

Practice Test

1. Which of the following statements are true about Default? [Choose 3]
    A. You can create a default in the current database only.
    B. You can bind a default to a system datatype.
    C. You can bind a default to a timestamp column.
    D. You can bind a default to an IDENTITY column or to a user-defined datatype with the IDENTITY property, but Adaptive Server ignores such defaults and assigns value that is greater than the last IDENTITY value assigned.
    E. If a default already exists on a column, you must remove it before binding a new default.

2. Which of the following statements are NOT TRUE about RULE?
    A. The rule definition can contain any expression that is valid in a where clause, and can include arithmetic operators, comparison operators, like, in, between, and so on.
    B. The rule definition can reference any column or other database object directly.
    C. Built-in functions that do not reference database objects *can* be included.
    D. use **sp_bindrule** to link the rule to a column or user-defined datatype.

Section 11 - Transaction Management and Locking

11.1 Describe the behavior of transactions and transaction management commands

Adaptive Server automatically manages all data modification commands, including single-step change requests, as transactions. By default, each *insert, update,* and *delete* statement is considered a single transaction.
Transaction commands:
begin transaction: marks the beginning of the transaction block.
Syntax:
begin {transaction | tran} [*transaction_name*]

save transaction: marks a savepoint within a transaction
Syntax:
save {transaction | tran} *savepoint_name*
A **savepoint** is a marker that a user puts inside a transaction to indicate a point to which it can be rolled back. You can commit only certain portions of a batch by rolling back the undesired portion to a savepoint before committing the entire batch.

commit: commits the entire transaction
Syntax:
commit [transaction | tran | work] [*transaction_name*]

rollback: rolls a transaction back to a savepoint or to the beginning of a transaction
Syntax:
rollback [transaction | tran | work] [*transaction_name* | *savepoint_name*]
You can cancel or roll back a transaction with the rollback transaction command any time before commit transaction has been given. Using savepoints, you can cancel either an entire transaction or part of it. However, you cannot cancel a transaction after it has been committed.

The begin transaction and commit transaction commands tell Adaptive Server to process any number of individual commands as a single unit. Rollback transaction undoes the transaction, either back to its beginning, or back to a **savepoint**. You define a savepoint inside a transaction using save transaction.
Transactions give you control over transaction management. In addition to grouping SQL statements to behave as a single unit, they improve performance, since system overhead is incurred once per transaction, rather than once for each individual command.
Note: Any user can define a transaction. No permission is required for any of the transaction commands.

You can use certain data definition language commands (for example CREATE table, grant and alter table) in transactions by setting the **ddl in tran** database option to true. If ddl in tran is true

in the model database, you can issue the commands inside transactions in all databases created after ddl in tran was set to true in **model**.
Syntax: set ddl in tran to true
sp_dboption database_name,"ddl in tran", true

Note: Avoid using data definition language commands on tempdb within transactions; doing so can slow performance to a halt.

You cannot use system procedures sp_helpdb, sp_helpdevice, sp_helpindex, sp_helpjoins, sp_helpserver, sp_lookup, and sp_spaceused (because they create temporary tables) sp_configure and System procedures that change the master database

Note: rollback transaction or save transaction does not affect Adaptive Server and does not return an error message if the transaction is not currently active.

Here is how you can use the save transaction and rollback transaction commands:

```
begin tran
statements                          Group A
save tran mytran
statements                          Group B
rollback tran mytran                Rolls back group B
statements                          Group C
commit tran                         Commits groups A and C
```

@@transtate: The global variable @@transtate keeps track of the current state of a transaction. It may contain following values

Value	Description
0	Transaction in progress. A transaction is in effect; the previous statement executed successfully.
1	Transaction succeeded. The transaction completed and committed its changes.
2	Statement aborted. The previous statement was aborted; no effect on the transaction.
3	Transaction aborted. The transaction aborted and rolled back any changes.

Example:
begin transaction
insert into publishers (pub_id) values ("9999")
(1 row affected)
select @@transtate

0
(1 row affected)
commit transaction
select @@transtate

1

> **Note:** Adaptive Server does not clear @@transtate after every statement. It changes @@transtate only in response to an action taken by a transaction. Syntax and compile errors **do not** affect the value of @@transtate.

Nesting Transactions:
You can nest transactions within other transactions. When you nest begin transaction and commit transaction statements, the outermost pair actually begin and commit the transaction. The inner pairs just keep track of the nesting level. Adaptive Server does not commit the transaction until the commit transaction that matches the outermost begin transaction is issued. Normally, this transaction "nesting" occurs as stored procedures or triggers that contain begin/commit pairs call each other.

The @@trancount global variable keeps track of the current nesting level for transactions. An initial implicit or explicit begin transaction sets @@trancount to 1. Each subsequent begin transaction increments @@trancount, and a commit transaction decrements it. Firing a trigger also increments @@trancount, and the transaction begins with the statement that causes the trigger to fire. Nested transactions are not committed unless @@trancount equals 0.

11.2 Describe behavior of locks

Locking is a concurrency control mechanism: it ensures the consistency of data within and across transactions. Locking is needed in a multiuser environment, since several users may be working with the same data at the same time.

Lock contention: Locking affects performance when one process holds locks that prevent another process from accessing needed data. The process that is blocked by the lock sleeps until the lock is released. This is called *lock contention*.

Deadlock: A **deadlock** occurs when two user processes each have a lock on a separate page or table and each wants to acquire a lock on the same page or table held by the other process. The transaction with the least accumulated CPU time is killed and all of its work is rolled back.

Adaptive Server supports locking at the table, page, and row level.
Adaptive Server provides these locking schemes:

Locking	Description
Allpages	locks datapages and index pages
Datapages	which locks only the data pages
Datarows	which locks only the data rows

Allpages locking: Allpages locking locks both **data pages** and **index pages**. When a query updates a value in a row in an allpages-locked table, the data page is locked with an **exclusive lock**. Any index pages affected by the update are also locked with **exclusive locks**. These locks are transactional, meaning that they are held until the end of the transaction.

In many cases, the concurrency problems that result from allpages locking arise from the index page locks, rather than the locks on the data pages themselves. Data pages have longer rows than indexes, and often have a small number of rows per page. If index keys are short, an index page can store between 100 and 200 keys. An exclusive lock on an index page can block other users who need to access any of the rows referenced by the index page, a far greater number of rows than on a locked data page.

Datapages locking: In datapages locking, entire data pages are still locked, but index pages are not locked. When a row needs to be changed on a data page, that page is locked, and the lock is held until the end of the transaction. The updates to the index pages are performed using **latches**, which are non transactional. **Latches are held only as long as required to perform the physical changes to the page and are then released immediately.** Index page entries are implicitly locked by locking the data page. No transactional locks are held on index pages.

Datarows locking: In datarows locking, row-level locks are acquired on individual rows on data pages. **Index rows and pages are not locked.** When a row needs to be changed on a data page, a non transactional latch is acquired on the page. The latch is held while the physical change is made to the data page, and then the latch is released. The lock on the data row is held until the end of the transaction. The index rows are updated, using latches on the index page, but are not locked. Index entries are implicitly locked by acquiring a lock on the data row.

> **Note:** Page or row locks are less restrictive (or smaller) than table locks. A page lock locks all the rows on data page or an index page; a table lock locks an entire table. A row lock locks only a single row on a page. Adaptive Server uses **page** or **row** locks whenever possible to reduce **contention** and to **improve concurrency**.
> **Note:** Adaptive Server uses a table lock to provide more efficient locking when an entire table or a large number of pages or rows will be accessed by a statement. Locking strategy is directly tied to the **query plan**, so the query plan can be as important for its locking strategies as for its I/O implications.

Lock promotion threshold:
To avoid the overhead of managing hundreds of locks on a table, Adaptive Server uses a setting. Once a scan of a table accumulates more page or row locks than allowed by the lock promotion threshold, Adaptive Server tries to issue a table lock. If it succeeds, the page or row locks are no longer necessary and are released.

Page and row locks: The following describes the types of page and row locks:
- **Shared locks:** Adaptive Server applies **shared lock**s for read operations. If a shared lock has been applied to a data page or data row or to an index page, other transactions can also acquire a shared lock, even when the first transaction is active. However, no transaction can acquire an exclusive lock on the page or row until all shared locks on the page or row are released. This means that many transactions can simultaneously read the page or row, but no transaction can change data on the page or row while a shared lock

exists. Transactions that need an exclusive lock wait or "block" for the release of the shared locks before continuing.

By default, Adaptive Server releases shared locks after it finishes scanning the page or row. It does not hold shared locks until the statement is completed or until the end of the transaction unless requested to do so by the user.

- **Exclusive locks:** Adaptive Server applies an **exclusive lock** for a data modification operation. When a transaction gets an exclusive lock, other transactions cannot acquire a lock of any kind on the page or row until the exclusive lock is released at the end of its transaction. The other transactions wait or "block" until the exclusive lock is released.
- **Update locks**: Adaptive Server applies an **update lock** during the initial phase of an update, delete, or fetch (for cursors declared for update) operation while the page or row is being read. The update lock allows **shared locks** on the page or row, but does **not allow** other **update** or **exclusive locks**.

  Note: Update locks help avoid deadlocks and lock contention.

Note: In general, read operations acquire shared locks, and write operations acquire exclusive locks. For operations that delete or update data, Adaptive Server applies page-level or row-level exclusive and update locks only if the column used in the search argument is part of an **index**. If no index exists on any of the search arguments, Adaptive Server must acquire a **table-level lock**.

Examples: Page locks and row locks

Statement	All pages locked table	Datarows locked table
select balance from account where acct_number = 25	Shared page lock	Shared row lock
insert account values (34, 500)	Exclusive page lock on data page and exclusive page lock on leaflevel index page	Exclusive row lock
delete account where acct_number = 25	Update page locks followed by exclusive page locks on data pages and exclusive page locks on leaflevel index pages	Update row locks followed by exclusive row locks on each affected row
update account set balance = 0 where acct_number = 25	Update page lock on data page and exclusive page lock on data page	Update row lock followed by exclusive row lock

Table locks: The following describes the types of table locks.
- **Intent lock:** An **intent lock** indicates that page-level or row-level locks are currently held on a table. Adaptive Server applies an intent table lock with each shared or exclusive page or row lock, so an intent lock can be either an **exclusive lock** or a **shared lock**. Setting an intent lock prevents other transactions from subsequently acquiring conflicting table-level locks on the table that contains that locked page. An intent lock is held as long as page or row locks are in effect for the transaction.

- **Shared lock**: This lock is similar to a shared page or lock, except that it affects the entire table. Adaptive Server applies a shared table lock for a select command with a **holdlock** clause if the command does not use an index.
  Note: A **create nonclustered index** command also acquires a **shared table lock**.
- **Exclusive lock**: This lock is similar to an exclusive page or row lock, except it affects the entire table. update and delete statements require exclusive table locks if their search arguments do not reference indexed columns of the object.
  Note: Adaptive Server applies an **exclusive table lock** during a **create clustered index** command.

Lock duration:
The lock duration depends on the isolation level and the type of query. Lock duration can be one of the following:
- Scan duration: Locks are released when the scan moves off the row or page, for row or page locks, or when the scan of the table completes, for table locks.
- Statement duration: Locks are released when the statement execution completes.
- Transaction duration: Locks are released when the transaction completes.

Demand locks:
Adaptive Server sets a **demand lock** to indicate that a transaction is next in the queue to lock a table, page, or row. Since many readers can hold shared locks on a given page, row, or table, tasks that require exclusive locks are queued after a task that already holds a shared lock. Adaptive Server allows up to three readers' tasks to skip over a queued update task.
After a write transaction has been skipped over by three tasks or families (in the case of queries running in parallel) that acquire shared locks, Adaptive Server gives a demand lock to the write transaction.
As soon as the readers queued ahead of the demand lock release their locks, the write transaction acquires its lock and is allowed to proceed. The read transactions queued behind the demand lock wait for the write transaction to finish and release its exclusive lock.

Latches:
Latches are non transactional synchronization mechanisms used to guarantee the physical consistency of a page. While rows are being inserted, updated or deleted, only one Adaptive Server process can have access to the page at the same time. Latches are used for **datapages** and **datarows** locking but not for **allpages locking**.
The most important distinction between a lock and a latch is the duration:
- A lock can persist for a long period of time: while a page is being scanned, while a disk read or network write takes place, for the duration of a statement, or for the duration of a transaction.
- A latch is held only for the time required to insert or move a few bytes on a data page, to copy pointers, columns or rows, or to acquire a latch on another index page.

Section 11 - Transaction Management and Locking

Isolation levels affect locking:
You can choose the isolation level for all select queries during a session, or you can choose the isolation level for a specific query or table in a transaction.
At all isolation levels, all updates acquire **exclusive locks** and **hold** them for the duration of the transaction

Note For tables that use the allpages locking scheme, requesting isolation level 2 also enforces isolation level 3.

Specifying the locking scheme for a table:
You can specify locking schemes using following ways:

Option	Description
sp_configure	to specify a server-wide default locking scheme
Create table	specify the locking scheme for newly created tables
Alter table	change the locking scheme for a table to any other locking scheme
select into	to specify the locking scheme for a table created by selecting results from other tables

Specifying a server-wide locking scheme by using sp_configure:
Syntax:
sp_configure "lock scheme", 0,
{allpages | datapages | datarows}
Example:
sp_configure "lock scheme", 0, allpages

Specifying a locking scheme with *create table:*
Syntax:
create table *table_name* (*column_name_list*)
[lock {datarows | datapages | allpages}]
Example:
create table employee_new
(emp_id char(4) not null,
emp_name varchar(50) null,
status int not null)
lock datarows

Note: Specifying the locking scheme with create table overrides the default server-wide setting.

Changing a locking scheme with *alter table:*
Syntax:
alter table *table_name*
lock {allpages | datapages | datarows}
Example:

alter table employee_new lock datapages

> **Note:** Changing from allpages locking to data-only locking requires copying the data rows to new pages and re-creating any indexes on the table.
> **Note:** Changing from datapages locking to datarows locking or vice versa does not require copying data pages and rebuilding indexes.

Specifying a locking scheme with *select into:*
Syntax:
select [all | distinct] *select_list*
into [[*database*.]*owner*.]*table_name*
lock {datarows | datapages | allpages}
from ...
Example:
*select * into employee_test*
   lock allpages
from employee_new
Note: If you do not specify a locking scheme with select into, the new table uses the **server-wide default locking scheme**, as defined by the configuration parameter lock scheme.

Readpast locking: Readpast locking allows **select** and **readtext** queries to silently skip all **rows** or **pages** locked with incompatible locks. The queries do not block, terminate, or return error or advisory messages to the user. It is largely designed to be used in queue-processing applications.

11.3   Describe transaction logging; lock blocking, diagnosis and resolution of deadlocks

Transaction log:
Every change to a database, whether it is the result of a single update statement or a grouped set of SQL statements, is recorded in the system table syslogs. This table is called the **transaction log**.

Some commands that change the database are not logged, such as truncate table, bulk copy into a table that has no indexes, select into, writetext, and dump transaction with no_log.
The transaction log records update, insert, or delete statements on a momentto- moment basis. When a transaction begins, a begin transaction event is recorded in the log. As each data modification statement is received, it is recorded in the log.
The change is always recorded in the log before any change is made in the database itself. This type of log, called a write-ahead log, ensures that the database can be recovered completely in case of a failure.
Failures can be due to hardware or media problems, system software problems, application software problems, program-directed cancellations of transactions, or a user decision to cancel the transaction.

In case of any of these failures, the transaction log can be played back against a copy of the database restored from a backup made with the dump commands.

Adaptive Server's dynamic dump allows the database and transaction log to be backed up while use of the database continues. Make frequent backups of your database transaction log. The more often you back up your data, the smaller the amount of work lost if a system failure occurs. The owner of each database or a user with the ss_oper role is responsible for backing up the database and its transaction log with the dump commands, though permission to execute them can be transferred to other users. Permission to use the load commands, however, defaults to the Database Owner and cannot be transferred.

Deadlocks:
Simply stated, a **deadlock** occurs when two user processes each have a lock on a separate data page, index page, or table and each wants to acquire a lock on same page or table locked by the other process. When this happens, the first process is waiting for the second release the lock, but the second process will not release it until the lock on the first process's object is released.
When tasks deadlock in Adaptive Server, a deadlock detection mechanism rolls back one of the transactions, and sends messages to the user and to the Adaptive Server error log. It is possible to induce application-side deadlock situations in which a client opens multiple connections, and these client connections wait for locks held by the other connection of the same application. These are not true server-side deadlocks and cannot be detected by Adaptive Server deadlock detection mechanisms

Application deadlock example
Some developers simulate cursors by using two or more connections from DB-Library™. One connection performs a select and the other connection performs updates or deletes on the same tables. This can create application deadlocks.
Example:
- Connection A holds a shared lock on a page. As long as there are rows pending from Adaptive Server, a shared lock is kept on the current page.
- Connection B requests an exclusive lock on the same pages and then waits.
- The application waits for Connection B to succeed before invoking the logic needed to remove the shared lock. But this never happens. Since Connection A never requests a lock that is held by Connection B, this is not a server-side deadlock.

Server task deadlocks:
Example:

T19	Event Sequence	T20
begin transaction	T19 and T20 start.	begin transaction
update savings set balance = balance - 250 where acct_number = 25	T19 gets exclusive lock on savings while T20 gets exclusive lock on checking.	
		Update checking set balance = balance - 75 where acct_number = 45
update checking set balance = balance + 250 where acct_number = 45	T19 waits for T20 to release its lock while T20 waits for T19 to release its lock; deadlock occurs.	
commit transaction		Update savings set balance = balance + 75 where acct_number = 25

Adaptive Server checks for deadlocks and chooses the user whose transaction has accumulated the least amount of CPU time as the victim. Adaptive Server rolls back that user's transaction, notifies the application program of this action with message number 1205, and allows the other process to move forward.

11.4   Describe the effect of transaction isolation levels

Adaptive Server provides the following options to support SQL-standardscompliant transactions:

option	Description
transaction mode	lets you set whether transactions begin with or without an implicit begin transaction statement.
isolation level	refers to the degree to which data can be accessed by other users during a transaction.

Transaction mode:
@@tranchained display current transaction mode.
Example:
select @@tranchained
if above returns 0 then transaction mode is **unchained** and if returns 1 then transaction mode is **chained**.
Note: You can set chained on and off by using following commands:

Section 11 - Transaction Management and Locking

set chained on
set chained off
Adaptive Server supports the following transaction modes:

Chained mode: Implicitly begins a transaction before any data retrieval or modification statement. These statements include: **delete, insert, open, fetch, select, and update**. You must still explicitly end the transaction with commit transaction or rollback transaction.
Example:
set chained on
insert into employee
values (106, 'Steve', '01 Jan 1973', 1)
begin transaction
delete from employee where emp_id = 106
rollback transaction

*select * from employee*

emp_id	emp_name	dob	status
102	Mike	Nov 25 1979 12:00AM	1
103	Salman	Jan 1 1980 12:00AM	0
101	Abhisek	Jun 25 1983 12:00AM	1
104	Steve	Jan 1 1973 12:00AM	1

In above example, ASE implicitly executes *begin transaction* statement just before the insert command and rollback whole transaction (including *insert statement*).

Unchained mode: The default mode. Requires explicit begin transaction statements paired with commit transaction or rollback transaction statements to complete the transaction.
Example: The rollback affects only the delete statement, so employee still contains the inserted row.
insert into employee
values (105, 'Thomas', '02 Jan 1973', 1)
begin transaction
delete from employee where emp_id = 105
rollback transaction

*select * from employee*

emp_id	emp_name	dob	status
102	Mike	Nov 25 1979 12:00AM	1
103	Salman	Jan 1 1980 12:00AM	0
101	Abhisek	Jun 25 1983 12:00AM	1
104	Steve	Jan 1 1973 12:00AM	1
105	Thomas	Jan 2 1973 12:00AM	1

Note: Although chained mode implicitly begins transactions with data retrieval or modification statements, you can nest transactions only by explicitly using begin transaction statements.

Isolation level:
The ANSI SQL standard defines four levels of isolation for transactions. Each isolation level specifies the kinds of actions that are not permitted while concurrent transactions are executing. Higher levels include the restrictions imposed by the lower levels:
- **Level 0:** ensures that data written by one transaction represents the actual data. It prevents other transactions from changing data that has already been modified (through an insert, delete, update, and so on) by an uncommitted transaction. The other transactions are blocked from modifying that data until the transaction commits. However, other transactions can still read the uncommitted data, which results in **dirty reads**.
- **Level 1:** prevents **dirty reads**. Such reads occur when one transaction modifies a row, and a second transaction reads that row before the first transaction commits the change. If the first transaction rolls back the change, the information read by the second transaction becomes invalid. This is the **default isolation level** supported by Adaptive Server.
- **Level 2:** prevents **nonrepeatable reads**. Such reads occur when one transaction reads a row and a second transaction modifies that row. If the second transaction commits its change, subsequent reads by the first transaction yield different results than the original read.
   Adaptive Server supports this level for **data-only-locked** tables. It is **not** supported for allpages-locked tables.
- **Level 3:** ensures that data read by one transaction is valid until the end of that transaction, preventing **phantom rows**. Adaptive Server supports this level through the **holdlock** keyword of the select statement, which applies a read-lock on the specified data. **Phantom** rows occur when one transaction reads a set of rows that satisfy a search condition, and then a second transaction modifies the data (through an insert, delete, update, and so on). If the first transaction repeats the read with the same search conditions, it obtains a different set of rows.

You can set the isolation level for your session by using the transaction isolation level option of the set command.
set transaction isolation level 0

The global variable @@isolation contains the current isolation level of your Transact-SQL session.

Note: The **ANSI SQL standard** requires that **level 3** be the **default** isolation for all transactions.
Note: If you also use the chained transaction mode, that isolation level remains in effect for any data retrieval or modification statement that implicitly begins a transaction. In both cases, this can lead to concurrency problems for some applications, since more locks may be held for longer periods of time.

Changing the isolation level for a query:

You can change the isolation level for a query by using the at isolation clause with the select or readtext statements. The at isolation clause supports isolation levels 0 (read uncommitted), 1(read committed), and 3 (serializable). It does not support isolation level 2.
Example:
*select **
from titles
at isolation read uncommitted
or
*select **
from titles
at isolation 0

Note: The *at isolation* clause is valid only for single select and readtext queries or in the declare cursor statement.

Isolation level precedences: The following describes the precedence rules as they apply to the different methods of defining isolation levels:
1. The holdlock, noholdlock, and shared keywords take precedence over the **at isolation** clause and **set transaction isolation level option**, except in the case of **isolation level 0**.
For example:
/* This query executes at isolation level 3 */
select *
from titles holdlock
at isolation read committed
create view authors_nolock
as select * from authors noholdlock
set transaction isolation level 3
/* This query executes at isolation level 1 */
select * from authors_nolock

2. The at isolation clause takes precedence over the set transaction isolation level option. For example:
set transaction isolation level 2
/* executes at isolation level 0 */
select * from publishers
at isolation read uncommitted
You cannot use the **read uncommitted** (isolation level 0) option of at isolation in the same query as the holdlock, noholdlock, and shared keywords.

3. The transaction isolation level 0 option of the set command takes precedence over the holdlock, noholdlock, and shared keywords.
For example:
set transaction isolation level 0
/* executes at isolation level 0 */

select *
from titles holdlock
Adaptive Server issues a warning before executing the above query.

Cursors and isolation levels:
- Level 0 – Adaptive Server uses **no locks** on base table pages that contain a row representing a current cursor position. Cursors acquire no read locks for their scans, so they do not block other applications from accessing the same data. However, cursors operating at this isolation level are not updatable, and they require a unique index on the base table to ensure the accuracy of their scans.
- Level 1 – Adaptive Server uses a **shared** or **update** lock on base table pages that contain a row representing a current cursor position. The page remains locked until the current cursor position moves off the page (as a result of fetch statements), or the cursor is closed. If an index is used to search the base table rows, it also applies shared or update locks to the corresponding index pages. This is the default locking behavior for Adaptive Server.
- Level 3 – Adaptive Server uses a **shared** or **update** lock on any base table pages that have been read in a transaction on behalf of the cursor. In addition, the locks are held until the transaction ends, as opposed to being released when the data page is no longer needed. The holdlock keyword applies this locking level to the base tables, as specified by the query on the tables or views.

Note: Isolation level 2 is not supported for cursors.

Stored procedures and isolation levels: The Sybase system procedures always operate **at isolation level 1**, regardless
of the isolation level of the transaction or session. User stored procedures operate at the isolation level of the transaction that executes it. If the isolation level changes within a stored procedure, the new isolation level remains in effect only during the execution of the stored procedure.

Triggers and isolation levels: Since triggers are fired by data modification statements (like insert), all triggers execute at either the transaction's isolation level or isolation level 1, **whichever is higher**. So, if a trigger fires in a transaction at level 0, Adaptive Server sets the trigger's isolation level to 1 before executing its first statement.

11.5 Define methods for reducing lock contention

To help reduce lock contention between update and select queries:
- Use datarows or datapages locking for tables with lock contention due to updates and selects.
- If tables have more than **32** columns, make the first 32 columns the columns that are most frequently used as search arguments and in other query clauses.
- Select only needed columns. Avoid using **select *** when all columns are not needed by the application.

- Use any available predicates for select queries. When a table uses datapages locking, the information about updated columns is kept for the entire page, so that if a transaction updates some columns in one row, and other columns in another row on the same page, any select query that needs to access that page must avoid using any of the updated columns.

11.6   Describe how ASE resolves a deadlock

Adaptive Server checks for deadlocks and chooses the user whose transaction has accumulated the least amount of CPU time as the victim. Adaptive Server rolls back that user's transaction, notifies the application program of this action with message number **1205**, and allows the other process to move forward.

Summary

You read about database locking concept in this section.

- Adaptive Server automatically manages all data modification commands, including single-step change requests, as transactions. By default, each *insert, update,* and *delete* statement is considered a single transaction.

- A **savepoint** is a marker that a user puts inside a transaction to indicate a point to which it can be rolled back.

- The begin transaction and commit transaction commands tell Adaptive Server to process any number of individual commands as a single unit. Rollback transaction undoes the transaction, either back to its beginning, or back to a **savepoint**.

- LOCKING ensures the consistency of data within and across transactions.

- A **deadlock** occurs when two user processes each have a lock on a separate page or table and each wants to acquire a lock on the same page or table held by the other process.

- Adaptive Server supports locking at the table, page, and row level.

- Adaptive Server provides these locking schemes:
    - Allpages
    - Datapages
    - Datarows

- Adaptive Server sets a **demand lock** to indicate that a transaction is next in the queue to lock a table, page, or row. Since many readers can hold shared locks on a given page, row, or table, tasks that require exclusive locks are queued after a task that already holds a shared lock.

- Latches are non transactional synchronization mechanisms used to guarantee the physical consistency of a page.

- Every change to a database, whether it is the result of a single update statement or a grouped set of SQL statements, is recorded in the system table syslogs. This table is called the **transaction log**.

- Adaptive Server supports the following transaction modes:
    - Chained mode
    - Unchained mode

- The ANSI SQL standard defines four levels of isolation for transactions.

- Isolation levels:

    Level 0, Level 1, Level 2, Level 3

Practice Test

1. If global variable @@transtate return 0 value, it means?
    A. Transaction succeeded. The transaction completed and committed its changes.
    B. Transaction in progress. A transaction is in effect; the previous statement executed successfully.
    C. Statement aborted. The previous statement was aborted; no effect on the transaction.
    D. Statement aborted. The previous statement was aborted; no effect on the transaction.

2. The @@trancount global variable keeps track of the?
    A. rows count
    B. tansaction counts
    C. Current nesting level for transactions
    D. None of the above

3. Which of the following statements is true for deadlock?
    A. The transaction with the least accumulated CPU time is killed and all of its work is rolled back.
    B. The transaction with the max accumulated CPU time is killed and all of its work is committed.
    C. The transaction with the least accumulated CPU time is killed and all of its work is committed.
    D. None of the above

4. Intent lock can be?
    A. An exclusive lock
    B. A shared lock
    C. Both A and B
    D. None of the above

5. Every change to a database, whether it is the result of a single update statement or a grouped set of SQL statements, is recorded in the system table?
    A. sysstatistics
    B. syslogs
    C. sysprocedures
    D. syscomments

6. Which of the following global variable displays current transaction mode?
    A. @@tranmode
    B. @@tranchanged
    C. @@mode
    D. @@chained

7. ASE notified which message number in case of deadlock?
    A. 100
    B. 1207
    C. -1
    D. 1205

Section 12 - Joins, Subqueries, and Unions

12.1 Define the different types of joins

JOIN:

A **join** operation compares two or more tables (or views) by specifying a column from each, comparing the values in those columns row by row, and linking the rows that have matching values.

When you join two or more tables, the columns being compared must have similar values—that is, values using the same or similar datatypes. You can embed a join in a **select, update, insert, delete,** or **subquery**.

Syntax:

start of select, update, insert, delete, or subquery
from {table_list | view_list}
where [not]
[table_name. | view_name.]column_name join_operator
[table_name. | view_name.]column_name
[{and | or} [not]
[table_name.|view_name.]column_name join_operator
[table_name.|view_name.]column_name]...
End of select, update, insert, delete, or subquery

Example:
select f_name, l_name,dob from employee, emp_dept
where employee.city = emp_dept.city

You can use alias as well instead of full table name

Example:
select f_name, l_name,dob from employee emp, emp_dept dept
where emp.city = dept.city

Note: if "*" is used (like select * from), the columns in the results are displayed in the order in which they were stated in the create statement that created the table.

At most, a query can reference 50 tables and 46 worktables (such as those created by aggregate functions). The 50-table limit includes:

- Tables (or views on tables) listed in the from clause
- Each instance of multiple references to the same table (self-joins)
- Tables referenced in subqueries
- Tables being created with into
- Base tables referenced by the views listed in the from clause

Join Operators: = (Equal to), > (Greater than), >= (Greater than or equal to), <(Less than), <=(Less than or equal to), != (Not equal to), !> (Less than or equal to), !< (Greater than or equal to)

Note: Joins that use the relational operators are collectively called **theta joins**.

Outer Join operator: The outer join operators are Transact-SQL extensions

Operator	Description
*=	Include in the results all the rows from the first table, not just the ones where the joined columns match.
=*	Include in the results all the rows from the second table, not just the ones where the joined columns match.

Note: The columns being joined must have the same or compatible datatypes. You can use **convert** function when comparing columns whose datatypes cannot be implicitly converted. If the datatypes used in the join are compatible, Adaptive Server automatically converts them.
Example: Assuming *value* column in *dummy* table is of varchar type.
Where employee.emp_id = convert(int, dummy.value)
Note: You cannot use joins for columns containing **text** or **image** values. You can, however, compare the lengths of text columns from two tables with a where clause. For example:
where datalength(textab_1.textcol) > datalength(textab_2.textcol)
Note: Join expressions are usually connected with and, although or is also legal.

Join processing:
Step1. Produce Cartesian product of the tables:

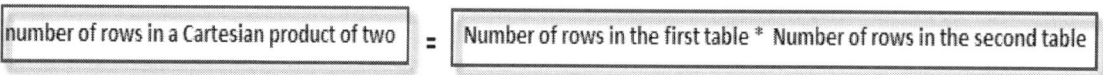

For example there are 10 rows in table1 and 2 rows in table2 and if you run below query, It will display 20 rows.
Select * from table1, table2
Note: This Cartesian product does not contain any particularly useful information.
Step2: Eliminates the rows that do not satisfy the join by using the conditions in the where clause
You must include a where clause in the join, which specifies the columns to be matched and the basis on which to match them. It may also include other restrictions.
For example, the where clause in the example cited (the Cartesian product of the authors table and the publishers table) eliminates from the results all rows in which the author's city is not the same as the publisher's city:
where authors.city = publishers.city

Equi Joins: Joins based on equality (=) are called **equijoins**. Equijoins compare the values in the columns being joined for equality and then include all the columns in the tables being joined in the results.
Example:
*select * from employee, emp_dept*
where employee.city = emp_dept.city

Natural Joins: Above mentioned equi join will display city column twice(identical). There is no point of repeating same information (from city columns), one of these column can be eliminated. This is called natural join.

Section 12 - Joins, Subqueries, and Unions   255

Example:
select f_name, l_name,dob, employee.city from employee, emp_dept
where employee.city = emp_dept.city

Self-joins: Joins that compare values within the same column of one table are called selfjoins. For example: As per below image emp_transactions has transactions of employee, for every transaction there is a type: C (Credit) or D (Debit).

emp_transactions

emp_id	tran_amount	type
101	2000	D
101	1000	C
102	1000	D
102	3000	C

Now if we want to display credit and debit transaction amount in one row for every employee, we can write a query as below.
select emp_debit.emp_id, emp_debit.tran_amount debit_amount, emp_credit.tran_amount credit_amount from emp_transactions emp_debit, emp_transactions emp_credit
where emp_debit.type = 'D'
and emp_credit.type='C'
and emp_debit.emp_id = emp_credit.emp_id
And result will be as below:

emp_id	debit_amount	credit_amount
101	2000	1000
102	1000	3000

You can user any join operators like <, != etc.

Outer Joins: Joins that include all rows, regardless of whether there is a matching row, are called **outer joins**. Adaptive Server supports both left and right outer joins.

Note: Sybase supports both Transact-SQL and ANSI outer joins.

T-SQL left and right outer joins: Use *= for left outer join and =* for right outer join
Example(left outer join): Will display all the rows from *employee* table, even if values of *id* column of *employee* table does not match with value of *emp_id* column of *emp_dept* table. For non matching rows *dept.dept_id* column's value will be NULL.
select emp.f_name, dept.dept_id from employee emp, emp_dept dept
*where emp.id *= dept.emp_id*

ANSI outer joins: Use the keywords left join and right join to indicate a left and right join, respectively.
Example:
select emp.f_name, dept.dept_id from employee emp left join emp_dept dept
on emp.id = dept.emp_id

Inner and outer tables:
The terms **outer table** and **inner table** describe the placement of the tables in an outer join:
- In a *left join*, the **outer table** and **inner table** are the left and right tables respectively. The outer table and inner table are also referred to as the rowpreserving and null-supplying tables, respectively.
- In a *right join*, the outer table and inner table are the right and left tables respectively.

For example, in the queries below, T1 is the outer table and T2 is the inner table:
T1 left join T2
T2 right join T1
Or, using Transact-SQL syntax:
T1 *= T2
T2 =* T1

Outer join restrictions: If a table is an **inner member** of an outer join, it cannot participate in *both* an outer join clause and a regular join clause.

Views used with outer joins:
If you define a view with an outer join, then query the view with a qualification on a column from the inner table of the outer join, the results may not be what you expect. The query returns all rows from the inner table. Rows that do not
meet the qualification show a null value in the appropriate columns of those rows.
The following rules determine what types of updates you can make to columns through join views:
- delete statements are not allowed on join views.
- insert statements are not allowed on join views created with check option.
- update statements are allowed on join views with check option. The update fails if any of the affected columns appear in the where clause, in anexpression that includes columns from more than one table.
- If you insert or update a row through a join view, all affected columns must belong to the same base table.

Nested ANSI outer joins: Nested outer joins use the result set of one outer join as the table reference for another.
Example:
select t.title_id, title, ord_num, sd.stor_id, stor_name
from (salesdetail sd
left join titles t
on sd.title_id = t.title_id) /*join #1*/
left join stores
on sd.stor_id = stores.stor_id /*join #2*/
title_id title ord_num stor_id stor_name

- If the first outer join becomes an operator of the second outer join, this query is a **left-nested outer join**(above example is a **left-nested outer join**)

- If the second outer join is used as the table reference for the first outer join, this query is a **right-nested outer join**.

ANSI inner joins: Joins that produce a result set that includes only the rows of the joining tables that meet the restriction are called **inner joins**. Rows that do not meet the join restriction are not included in the joined table.

Syntax:
select *select_list*
from *table1* inner join *table2*
on *join_condition*
Example:
select title, price, advance, royaltyper
from titles inner join titleauthor
on titles.title_id = titleauthor.title_id

Note: If a joined table is used as a table reference in an ANSI inner join, it becomes a **nested** inner join. ANSI nested inner joins follow the same rules as ANSI outer joins.

NULL Values affect joins: Null values in tables or views being joined never match each other. Since bit columns do not permit null values, a value of 0 appears in an outer join when there is no match for a bit column in the inner table.

The result of a join of null with any other value is null. Because null values represent unknown or inapplicable values, Transact-SQL has no reason to believe that one unknown value matches another.

Note: sp_helpjoins to find the likely join columns.

The column pairs that **sp_helpjoins** displays come from two sources. First, sp_helpjoins checks the **syskeys** table in the current database to see if any foreign keys have been defined on the two tables with **sp_foreignkey**, and then checks to see if any common keys have been defined on the two tables with **sp_commonkey**. If it does not find any common keys there, the procedure applies less restrictive criteria to identify any keys that may be reasonably joined. It checks for keys with the same user datatypes, and if that fails, for columns with the same name and datatype.

12.2   Describe the union and union all command

Union and Union all:
Union: Returns a single result set that combines the results of two or more queries. Duplicate rows are eliminated from the result set unless the all keyword is specified.
Suntax:
select [top *unsigned_integer*] *select_list*
[into *clause*] [from *clause*] [where *clause*]
[group by *clause*] [having *clause*]
[union [all]
select [top *unsigned_integer*] *select_list*

[from *clause*] [where *clause*]
[group by *clause*] [having *clause*]]...
[order by *clause*]
[compute *clause*]
Example:
select stor_id, stor_name from sales
union
select stor_id, stor_name from sales_east

- The maximum number of subqueries within a single side of a union is **50**.
- The total number of tables that can appear on all sides of a union query is **256**.
- The **order by** and **compute** clauses are allowed only at the end of the union statement to define the order of the final results or to compute summary values.
- The **group by** and **having clauses** can be used only within individual queries and cannot be used to affect the final result set.
- The default evaluation order of a SQL statement containing union operators is **left-to-right**.
- Corresponding columns in the select lists of union statements must occur in the same order, because union compares the columns one-to-one in the order given in the individual queries.

Union all: Returns a single result set that combines the results of two or more queries. Duplicate rows are not eliminated from the result set.
select stor_id, stor_name from sales
union all
select stor_id, stor_name from sales_east

12.3   Describe subqueries

SUBQUERIES: You can use subqueries to handle query requests that are expressed as the results of other queries. Subqueries, also called **inner queries.** Select statements that contain one or more subqueries are sometimes called **nested queries** or **nested select statements**.

> **Note:** The result of a subquery that returns no values is NULL. If a subquery returns NULL, the query failed.

Example:
select title, price from titles
where price = (select price from titles
where title = "Straight Talk About Computers")

You can use column names in Subquery in following ways:

Section 12 - Joins, Subqueries, and Unions   259

Specify only column name without mentioning table name with column name i.e. employee.emp_id):

select emp_name
from employee
where emp_id in (select emp_id from emp_dept where dept_id = 1)

Note: Column names in a statement are implicitly qualified by the table referenced in the from clause at the same level.

Specify table name with column name:

select emp_name
from employee
where employee.emp_id in (select emp_dept. emp_id from emp_dept where emp_dept.dept_id = 1)

Specify correlation names (alias):

select emp.emp_name
from employee emp
where emp.emp_id in (select dept. emp_id from emp_dept dept where dept.dept_id = 1)

Multiple levels of nesting: A subquery can include one or more subqueries. You can nest up to **50 subqueries** in a statement.

Example: To find the names of employee whose department is in 'Singapore' city.

select emp_name
from employee
where emp_id in
    (select emp_id from emp_dept dept
        where dept_id in
          (select dept_id
          from dept_city
          where city = 'Singapore'))

Note: You can also write a query by using join to achieve above scenario.

You can use subqueries in update, delete and insert statement as well.

Subquery in update: Example:

update employee set emp_name = emp_name + 'Singapore'
    where emp_id in (select emp_id from emp_dept dept
        where dept_id in
        (select dept_id
        from dept_city
        where city = 'Singapore'))

Subquery in delete: Example:

delete employee
    where emp_id in (select emp_id from emp_dept dept
        where dept_id in
        (select dept_id
        from dept_city

where city = 'Singapore'))

Subqueries in conditional statements: You can use subqueries in conditional statements.
Example:
if exists (select title_id from titles where type = "business")
begin
delete salesdetail
where title_id in
(select title_id from titles
where type = "business")
end

In Transact-SQL, you can substitute a subquery almost anywhere you can use an expression in a select, update, insert, or delete statement.
Example: The following statement selects the book titles that have had more than 5000 copies sold, lists their prices, and the price of the most expensive book:
select title, price, (select max(price) from titles)
from titles
where total_sales > 5000

Note: You cannot use a subquery in an **order by** list or as **an expression in the values list in an insert statement.**

Types of subqueries:
There are two basic types of subqueries:

Type of Subqueries	Description
Expression subqueries	Are introduced with an **unmodified** comparison operator, must return a **single value**, and can be used almost anywhere an expression is allowed in SQL.
Quantified predicate	Operate on lists introduced with **in** or with a comparison operator modified by **any** or **all**. Quantified predicate subqueries return 0 or more values. This type is also used as an existence test, introduced with exists.

Subqueries of either type are either noncorrelated or correlated (repeating).

Type of Subqueries	Description
noncorrelated	Can be evaluated as if it were an independent query. Conceptually, the results of the subquery are substituted in the main statement, or outer query. This is not how Adaptive Server actually processes statements with subqueries. Noncorrelated subqueries can alternatively be stated as joins and are processed as joins by Adaptive Server.
correlated	Cannot be evaluated as an independent query, but can reference columns in a table listed in the from list of the outer query.

Expression subqueries: Expression subqueries include:
- Subqueries in a select list (introduced with in)

Section 12 - Joins, Subqueries, and Unions

- Subqueries in a where or having clause connected by a comparison operator (=, !=, >, >=, <, <=)

Example:
select emp_name
from employee
where emp_id in (select emp_id from emp_dept where dept_id = 1)

Using *group by* and *having* in expression subqueries: Because subqueries that are introduced by unmodified comparison operators must return a single value, they cannot include group by and having clauses unless you know that the group by and having clauses will return a single value. For example, this query finds the books that are priced higher than the lowest priced book in the trad_cook category:
select title from titles
where price > (select min(price)
from titles
group by type
having type = "trad_cook")

Quantified predicate subqueries: There are three types of quantified predicate subqueries:
any/all subqueries: Subqueries introduced with a modified comparison operator, which may include a group by or having clause.
Example:
select emp_name from employee where
emp_id > all (select emp_id from emp_dept where dept_id in (1))

Note: > *all* means greater than every value, or greater than the maximum value. For example: > all (1,2,3) means grater then 3.

select emp_name from employee where
emp_id > any (select emp_id from emp_dept where dept_id in (1))
Note: > *any* means greater than at least one value, or greater than the minimum value. Therefore, > any (1, 2, 3) means greater than 1.

Note: if the set returned by the inner query contains a NULL, the query returns 0 rows. This is because NULL stands for "value unknown," and it is impossible to tell whether the value you are comparing is greater than an unknown value.
For example if one of the *emp_id* is NULL in above mentioned subquery, it will return 0 rows.
Note: If you introduce a subquery with all and a comparison operator does not return any values, the entire query **fails**.

Note: The = any operator is an existence check; it is equivalent to in.

in/not in subqueries: Example: *in*

select pub_name from publishers
where pub_id in
(select pub_id
from titles
where type = "business")

This statement is evaluated in two steps. The inner query returns the identification numbers of the publishers who have published business books, 1389 and 0736. These values are then substituted in the outer query, which finds the names that go with the identification numbers in the publishers table.

Example: **not in**
select pub_name from publishers
where pub_id not in
(select pub_id
from titles
where type = "business")

Note: if the set returned by the inner query contains no matching value, but it does contain a NULL, the not in returns UNKNOWN. This is because NULL stands for "value unknown," and it is impossible to tell whether the value you are looking for is in a set containing an unknown value. The outer query discards the row.

exists/not exists subqueries. Example:
select pub_name from publishers
where exists
*(select * from titles*
where pub_id = publishers.pub_id
and type = "business")

A subquery that is introduced with exists is different from other subqueries, in these ways:
- The keyword exists is not preceded by a column name, constant, or other expression.
- The subquery exists evaluates to TRUE or FALSE rather than returning any data.
- The select list of the subquery usually consists of the asterisk (*). You need not specify column names, since you are simply testing for the existence or nonexistence of rows that meet the conditions specified in the subquery. Otherwise, the select list rules for a subquery introduced with exists are identical to those for a standard select list.

not exists is just like exists except that the where clause in which it is used is satisfied when no rows are returned by the subquery.
Example:
select pub_name from publishers
where not exists
*(select * from titles*
where pub_id = publishers.pub_id

Section 12 - Joins, Subqueries, and Unions   263

and type = "business")

A SQL derived table can be used in a subquery from clause: Example
select pub_name from publishers where "business" in
(select type from
(select type from titles, publishers where titles.pub_id = publishers.pub_id)
dt_titles)

Subquery restrictions: A subquery is subject to the following restrictions:
- The *subquery_select_list* can consist of only one column name, except in the exists subquery, where an (*) is usually used in place of the single column name.
- Subqueries **can be nested** inside the where or having clause of an outer select, insert, update, or delete statement, inside another subquery, or in a select list. Alternatively, you can write many statements that contain subqueries as joins; Adaptive Server processes such statements as joins.
- In Transact-SQL, a subquery can appear almost anywhere an expression can be used, if it returns a **single value**.
- A subquery can appear almost anywhere an expression can be used. SQL derived tables can therefore be used in the from clause of a subquery wherever the subquery is used.
- You cannot use subqueries in an **order by, group by**, or **compute by** list.
- You cannot include a **for browse** clause in a subquery.
- You cannot include a **union** clause in a subquery unless it is part of a **derived table expression** within the subquery.
- The select list of an inner subquery introduced with a comparison operator can include only one expression or column name, and the subquery must return a single value. The column you name in the where clause of the outer statement must be **join-compatible** with the column you name in the subquery select list.
- You cannot include **text, unitext,** or **image** datatypes in subqueries.
- Subqueries cannot manipulate their results internally, that is, a subquery cannot include the order by clause, the compute clause, or the into keyword.
- Correlated (repeating) subqueries are not allowed in the select clause of an updatable cursor defined by declare cursor.
- There is a limit of **50** nesting levels.
- The maximum number of subqueries on each side of a union is **50**.
- The where clause of a subquery can contain an aggregate function only if the subquery is in a having clause of an outer query and the aggregate value is a column from a table in the from clause of the outer query.
- The result expression from a subquery is subject to the same limits as for any expression. The maximum length of an expression is **16K**.

12.4   **Describe join costing and subquery optimization**

SUBQURY OPTIMIZATION: subqueries use the following optimizations to improve performance:
- Flattening: converting the subquery to a join
- Materializing: storing the subquery results in a worktable
- Short circuiting: placing the subquery last in the execution order
- Caching subquery results: recording the results of executions

Summary

You read about joins, subqueries, and unions in this section.

- A **join** operation compares two or more tables (or views) by specifying a column from each, comparing the values in those columns row by row, and linking the rows that have matching values.

- The columns being joined must have the same or compatible datatypes.

- **Equi Joins:** Joins based on equality (=) are called **equijoins**. Equijoins compare the values in the columns being joined for equality and then include all the columns in the tables being joined in the results.

- **Natural Joins:** Above mentioned equi join will display city column twice(identical). There is no point of repeating same information (from city columns), one of these column can be eliminated. This is called natural join.

- **Self-joins:** Joins that compare values within the same column of one table are called selfjoins.

- **Outer Joins:** Joins that include all rows, regardless of whether there is a matching row, are called **outer joins**.

- **Union:** Returns a single result set that combines the results of two or more queries. Duplicate rows are eliminated from the result set.

- **Union all:** Returns a single result set that combines the results of two or more queries. Duplicate rows are not eliminated from the result set.

- **SUBQUERIES:** You can use subqueries to handle query requests that are expressed as the results of other queries. Subqueries, also called **inner queries.**

- A subquery can include one or more subqueries. You can nest up to **50 subqueries** in a statement.

- **SUBQURY OPTIMIZATION:** subqueries use the following optimizations to improve performance:
    - Flattening: converting the subquery to a join
    - Materializing: storing the subquery results in a worktable
    - Short circuiting: placing the subquery last in the execution order
    - Caching subquery results: recording the results of executions

Practice Test

1. Which of the following command returns a single result set that combines the results of two or more queries?
    A. Union
    B. Outer join
    C. OR
    D. WHERE

2. Which of the following command returns a single result set that combines the results of two or more queries?
    A. Union
    B. Outer join
    C. OR
    D. WHERE

3. Which of the following statements are allowed only within individual queries and cannot be used to affect the final result set?
    A. GROUP BY
    B. ORDER BY
    C. COMPUTE
    D. HAVING

4. The default evaluation order of a SQL statement containing union operators is?
    A. left-to-right
    B. right-to-right
    C. top-to-bottom
    D. bottom-to-top

5. You can next up to ___ subqueries in a statement?
    A. 50
    B. Unlimited
    C. 256
    D. 100

Section 13 - Optimizer Statistics

13.1 Describe table-level and distribution statistics

Adaptive Server's cost-based optimizer uses statistics about the tables, indexes, and columns named in a query to estimate query costs. It chooses the access method that the optimizer determines has the least cost. But this cost estimate cannot be accurate if statistics are not accurate.

Running the update statistics commands requires system resources. Like other maintenance tasks, it should be scheduled at times when load on the server is light. In particular, update statistics requires table scans or leaf-level scans of indexes, may increase I/O contention, may use the CPU to perform sorts, and uses the data and procedure caches.

When you create an index, a **histogram** is generated for the leading column in the index. Examples in earlier sections have shown how statistics for other columns can increase the accuracy of optimizer statistics.

update statistics:
The update statistics commands create statistics, if there are no statistics for a particular column, or replaces existing statistics if they already exist. The statistics are stored in the system tables **systabstats** and **sysstatistics**.
Syntax:
For Table:
update statistics *table_name*
[[*index_name*] | [(*column_list*)]]
[using *step* values]
[with *consumers* = *consumers*]

For Index:
update index statistics *table_name* [*index_name*]
[using *step* values]
[with *consumers* = *consumers*]

For All (Table and Index):
update all statistics *table_name*

The effects of the commands and their parameters are:

For update statistics	
table_name	Generates statistics for the leading column in each index on the table.
table_name index_name	Generates statistics for all columns of the index.
table_name (column_name)	Generates statistics for only this column.
table_name (column_name, column_name...)	Generates a **histogram** for the leading column in the set, and multi column **density values** for the prefix subsets.
For update index statistics	
table_name	Generates statistics for all columns in all indexes on the table.
table_name index_name	Generates statistics for all columns in this index.
For update all statistics:	
table_name	Generates statistics for all columns of a table.

- Dropping an index does not drop the statistics for the index.
- If you want to remove the statistics after dropping an index, you must explicitly delete them with delete statistics.
- *Update all statistics* updates **histograms** for all columns in a table. Truncating a table does not delete the column-level statistics in **sysstatistics**. Since truncate table does not delete the column-level statistics, there is no need to run update statistics after the table is reloaded, if the data is the same.
- You can drop and re-create indexes without affecting the index statistics, by specifying 0 for the number of steps in the with statistics clause to create index. This create index command does not affect the statistics in **sysstatistics**:

    create index title_id_ix on titles(title_id)
    with statistics using 0 values

    This allows you to re-create an index without overwriting statistics that have been edited with optdiag.
- If two users attempt to create an index on the same table, with the same columns, at the same time, one of the commands may fail due to an attempt to enter a duplicate key value in sysstatistics.

Good candidates for column statistics are:
- Columns frequently used as search arguments in **where** and **having** clauses
- Columns included in a **composite index**, and which are not the leading columns in the index, but which can help estimate the number of data rows that need to be returned by a query.

Examples:
This command adds statistics for the price column in the titles table:
    update statistics titles (price)
This command specifies the number of histogram steps for a column:
    update statistics titles (price) using 50 values

This command adds a **histogram** for the titles.pub_id column and generates **density values** for the prefix subsets pub_id; pub_id, pubdate; and pub_id,pubdate, title_id:
> update statistics titles(pub_id, pubdate, title_id)

Note: Running update statistics with a table name updates **histograms** and **densities** for leading columns **for indexes only.** It does not update the statistics for **unindexed** columns. To maintain these statistics, you must run update statistics and specify the column name, or run update all statistics.

delete statistics:
Example: This example command deletes the statistics for the price column in the titles table.
delete statistics titles(price)
Note The delete statistics command, when used with a table name, removes all statistics for a table, even where indexes exist. You must run update statistics on the table to restore the statistics for the index.

Inaccurate row counts:
Row count values for the number of rows, number of forwarded rows, and number of deleted rows may be inaccurate, especially if query processing includes many rollback commands. If workloads are extremely heavy, and the housekeeper task does not run often, these statistics are more likely to be inaccurate.

Running update statistics corrects these counts in systabstats.
Running dbcc checktable or dbcc checkdb updates these values in memory.

When the housekeeper task runs, or when you execute **sp_flushstats**, these values are saved in **systabstats**.
Note The configuration parameter housekeeper free write percent must be set to 1 or greater to enable housekeeper statistics flushing.

The systabstats and sysstatistics tables store statistics for all tables, indexes, and any unindexed columns for which you have explicitly created statistics. In general terms:
Systabstats: stores information about the table or index as an object, that is, the size, number of rows, and so forth.
It is updated by query processing, data definition language, and update statistics commands.
Sysstatistics: stores information about the values in a specific column. It is updated by data definition language and update statistics commands.

The optdiag utility displays statistics from the **systabstats** and **sysstatistics** tables.
Syntax:
optdiag [binary] [simulate] statistics
{-i *input_file* |
database[.*owner*[.[*table*[.*column*]]]]
[-o *output_file*]}
[-U *username*] [-P *password*]

[-I *interfaces_file*]
[-S *server*]
[-v] [-h] [-s] [-T*flag_value*]
[-z *language*] [-J *client_charset*]
[-a *display_charset*]

Note: You can use optdiag to display statistics for an entire database, for a single table and its indexes and columns, or for a particular column.

Examples:
To display statistics for all user tables in the pubtune database, placing the output in the *pubtune.opt* file, use the following command:
optdiag statistics pubtune -Usa –Ppasswd -o pubtune.opt
This command displays statistics for the titles table and for any indexes on the table:
optdiag statistics pubtune..titles -Usa –Ppasswd -o titles.opt

13.2   Define the different types of statistics, such as cluster ratios, density values, and histograms

Table statistics:
This optdiag section reports basic statistics for the table.
Sample output for table statistics
Table owner: "dbo"
Statistics for table: "titles"
Data page count: 662
Empty data page count: 10 [Count of pages that have deleted rows only.]
Data row count: 4986.0000000000000000
Forwarded row count: 18.0000000000000000 [Number of forwarded rows in the table. **This value is always 0 for an APL table.**]
Deleted row count: 87.0000000000000000 [**This value is always 0 for an allpages-locked table.**]
Data page CR count: 86.0000000000000000 [A counter used to derive the data page cluster ratio.]
OAM + allocation page count: 5 [These statistics are used to estimate the cost of OAM scans on data-only-locked tables. **The value is maintained only on data-only-locked tables.**]
First extent data pages: 3 [**This information is maintained only for data-only-locked tables.**]
Data row size: 238.8634175691937287 [This value is updated only by update statistics, create index, and alter table...lock.]
Derived statistics:
Data page cluster ratio: 0.9896907216494846

Date Page CR Count: is used to compute the **data page cluster ratio**, which can help determine the effectiveness of **large I/O** for table scans and range scans. This value is updated only when you run **update statistics**.

Sample output for index statistics
Statistics for index: "title_id_ix" (nonclustered)
Index column list: "title_id"
Leaf count: 45
Empty leaf page count: 0
Data page CR count: 4952.0000000000000000
Index page CR count: 6.0000000000000000
Data row CR count: 4989.0000000000000000
First extent leaf pages: 0
Leaf row size: 17.8905999999999992 [Average size of a leaf-level row in the index.]
Index height: 1 [Index height, not including the leaf level.]
Derived statistics:
Data page cluster ratio: 0.0075819672131148
Index page cluster ratio: 1.0000000000000000
Data row cluster ratio: 0.0026634382566586

Sample output for column statistics
The following sample shows the statistics for the city column in the authors table:
Statistics for column: "city"
Last update of column statistics: Jul 20 1998 6:05:26:656PM
Range cell density: 0.0007283200000000
Total density: 0.0007283200000000
Range selectivity: default used (0.33)
In between selectivity: default used (0.25)

Cluster ratios:
When clustering is high, large I/O is effective. As the cluster ratios decline, effectiveness of large I/O drops rapidly. To refine I/O estimates, the optimizer uses a set of **cluster ratios**:
- For a table, the data page cluster ratio measures the **packing** and **sequencing of pages** on **extents**.
- For an index, the data page cluster ratio measures the **effectiveness of large I/O** for accessing the table using this index.
- The index page cluster ratio measures the **packing** and **sequencing** of **leaf-level index pages** on index extents

Data page cluster ratio:
The data page cluster ratio for a table measures the effectiveness of large I/O for table scans. Its use is slightly different depending on the locking scheme.
- For Allpages-lockes tables: For allpages-locked tables, a table scan or a scan that uses a clustered index to scan many pages follows the next-page pointers on each data page. **Immediately after the clustered index is created, the data page cluster ratio is 1.0**, and pages are ordered by page number on the extents. However, after updates and page splits, the page chain can be fragmented across the page chain
    Note: The data page cluster ratio for an allpages-locked table measures the effectiveness of large I/O for both **table scans** and **clustered index scans**.

- **On data-only-locked tables:** For data-only-locked tables, the data page cluster ratio measures how well the pages are packed on the extents. A cluster ratio of 1.0 indicates complete packing of extents, with the page chain ordered. **If extents contain unused pages, the data page cluster ratio is less than 1.0.**
  Optdiag reports two data page cluster ratios for data-only-locked tables with clustered indexes. The value reported for the table is used for table scans. The value reported for the clustered index is used for scans using the index.

Index page cluster ratio:
The index page cluster ratio measures the packing and sequencing of index leaf pages on extents for nonclustered indexes and clustered indexes on data-only-locked tables. For queries that need to read more than one leaf page, the leaf level of the index is scanned using next-page or previouspage pointers. If many leaf rows need to be read, 16K I/O can be used on the leaf pages to read one extent at a time. The index page cluster ratio measures fragmentation of the page chain for the leaf level of the index.

Histogram:
Histograms store information about the distribution of values in a column.
Sample output for histograms
Histogram for column: "city"
Column datatype: varchar(20)
Requested step count: 20
Actual step count: 20

Histogram output: A histogram is a set of cells in which each cell has a weight. Each cell has an upper bound and a lower bound, which are distinct values from the column. The weight of the cell is a floating-point value between 0 and 1, representing either:
- The fraction of rows in the table within the range of values, if the operator is <=, or
- The number of values that match the step, if the operator is =.

The optimizer uses the combination of **ranges, weights, and density values** to estimate the number of rows in the table that are to be returned for a query clause on the column.
Adaptive Server uses **equi-height histograms**, where the number of rows represented by each cell is approximately equal.

In histograms for columns with highly duplicated values, a single cell, called a **frequency cell**, represents the duplicated value. The weight of the frequency cell shows the percentage of columns that have matching values.

Dense frequency count: all the values for the column are contiguous integers.

In a histogram representing a column with a *sparse frequency count*, the highly duplicated values are represented by a step showing the discrete values with the = operator and the weight for the cell.

For tables with some values that are highly duplicated, and others that have distributed values, the histogram output shows a combination of operators and a mix of frequency cells and range cells.

Please see section: Identify guidelines for SARGs for Density values

13.3 Describe simulated statistics

Simulated statistics:
The optdiag utility command allows you to load **simulated statistics** and perform query diagnosis using those statistics. Since you can load simulated statistics even for tables that are empty, using simulated statistics allows you to perform tuning diagnostics in a very small database that contains only the tables and indexes. Simulated statistics **do not overwrite** any existing statistics when they are loaded, so you can also load them into an existing database. Once simulated statistics have been loaded, instruct the optimizer to use them (rather than the actual statistics):
set statistics simulate on
optdiag can generate statistics that can be used to simulate a user environment without requiring a copy of the table data. This permits analysis of query optimization using a very small database. For example, simulated statistics can be used:
• For Technical Support replication of optimizer problems
• To perform "what if" analysis to plan configuration changes

Note: In most cases, you will use simulated statistics to provide information to Technical Support or to perform diagnostics on a development server.
optdiag syntax for simulated statistics:
This command displays simulate-mode statistics for the pubtune database:
  optdiag simulate statistics pubtune -o pubtune.sim
If you want binary simulated output, use:
  optdiag binary simulate statistics pubtune -o pubtune.sim
To load these statistics, use:
  optdiag simulate statistics -i pubtune.sim

Simulated statistics output: Output for the simulate option to optdiag prints a row labeled "simulated" for each row of statistics, except histograms. You can modify and load the simulated values, while retaining the file as a record of the actual values.
If binary mode is specified, there are three rows of output:
- A binary "simulated" row
- A decimal "simulated" row, commented out
- A decimal "actual" row, commented out

If binary mode is not specified, there are two rows:
- A "simulated" row
- An "actual" row, commented out

Requirements for loading and using simulated statistics:

To use simulated statistics, you must issue the set statistics simulate on command before running the query.
Example:
set statistics simulate on
To accurately simulate queries:
- Use the same locking scheme and partitioning for tables
- Re-create any triggers that exist on the tables and use the same referential integrity constraints
- Set any non default cache strategies and any non default concurrency optimization values
- Bind databases and objects to the caches used in the environment you are simulating
- Include any set options that affect query optimization (such as set parallel_degree) in the batch you are testing
- Create any view used in the query
- Use cursors, if they are used for the query
- Use a stored procedure, if you are simulating a procedure execution

Note: Simulated statistics can be loaded into the original database, or into a database created solely for performing "what-if" analysis on queries.

simulated statistics in the original database : When the statistics are loaded into the original database, they are placed in separate rows in the **system tables**, and do not overwrite existing **nonsimulated statistics**. The **simulated statistics** are only used for sessions where the **set statistics simulate** command is in effect.

While simulated statistics are not used to optimize queries for other sessions, executing any queries by using simulated statistics may result in query plans that are not optimal for the actual tables and indexes, and executing these queries may adversely affect other queries on the system.

Dropping simulated statistics:
Loading simulated statistics adds rows describing cache configuration to the **sysstatistics** table in the **master database**. To remove these statistics, use **delete shared statistics**. **The command has no effect on the statistics in the database where the simulated statistics were loaded.** If you have loaded simulated statistics into a database that contains real table and index statistics, you can drop simulated statistics in one of these ways:
- Use delete statistics on the table which deletes all statistics, and run update statistics to re-create only the non simulated statistics.
- Use optdiag (without simulate mode) to copy statistics out; then run delete statistics on the table, and use optdiag (without simulate mode) to copy statistics in

Summary

You read about optimizer statistics in this section.

- Adaptive Server's cost-based optimizer uses statistics about the tables, indexes, and columns named in a query to estimate query costs. It chooses the access method that the optimizer determines has the least cost. But this cost estimate cannot be accurate if statistics are not accurate.

- The update statistics commands create statistics, if there are no statistics for a particular column, or replaces existing statistics if they already exist. The statistics are stored in the system tables **systabstats** and **sysstatistics**.

- This optdiag section reports basic statistics for the table.

- Date Page CR Count is used to compute the **data page cluster ratio**, which can help determine the effectiveness of **large I/O** for table scans and range scans. This value is updated only when you run **update statistics.**

- When clustering is high, large I/O is effective. As the cluster ratios decline, effectiveness of large I/O drops rapidly

- The data page cluster ratio for a table measures the effectiveness of large I/O for table scans.

- The index page cluster ratio measures the packing and sequencing of index leaf pages on extents for nonclustered indexes and clustered indexes on data-only-locked tables.

- Histograms store information about the distribution of values in a column.

- **Simulated statistics:** The optdiag utility command allows you to load **simulated statistics** and perform query diagnosis using those statistics. Since you can load simulated statistics even for tables that are empty, using simulated statistics allows you to perform tuning diagnostics in a very small database that contains only the tables and indexes.

- Loading simulated statistics adds rows describing cache configuration to the **sysstatistics** table in the **master database**. To remove these statistics, use **delete shared statistics. The command has no effect on the statistics in the database where the simulated statistics were loaded.**

Practice Test

1. When you create an index, a histogram is generated for the?

A. leading column in the table.
B. leading column in the index.
C. unused column in the index.
D. All of the above.

2. The statistics are stored in the
   A. systabstats
   B. sysstatistics
   C. Both A and B
   D. None of the above.

3. Which of the following is used to compute the data page cluster ratio?
   A. Data row size
   B. Forwarded row count
   C. Date Page CR Count:
   D. All of the above

4. In APL tables, immediately after the clustered index is created, the data page cluster ratio is?
   A. 0
   B. < 1
   C. 1
   D. > 1

5. Which of the following store information about the distribution of values in a column?
   A. Index page
   B. Clustered ratio
   C. Histogram
   D. None of the above

6. Which tools or methods can be used to determine the index page cluster ratio for a particular index? (Choose 2)
   A. optdiag utility
   B. direct query against sysattributes
   C. direct query against sysstatistics
   D. derived_stat()

Practice Test Answers

Section 1 - What's New in ASE 15

1. What conditions must be met before altering the partition strategy of a table from round-robin to a range partitioned table?
Answer: D

2. Global indexes can be clustered on
Answer: A

3. Scrollable Cursor can NOT be
Answer: C

4. Which of the following are TRUE about the cursor fetch statement? (Choose 2)
Answer: B, D

5. Which of the following statement is NOT true?
Answer: A

6. What is used to determine how many rows qualify for the search argument?
Answer: A

7. If a query should use Nested Loop Joins, what optimization goal setting is recommended?
Answer: C

Section 2 - ASE Performance and Tuning Basics

1. In sp_configure command, each configuration parameter has an associated display level and default is
Answer: C

2. Which of the following statements are true about MDA tables (Choose 3)?
Answer: A, C, D (The MDA tables report information about ASE at a low level.)

3. Provides the SQL text that is currently being executed.
Answer: C

4. The parser converts the text of the SQL statement to an internal representation called a
Answer: C

5. To see query plans, use:
Answer: C

Section 3 - Logical and Physical Design

1. There are three kinds of relationships between tables. Those are [Choose 3]
Answer: A,B,C

2. Which of the following structures can be used to enforce entity integrity? (Choose 2)
Answer: A, E

3. A **Foreign key** is a field (or fields) that points to the _____ of another table.
Answer: B

4. Which statements are TRUE. Defaults & rules... (Choose 2)
Answer: B, D

5. A derived table may be a [Choose 2]
Answer: B, C

6. What are not the advantages of normalization? [Choose 2]
Answer: C, E

7. Whatever denormalization techniques you use, you need to ensure data integrity by using?
Answer: D

Section 4 - ANSI SQL – DDL

1. Which of the following command can create a table in another database from your current database? (Assuming newdb is another database)
Answer: A

2. Which of the following database object you can create in a database other than the current database?
Answer: B, F

3. NULL value means?
Answer: C

4. A _____ is a portion of a device that is defined within ASE. It is used for the storage of specific types of
Answer: A

5. A data partition is an independent database object with a?
Answer: A

6. You can specify maximum _____ values in each list partition?
Answer: C

Section 5 - ANSI SQL

Practice Test Answers 279

1. Which of the following are NOT DML commands [Choose 2]?
Answer: B, F

2. Which of the following components of a 'select' statement will ALWAYS require a sort?
Answer: D

3. Which of the following are techniques of direct updates [Choose 3]?
Answer: A, B, D

4. What must an expression used in a function based index contain?
Answer: A

5. Which of the following is TRUE about materialized computed columns?
Answer: C

6. Which of the following statements is NOT TRUE regarding computed columns?
Answer: A

Section 6 - Query Access Methods

1. Point queries are queries which are having?
Answer: B

2. Which of the following would be best used in a heavy DSS workload environment?
Answer: D

3. If you create a table on Adaptive Server, but do not create a clustered index, the table is stored as a

Answer: C

4. Which of the following is a NOT performance benefit of using indexes?
Answer: E

5. Which of the following statements are true about Fast bcp? [Choose 2]
Answer: B, D

6. Which of the following commands are NOT True? [Choose 2]
Answer: A, B

Section 7 - Query Optimization

1. The __ operator is a binary operator that joins two data streams, based on row IDs generated for the same source table
Answer: C

2. Which of the following set command reports information about physical and logical I/O and the number of times a table was accessed?
Answer: A

3. Adaptive Server can generate an abstract plan for a query, and save the text and its associated abstract plan in?
Answer: B

4. Which of the following is not a parallel method?
Answer: D

5. A parallel query's degree of parallelism is the?
Answer: B

6. How to calculate *Minimum procedure cache size needed*?
Answer: B

Section 8 - Stored Procedures and Triggers

1. Which of the following statement is correct to execute a stored procedure *employee_proc*?
Answer: D

2. The maximum number of arguments for stored procedures is?
Answer: A

3. Which of the following statement are TRUE about stored procedures? [Choose 3]
Answer: A, B, D

4. When do triggers fire?
Answer: D

5. Which of the following command is correct to disable all the triggers on a table?
Answer: B

6. Which of the following commands trun on self-recursion for triggers?
Answer: B

Section 9 - Transact-SQL Statements

1. Which of the following can be including in CASE expression?
Answer: F

2. Which of the following keyword control the operation of the statements inside a while loop? [Choose 2]
Answer: A, C

Practice Test Answers

3. Which of the following statements is NOT true about the case expression?
Answer: D

4. If you think a particular query plan is unusual, you can use ___ to determine why the optimizer made the decision.
Answer: B

5. Which of the statements is true about Histogram?
Answer: C

6. Which of the following are types of Histogram? [Choose 2]
Answer: A, B

Section 10 - Data Integrity and Constraints

1. Which of the following statements are true about Default? [Choose 3]
Answer: A, D, E

2. Which of the following statements are NOT TRUE about RULE?
Answer: B

Section 11 - Transaction Management and Locking

1. If global variable @@transtate return 0 value, it means?
Answer: B

2. The @@trancount global variable keeps track of the?
Answer: C

3. Which of the following statements is true for deadlock?
Answer: A

4. Intent lock can be?
Answer: C

5. Every change to a database, whether it is the result of a single update statement or a grouped set of SQL statements, is recorded in the system table?
Answer: B

6. Which of the following global variable displays current transaction mode?
Answer: B

7. ASE notified which message number in case of deadlock?
Answer: D

Section 12 - Joins, Subqueries, and Unions

1. Which of the following command returns a single result set that combines the results of two or more queries?
Answer: A

2. Which of the following command returns a single result set that combines the results of two or more queries?
Answer: A

3. Which of the following statements are allowed only within individual queries and cannot be used to affect the final result set?
Answer: A, D

4. The default evaluation order of a SQL statement containing union operators is?
Answer: A

5. You can next up to ___ subqueries in a statement?
Answer: 50

Section 13 - Optimizer Statistics

1. When you create an index, a histogram is generated for the?
Answer: B

2. The statistics are stored in the
Answer: C

3. Which of the following is used to compute the data page cluster ratio?
Answer: C

4. In APL tables, immediately after the clustered index is created, the data page cluster ratio is?
Answer: C

5. Which of the following store information about the distribution of values in a column?
Answer: C

6. Which tools or methods can be used to determine the index page cluster ratio for a particular index? (Choose 2)
Answer: A, D

INDEX

@@cursor_rows, 16
@@error, 214
@@fatch_status, 16
@@isolation, 244
@@nestlevel, 194
@@rowcount, 117
@@textsize, 110
@@tranchained, 242
@@trancount, 235
@@transtate, 234
Abstract Plans, 171
, 85
   CREATE INDEX, 86
   CREATE TABLE, 85
Associative Tables, 60
Attributes, 57
Automatic Update Statistics, 24
   Datachange(), 24
Basic units of costing, 222
BCP commands, 141
Check Constraints, 225
Cluster ratio
   Data page cluster ratio, 269
   Index page cluster ratio, 270
Cluster ratios, 269
Computed columns, 129
   Deterministic Property, 131
   Materialized, 130
   Virtual, 130
CREATE INDEX
   Indexes on computed columns, 87
   Indexing with function-based indexes, 87
CREATE VIEW, 91
CURSORS, 114
Data access in ASE, 138
   Delete Operations, 139
   Insert Operations, 138
   Select operations, 138
   Update Operations, 140
Data Manipulation Commands(DML), 109
   DELETE, 113
   INSERT, 110
   SELECT, 109
   UPDATE, 112
Deadlock, 235
Deadlocks Resolution, 241
Default Constraint, 66

Defaults, 226
Deferred updates, 126
   Deferred index inserts, 127
Demand locks, 238
Denormalization techniques, 77
Density values, 221
Derived tables, 68
derived_stat, 170
Direct updates, 125
   Cheap direct updates, 125
   Expensive direct updates, 125
   In-place updates, 125
Domain integrity, 67
Dropping simulated statistics, 272
Entity, 57
Equi Joins, 252
Foreign keys, 62
Histogram, 270
Histogram cells, 221
Historical/Stateful MDA tables, 45
IDENTITY columns, 94
Important clauses of DML statements, 120
   GROUP BY AND HAVING, 121
   ORDER BY, 123
   WHERE, 120
Indexes on partitioned tables, 11
   Global Indexes, 11
   Local Indexes, 11
Inner joins
   ANSI inner joins, 255
Isolation level, 244
Join processing, 252
Join types, 29
   HASH JOIN, 32
   MERGE JOIN, 30
   NARY NESTED LOOP JOIN operator, 34
   NESTED LOOP JOIN, 29
Latches, 238
Lock contention, 235
Lock duration, 238
Lock promotion threshold, 236
Locking, 235
   Allpages locking, 235
   Datapages locking, 236
   Datarows locking, 236
MDA Tables, 42
minimally-logged operations, 143

INDEX

Natural Joins, 252
Nesting, 70
Nesting Transactions, 235
New Datatypes, 63
Normalization, 74
    Advantages, 74
    Fist Normal Form, 75
    Second Normal Form, 76
    Third Normal Form, 76
Null values, 93
Optimization goals, 26
optimization 'set' command tools, 169
    set forceplan, 170
    set parallel_degree, 170
    set prefetch, 170
    set showplan, 169
    set sort_merge, 170
    set statistics io, 169
    set statistics subquerycache, 169
    set statistics time, 170
    set table count, 170
Optimizing updates, 128
    Designing for direct updates, 128
    sp_sysmon while tuning updates, 128
Outer Joins, 253
Page and row locks, 236
    Exclusive locks, 237
    Shared locks, 236
    Update locks, 237
Parallel data access, 178
    Hash-based index scans, 178
    Hash-based table scans, 178
    Partition-based scans, 178
Parallel query optimization, 180
Parallel sorting, 181
Parallel sorting strategy, 181
Partition skew, 182
Partitioning strategies, 98
    Data partitions, 98
    Index partitions.
Partitioning types, 99
    Hash partitioning, 100
    List partitioning, 100
    Range partitioning, 99
    Round-robin partitioning, 101
Performance problems, 186
Primary Key, 61, 226
Procedure cache, 198
Programming Commands, 209
    , 137
    Covered Query, 137
    Point Query, 137

    Range Query, 137
    , 147
    OR strategy, 147
    Showplan, 149
Query Processing Metrics
    sp_metrics, 22
Query Processor Improvements, 51
Query Processor modules, 50
Relationships, 57
RULES, 228
SARGs, 216
    Guidelines for creating search arguments, 219
    Join transitive closure, 218
    Predicate transformation and factoring, 218
    Search argument syntax, 220
    Search argument transitive closure, 217
    Statistics for SARGS, 220
scrollable cursors, 14
    Insensitive scrollable cursors, 17
    Semisensitive scrollable cursors, 18
Self-joins, 253
Serial query optimization, 180
Simulated statistics, 271, 273
sp_cachestrategy, 170
sp_configure, 39
sp_showplan, 51
    , 191
    Create procedure, 191
    Execute, 191
    Parameters, 193
    Permissions, 192
    proc_role function, 196
    Procedure Groups, 194
    Restrictions, 197
    Return parameters, 196
    Temporary tables in stored procedures, 195
SUBQUERIES, 256, 263
Subquery restrictions, 261
SUBQURY OPTIMIZATION, 187, 262, 263
    Flattening methods, 187
Table locks, 237
    Exclusive lock, 238
    Intent lock, 237
    Shared lock, 238
Table statistics, 268
Temporary tables, 96
Transaction commands, 233
Transaction log, 240
Transaction mode, 242
    Chained mode, 243
    Unchained mode, 243
Trigger, 200

INDEX

Create trigger, 200
Nesting triggers, 204
Rollback triggers, 202
self-recursion Trigger, 204
SQL statements that are not allowed in triggers, 206
Trigger restrictions, 205

UpdateTrigger, 201
Use of Trigger, 205
Union, 255
Union all, 256, 263
Update statistics, 265
Worker process model, 177
    Parallel query execution, 177

Printed in Great Britain
by Amazon.co.uk, Ltd.,
Marston Gate.